Eunice Dauterman Maguire, Henry P. Maguire,
and Maggie J. Duncan-Flowers

Art and Holy Powers in the Early Christia

with contributions by
Anna Gonosová and Barbara Oehlschlaeger-Garvey

Illinois Byzantine Studies II

Krannert Art Museum
University of Illinois at Urbana-Champaign

University of Illinois Press
Urbana and Chicago

This publication has been made possible in part by grants from the National Endowment for the Humanities, a Federal agency, and from the Research Board of the University of Illinois at Urbana-Champaign.

Manufactured in the United States of America

P 5 4 3 2 1

This book is printed on acid-free paper.

Library of Congress Cataloging-in-Publication Data

Maguire, Eunice Dauterman.

Art and holy powers in the early Christian house / Eunice Dauterman Maguire, Henry P. Maguire, and Maggie J. Duncan-Flowers; with contributions by Anna Gonosová and Barbara Oehlschlaeger-Garvey.

p.   cm.—(Illinois Byzantine studies; 2)

"Published in conjunction with the exhibition Art and holy powers in the early Christian house, shown at the Krannert Art Museum of the University of Illinois at Urbana-Champaign from 25 August to 1 October 1989, and at the Kelsey Museum of Archaeology of the University of Michigan in Ann Arbor from 27 October 1989 to 29 April 1990"—Pref.

Bibliography: p.

Includes index.

ISBN 0–252–06095–4 (alk. paper)

1. Decorative arts, Early Christian—Themes, motives—Exhibitions. I. Maguire, Henry, 1943– . II. Duncan-Flowers, Maggie J. III. Krannert Art Museum. IV. Kelsey Museum of Archaeology. V. Title. VI. Series.

NK715.M34   1989   89–32069
745'.09'21—dc20   CIP

There were two worlds, the world of workaday reality and the world of the spirit. These two worlds ceaselessly looked for one another.

V. S. Naipaul, *The Crocodiles of Yamoussoukro*

Contents

Lenders to the Exhibition

The Cleveland Museum of Art, Cleveland, Ohio

Indiana University Art Museum, Bloomington, Indiana

Kelsey Museum of Archaeology, University of Michigan, Ann Arbor, Michigan

Krannert Art Museum, University of Illinois, Champaign, Illinois

Malcove Collection, University of Toronto, Toronto, Ontario

The Metropolitan Museum of Art, New York

Museum of Fine Arts, Boston, Massachusetts

Private Collection

Rare Book and Special Collections Library, University of Illinois,
    Champaign, Illinois

Royal Ontario Museum, Toronto, Ontario

University of Chicago, Chicago, Illinois

Virginia Museum of Fine Arts, Richmond, Virginia

World Heritage Museum, University of Illinois, Champaign, Illinois

This book is being published in conjunction with the exhibition Art and Holy Powers in the Early Christian House, organized by the Krannert Art Museum of the University of Illinois at Urbana-Champaign and shown there from 25 August to 1 October 1989, and subsequently shown at the Kelsey Museum of Archaeology of the University of Michigan in Ann Arbor from 27 October 1989 to 29 April 1990. The purpose of both the book and the exhibition is to present the domestic art of people who lived in the Early Christian period, primarily from the third to the seventh centuries, and to show how that art represents the interpenetration of two kinds of reality: the visible, which obeyed physical laws, and the unseen, which coexisted with the visible, and which was subject to the operations of benificent powers and malevolent demons.

      The book contains an introduction and nine sections corresponding to the nine divisions of objects on display. The introductory essay develops the theme of the two realities of the early Christians by explaining the meanings and functions of the motifs adorning household objects. These motifs, thought capable of affecting the invisible world, may be seen throughout the exhibition on different types of objects and in different media. The nine subsequent sections are devoted to nine aspects of daily life. In each section a short essay setting the exhibited objects into context precedes the entries on the individual pieces. Many of the objects are published here for the first time.

      All of the introductions in this book are by Eunice Dauterman Maguire and Henry Maguire; all of the entries are by Maggie Duncan-Flowers, except for numbers 1-2, 4-5, and 68-76, which are by Anna Gonosová, numbers 6, 29, 56, 118, 132, and 134-37, which are by Eunice and Henry Maguire, and number 101, which is by Barbara Oehlschlaeger-Garvey. We composed numbers 33-34, 63-64, 84-89, 97, 100, 126-29, 133, and 138 from data provided by Paul Denis of the Royal Ontario Museum, Toronto, to whom we are extremely grateful. His own fuller publication of these pieces is forthcoming.

      Throughout the book, dimensions are given in centimeters. The following abbreviations have been used: H. for height, L. for length, W. for width, and D. for diameter.

Eunice Dauterman Maguire
Henry Maguire

Acknowledgments

We would like to record here our gratitude to all those individuals and institutions who have helped to make our project not just a possibility but a reality. First, we are indebted to the funding agencies: to the National Endowment for the Humanities for supporting both the planning and the implementation of this exhibition; and to the Research Board of the University of Illinois for providing assistance toward the writing of the book. Second, we are deeply grateful to many individuals at lending institutions, who gave generously of their time and expertise when we visited their collections or corresponded with them. In particular, as organizers of the exhibition, we would like to thank Jean-Michel Tuchscherer and Deborah Kraak of the Boston Museum of Fine Arts, Patrick M. de Winter and Anne W. Wardwell of The Cleveland Museum of Art, Adriana Calinescu of the Indiana University Art Museum at Bloomington, Margaret Frazer, Carolyn Kane, and Nobuko Kajitani of The Metropolitan Museum of Art in New York, Sheila D. Campbell, curator of the Malcove Collection at the Pontifical Institute of Mediaeval Studies in Toronto, Paul Denis, John Hayes, and Louise W. Mackie of the Royal Ontario Museum at Toronto, Franklin I. Gamwell and Kathleen Shelton of the University of Chicago, Pinkney Near of the Virginia Museum of Fine Arts in Richmond, and Barbara Bohen and Carol Knauss of the World Heritage Museum of the University of Illinois at Urbana-Champaign. In addition, we are grateful for the assistance of Peter Barnet of The Detroit Institute of Arts, Susan Boyd of Dumbarton Oaks, David Buckton of The British Museum in London, Bertrand Davezac and Mary Kadish of the Menil Foundation in Houston, Susan B. Matheson of the Yale University Art Gallery in New Haven, Karel Otavsky of the Abegg-Stiftung at Riggisberg, James A. Sauer of The University Museum at the University of Pennsylvania in Philadelphia, and Slobodan Ćurčić of Princeton University.

Anna Gonosová and Gary Vikan have acted as consultants to this exhibition, sharing with us their advice and special expertise. We are extremely thankful to them both. Several other individuals have assisted us with their expert knowledge of particular areas, especially Leila Abdel-Malek, Susan H. Auth, Charalambos Bakirtzis, Robert Bianchi, John Nesbitt, and Thelma Thomas.

Our particular thanks go to Stephen Prokopoff, director of the Krannert Art Museum, who invited us to undertake this project; he has been generous with his advice throughout. We have also been greatly aided by George Dimock, the assistant director, and by Kathleen Jones, the registrar, who have selflessly helped the project at every stage.

For her tireless work on the catalogue, we owe a special debt of gratitude to Maggie J. Duncan-Flowers, who also aided us greatly in planning the exhibition. We also thank Anna Gonosová and Barbara Oehlschlaeger-Garvey for their contributions to this volume. For assistance in the production stage, we are indebted to our copy editor, Carol Bolton Betts, and to our graphic designer, David Colley.

Finally, we are grateful to Elaine K. Gazda, director of the Kelsey Museum of Archaeology, for her enthusiastic cooperation from the outset. The Kelsey has not only agreed to host this exhibition, but has lent to the display many of its finest and most interesting objects. We thank the staff at the Kelsey for their valuable assistance, especially Marti Lu Allen, Barbara May, Robin Meador-Woodruff, and Amy Rosenberg.

Eunice Dauterman Maguire
Henry Maguire

Fig. 1. Washington, D.C., Textile Museum,
Tapestry Weave.
Wealth-bringing Woman.

Fig. 2. Washington, D.C., Textile Museum,
Tapestry Weave.
Gorgon Enclosed by Interlace.

The Time and Place

The period of the fourth to the seventh centuries A.D., which corresponds to the dissolution of the Roman Empire, was also the first epoch in western history in which the dominant religion and culture were Christian. For the first time Christianity molded the thoughts and actions of people at all levels of society, over a wide geographical area ranging from Britain in the north to Mediterranean Africa in the south, from Spain in the west to Syria in the east. This age saw the first attempts to create societies that were Christian in their structure and governance, attempts that have continued to have repercussions to the present day. It was a time when the emperor ruled as the representative of God on earth, when the local administration of cities passed increasingly into the hands of bishops, when Christianity reached into every facet of people's lives, and when artists produced the first masterpieces of Christian art.

Although the Early Christian era is long past, archaeological excavations carried out during the past century allow us to reconstruct in extraordinary detail the everyday lives of the people who lived around the Mediterranean during that period. Through beautifully preserved objects such as furniture, lamps, baskets, tableware, clothing, jewelry, amulets, medical necessities, and items of personal care, we can see today the rich texture of daily life during these centuries and understand how ordinary people from different social classes thought and felt. The purpose of this exhibition is to display the material experience of that first Christian civilization, and the ways by which individuals gave significance and meaning to their day-to-day existence.

Today the best-known works of art of the Early Christian era are the mosaics and elaborately worked fittings of ecclesiastical buildings such as the churches and baptisteries of Ravenna. But there was another, more intimate aspect of Early Christian art, which this exhibition explores. Like the officially commissioned monuments of the church, the applied arts found in private houses from the fourth to the seventh centuries strike the modern viewer with their visual richness. In addition, they possess more immediate qualities: It is often easier for people of the twentieth century to relate to personal items of the late antique period, such as decorated combs, pieces of clothing, and children's toys, than it is for them to respond to the more complex art of the early church, more heavily laden with theology and political ideology, and more remote from the concerns of modern society. The objects from the daily lives of the early Christians give us a direct avenue for entering their rich, intricate culture. It could even be said that material culture provides a better view of the mentality of these individuals than do texts such as the writings of the church fathers, for domestic objects and their imagery provide an insight into the attitudes and artistic concerns of ordinary people, including those who could not read or write. The written materials reflect only the reactions of the educated, who were a small proportion of the total population.

1

In his *Tricennial Oration in Praise of Constantine* , composed to honor the emperor who had given official status to Christianity, the fourth-century bishop Eusebius wrote: ". . . two kinds of nature have been entangled in us, I mean the spiritual and the physical, the one composed of that which is visible to all and the other of that which is invisible" (*Oratio de laudibus Constantini,* VII, 1; trans. Drake, p. 95). The objects of daily life shown in this exhibition illustrate both worlds of the early Christians, the physical and the spiritual. On the one hand, the early Christians lived in the concrete world of visible cause and effect. But alongside this world they inhabited another realm, composed of invisible powers. Some of these powers—those of the holy men, of the saints, of the angels, and of God himself—were benificent; but others—the powers of a multitude of demons and evil spirits—were malevolent. "The invisible enemies were the soul-destroying demons," wrote Eusebius, "surely fiercer than any barbarians." These unseen forces could influence the physical world in ways that were visible, for example, causing illness or misfortune, or bringing health and prosperity. Conversely, it was possible for people and objects in the physical world to affect the spiritual world: the invisible powers could be invoked and controlled. For this reason, many of the objects used in Early Christian households had a dual function. On one level, the artifacts worked in a material sense, in that they were designed to perform tasks in the physical world; a lock and key, for example, would be designed to provide security from theft (catalogue nos. 29 and 32), or a garment to keep a person warm (nos. 68 and 69). But, at another level, material objects could be designed to operate in the world of spirits, when they were marked with motifs or images that evoked or affected the powers of the unseen world. A key might incorporate a cross into its design (no. 87), a sign whose power to ward off evil was potent but invisible. Likewise, a tunic might be woven with images of victorious horsemen (no. 68), a motif endowed with the power to destroy demons and to win prosperity for the wearer. Many objects, therefore, were designed to "work" in each of the two worlds, seen and unseen. In most cases, the function of the object in the visible world is much more obvious to the modern viewer than its function in the invisible. An Early Christian tunic can still be recognized as a piece of clothing, even if fashions have changed over the millennium and a half since it was made. But the motifs that were embroidered into its fabric may strike the twentieth-century observer as pure and fanciful decoration, while to the Early Christian wearer they were not just ornaments but also important assurances of prosperity and security.

The designs that appear on the domestic arts of the early Christians can be divided into two broad categories, those that were of a non-Christian character, and those that were essentially Christian in nature. Both classes of design, however, had the same functions: to adorn the object and to make it as effective in the spirit world as it was in the physical. Within the non-Christian designs a further distinction can be made, for some were intended to protect from evil, while others were supposed to attract good fortune. These two categories of design, the protecting and the attracting, are well illustrated by two fragments of weaving from Egypt, a square panel and a circular medallion now preserved in the Textile Museum in Washington, D.C. (figs. 1 and 2).

Each textile is an example of tapestry weave in wool and linen, measuring about twelve and a half inches across, and each was originally part of a larger fabric, such as a cushion cover. Each of the designs portrays a woman. In the square panel (fig. 1), she is richly dressed, her hair bound by a jeweled diadem, and her face framed by heavy gold earrings; she is enclosed by a border containing stylized plants and flowers (Trilling, p. 33). In the circular medallion (fig. 2), the woman at the center of the composition is a mythical monster, a Gorgon, with a mass of writhing snakes in her hair. She is framed by a tangle of knotted inter-lace (Trilling, p. 81). Of these two females, the one who is richly dressed and framed by flowers was intended to *bring* prosperity and good luck, while the Gorgon with her enclosure of knots was supposed to *repel* misfortune and evil. The role of the Gorgon as an apotropaic, or protective, device goes back to the ancient myth of Perseus, who cut off Medusa's head and used it as a charm with which to turn his enemies to stone; on the other hand, the richly dressed woman could be associated with a number of female personifications who conveyed to the early Christians assurances of fertility and the blessings of good fortune, as we will show below.

In the following pages we will first consider the apotropaic designs, which deflected misfortune, before moving on to the other group of motifs, the images which attracted wealth and well-being to the object's owner or wearer. Finally, we will consider the designs that were explicitly Christian.

Protective Designs

Knots and Interlaces

In antiquity and in the Middle Ages knots of various kinds were widely be-lieved to provide security from harm (Gombrich, p. 263). Their force in the supernatural world was expressed in the Greek language itself, for the verb katadeō meant both to bind physically and to bind by spells, or to enchant (Dinkler, pp. 73-86). The apotropaic function of knots is graphically illustrated by a floor mosaic recently discovered in the nave of a church at Shuneh-Nimrīn, in Jordan (fig. 3), one of whose panels shows a knot surrounded by the inscrip-tion METH ĒMŌN O THEOS, or "God with us" (Piccirillo, p. 94). Both the knot and the invocation are enclosed in an octagon, itself a shape with protective properties, as we shall show below. The most recognizable of the apotropaic knots was the so-called knot of Hercules, which corresponds to the modern reef knot. In ancient portrayals of Hercules, the hero was usually shown with the paws of his lion's skin tied around his chest by means of this knot. The knot was thought to be capable of protecting from danger in battle, and so generals used it to fasten their sashes over their cuirasses. It was believed to prevent infection, prompting doctors to employ it to tie bandages (Kalavrezou-Maxeiner, pp. 95-96). It was also used to ensure fertility: "The husband undoes this girdle," wrote the grammarian Festus, speaking of the bridegroom removing his bride's marriage belt, "which is fastened with a Herculean knot as a good omen, in order that he himself may be as fortunate in producing children as was Hercu-les, who left seventy children" (*De significatione verborum*, 63). The Herculean knot, therefore, was a general talisman of security and good luck in the pagan

Fig. 3. Shuneh-Nimrīn, Church, Floor Mosaic in Nave. Knot with Inscription: "God with Us."

3

Fig. 4. Cairo, Coptic Museum, Gravestone.

world. A splendid example of its use is a fourth-century silver mirror with its handle formed by the knot (no. 118). As will be seen below, the mirror itself could be a talisman which protected its holder. Though its derivation was pagan, the sign of the Herculean knot found its way into Christian contexts; it was used, for example, as a tutelary device on the stone screens that protected the sacred precincts defined by the chancels of churches (e.g., Boston Museum of Fine Arts, inv. no. 1978.499), and it was used to protect gravestones. An Egyptian stone relief now in the Coptic Museum in Cairo (fig. 4), displays the Hercules knot beside the inscription EIS THEOS ("One God"). (The same phrase appears on amulets, to give protection.) On the relief the knot is tied with the stems of a vine, a plant rich in Christian symbolism (Strzygowski, p. 108).

A second type of knot with apotropaic powers was the so-called knot of Solomon. The Solomonic knot has at its core two looped bands which interlace with each other to form a cross. This basic design may be made more complicated by the addition of other bands which interweave with the central cross (Zischka, pp. 41-48). An example of a simple Solomonic knot can be seen engraved on a bronze belt-buckle (no. 101). Like the Herculean knot, the Solomonic knot was used, both in its simple and its complex forms, to guard sacred places, such as the entrances to chancels or to holy shrines (Schiemenz, p. 114, pl. 16). The access to the stairway leading down to the grotto of Christ's birth under the Church of the Nativity in Bethlehem, for example, was protected by a fifth-century floor mosaic depicting, among other motifs, a knot of Solomon (Kitzinger, 1970, p. 645, figs. 2, 4). In private houses, also, the entrances to rooms were protected by floor mosaics depicting this knot (Kitzinger, 1970, p. 643, figs. 6-7). The knot appeared as an apotropaic device in many other contexts; for example, it was stamped onto the stoppers used to seal jars, in order to protect the contents (Badawy, pp. 345-46, fig. 5.52).

The Much-Suffering Eye

Belief in the power of the evil eye, the malevolent glance of an envious neighbor, has been widespread from antiquity until the present day (Maloney, passim; Russell, pp. 539-48). The evil eye might fall on any aspect of one's good fortune, whether house, possessions, health, or children, and cause harm; its strength posed a perpetual danger, requiring constant vigilance by those on whom it might fall. Small wonder that it was a standard procedure for letter writers, when they referred to their correspondents' children, to add the formula: "may the evil eye (or enchantment) not touch them." We know from the private correspondence preserved in Egyptian papyri that this hope was expressed by Christians as well as by pagans (Rea, p. 99; Browne, p. 79; Sijpesteijn, pp. 137-38).

A common visual device against the evil eye was the so-called "much-suffering eye," which was depicted on the floors of private houses, in wall paintings, and, above all, in amulets worn on the body. The "much-suffering eye" shows an eye, sometimes specifically identified in an inscription as "envy," being attacked by a variety of enemies, both animate and inanimate, such as daggers, spears, tridents, scorpions, snakes, birds, or wild beasts (Perdrizet, 1922, pp. 25-32, figs. 7-11). The name is derived from *The Testament of Solomon*, a popular magical treatise incorporating both Jewish and

Christian elements. According to the *Testament*, King Solomon was given a ring with an engraved stone by the Archangel Michael, who had been sent by "The Lord Sabaoth" (McCown, p. 10*). This seal gave Solomon power over all the demons, and enabled him to summon thirty-six of them before him in turn, forcing each of the evil spirits to reveal its name and the incantation or device that was effective against it. The thirty-fifth demon in this parade was responsible for the evil eye: "My name is Rhyx Phthenoth," it said, "I cast the glance of evil at every man. My power is annulled by the engraved image of the much-suffering eye" (McCown, p. 58*; Bonner, p. 97). An example of such an "engraved image of the much-suffering eye" can be seen in number 135 of this exhibition, a bronze amulet which shows the evil eye suffering, that is, being attacked by a trident and daggers, under an invocation to Jehovah Sabaoth and St. Michael, the two powers who had given Solomon his seal against the demons ("Jehovah Sabaoth Michael Help [The Wearer]"). Many other amulets engraved with the suffering eye survive from the Early Christian period, some also invoking Jehovah Sabaoth (e.g., Ćurčić and St. Clair, p. 81).

Concentric Circles

Objects of daily life from the Early Christian period are frequently marked with a repeated motif of a dot enclosed by a circle or by several concentric circles. In this exhibition, the visitor will find such circles decorating pectoral crosses (nos. 91 and 93), hair combs (nos. 113 and 114), weavers' combs (no. 79), lamps (no. 16), lampstands (no. 10), and dice (nos. 142-44). Many other objects of daily life were marked in this manner, especially those made of organic materials such as wood and bone, into which the circles could easily be incised or punched. Because artifacts made of organic materials have survived in great abundance in the dry climate of Egypt, the concentric circles have been associated especially with the Early Christian art of that country; however, objects of wood and bone surviving from excavations in northern countries, such as Germany, also frequently exhibit this design (e.g., fourth- and fifth-century combs from Trier; Paris, pp. 276-77, no. 240).

 Similar circles can also be found on buildings of the Early Christian period, especially in association with the entrances of fortifications. A lintel over a doorway of the sixth-century fort of the town of Umm el-Jimal in Jordan, for example, is carved with a wreath flanked by two circles, each enclosing a central boss (fig. 5). The original portal in the walls of the fortified monastery built by the Byzantine Emperor Justinian at Mount Sinai is protected by three projecting roundels inscribed with circles or concentric circles (Forsyth and Weitzmann, pl. 12b).

 The circled dots could serve several functions. For example, they could stand abstractly for animating features, such as the eyes and mouth on the child's wooden doll, number 147 in the exhibition, or they could represent the reflective shine of jewels, as on bronze crosses like numbers 91 and 93. In many contexts, however, there is strong evidence that the circles were apotropaic. A case in point is provided by amulets which have the circled dot as their sole design. In the Detroit Museum of Fine Arts, for example, there is a small stone shrine-shaped amulet from Egypt, designed to be worn around the neck, which is marked only with two dotted circles enclosed under a triangular

Fig. 5. Umm el-Jimal,
Doorway of the Fort.

Fig. 6. Detroit Museum of Fine Arts, Amulet.

gable (fig. 6). Since such amulets were presumably intended to protect the wearer, the dotted circle design must have been invested with some significance that went beyond pure decoration.

A clue to the meaning of the circled dots in the Early Christian period can be found on wooden hair combs. On some combs, small circular mirrors set into the wood take the place of the concentric circles (compare nos. 113 and 114 in this exhibition). Here the circled dots appear to complement the mirrors, even to be interchangeable with them in concept, since inset mirrors would have been more expensive and difficult to produce. In the ancient world, from the Hellenistic to the Byzantine period, the most common decoration for metal mirrors was a design of concentric rings or circles, engraved or embossed on the mirror's back or lid. A Roman example is number 119 in this exhibition (for other Roman examples, see Hayes, 1984, pp. 188-93, figs. 316-23; for a Byzantine example, see M. M. Mango, pp. 212-15, fig. 48.2). This kind of linear pattern was technically the simplest way to decorate a disk. The maker of the mirror would accurately form the circular outer rim by cutting or trimming the metal as it turned on a lathe. The point at which the metal was fixed to the lathe would be marked by a small depression, or dot, at its center. Fixed in this way on the lathe, the piece could be tooled by turning it to make circles within the perimeter. Concentric circles, then, became the characteristic decoration of circular mirrors.

A famous object of the Early Christian period provides further evidence that the concentric circles were signs for mirrors. On the fourth-century silver wedding casket of Projecta, there is a relief portraying the bride, a lady from an aristocratic Roman family, turning toward an attendant who holds up to her a mirror decorated with concentric rings (color plate I). But in this case, it is the reflective face of the mirror, not its back, that bears the circles. Obviously, this detail cannot be realistic, since the rings would interfere with the reflection. Rather, it must be that the silversmith has included the rings to indicate clearly the mirror's identity, demonstrating that the concentric circles in themselves were a sign which had the meaning of a mirror.

      For people of the ancient world, mirrors had the ability to reflect more than light. In classical mythology, the hero Perseus used his reflective shield to protect himself from the deadly gaze of the Gorgon Medusa. According to the *Geoponica*, a compilation of agricultural treatises, farmers reputedly could deflect hail from their crops by holding out a mirror to the threatening cloud (*Geoponica*, I, 14, 4). Even divine protection was imagined by similar means, as in a fifth-century mosaic in the Roman church of S. Maria Maggiore (Grabar, 1967, fig. 159), where a shining shield of light stands behind Moses and his companions to protect them from a hail of stones cast by the people of Israel (Numbers 14:10). The belief in the protective power of mirrors survived into the Middle Ages in the west, in legends such as that of Alexander killing the evil basilisk by placing a reflecting glass before it, so that its poison was turned back upon itself (*Gesta Romanorum*, tale 139). In the Early Christian period some mirrors were made for purely apotropaic purposes; that is, they were not used for grooming, but only for protection. In Syria, Palestine, and Egypt, mirrors were set into small shrine-like plaques of clay, plaster, metal, or stone, which could be displayed in houses, or, frequently, buried in tombs (Michon, pp. 161-65, figs. 1-4; Rahmani, pp. 54-59, pl. 16; New York, 1986, pp. 238-40). Some of the plaques are circular, with a decoration of concentric circles enclosing the central mirror, and with a hole at the top for suspension. Other plaques are shaped like fish or birds, or, more often, like miniature architectural shrines. An example of the latter is number 137 in this exhibition, a terra-cotta plaque now missing its two circular mirrors, but retaining the fixtures for them in two circles on its central axis. Like the amulet in Detroit (fig. 6), the shrine is given an architectural shape with a gabled top, and it is divided into two registers. In each register, the mirror appears between encircled dots. Two concentric rings encircle each dot in the gable, while the larger mirror below was placed within a square frame leaving room for only a single circle around each dot. Thus, the power of the actual mirrors was increased by the power of the mirror-cyphers (the circled dots) which flanked them. Beneath the triangular gable, and above the larger of the two mirrors, there is a niche with a scalloped head; this reinforces the architectural sense of the gable, and gives an added honorific position to the mirror beneath. The scallop-headed niche was elsewhere employed to exalt holy persons and the sign of the cross.

The Rayed Serpent

The designs that we have considered above, the knots, circles, mirrors, and the "suffering eye," were all apotropaic in a general sense; they were capable of deflecting a variety of ills. However, certain other devices had specific applications for particular medical problems. Preeminent among these was the image of the rayed serpent which, as we know from the famous Roman physician Galen, was already prescribed for illnesses of the stomach in a treatise attributed to "King Nechepsos," of about 150 B.C. Galen wrote:

> The testimony of some authorities attributes to certain
> stones a peculiar quality which is actually possessed by the
> green jasper. Worn as an amulet, it benefits the stomach and
> oesophagus. Some also set it in a ring, and engrave upon it
> the radiate serpent, just as King Nechepsos prescribed in his
> fourteenth book. I myself have made a satisfactory test of
> this stone. I made a necklace of small stones of that variety
> and hung it from my neck at just such a length that the stones
> touched the position of the cardiac orifice. They seemed just
> as beneficial even though they had not the design that
> Nechepsos prescribed. (*De simplicium medicamentorum tem-*
> *peramentis,* II, 19; trans. Bonner, 54)

Galen, then, determined by empirical experiment that it was the stone that
worked and not the device; nevertheless, well into the Byzantine period, rayed
serpents remained one of the most popular remedies against ailments of the
stomach and also of the womb. An amulet of the type described by Galen, but
dating to the Early Christian period, appears in this exhibition (no. 132). The
green stone, pierced to be hung on a necklace, is engraved on two sides with
rayed serpents; on the other two sides it bears the inscriptions AGIE and IAO
("Holy Jehovah"). On many amulets and items of personal jewelry the serpent
took the form of the Chnoubis, a snake with a lion's head. A treatise on engraved
stones, the *Peri Lithōn* of Socrates and Dionysius, gives the following prescrip-
tion for cutting an amulet of onyx: "Engrave on it a serpent coil with the upper
part or head of a lion, with rays. Worn thus it prevents pain in the stomach; you
will easily digest every kind of food" (Bonner, 55). On some amulets the
Chnoubis is accompanied by a charm addressed to the womb (Bonner, pp. 91,
217; Vikan, 1984, pp. 77-78, fig. 18). In these cases, the role of the Chnoubis
evidently was to ensure the tranquility of the womb and healthy childbirth.

   Toward the end of the Early Christian period, from the
seventh century, the Chnoubis appears to have been conflated with the Gorgon,
and takes on a new appearance. Instead of being shown as a snake with a lion's
head surrounded by rays, it assumes the form of a head ringed by tentacle-like
"rays" ending in snakes' heads. Such a Chnoubis/Gorgon can be seen on a lead
medallion (no. 133) in this exhibition, as well as on other rings and pendants
from the Byzantine world (Vikan, 1984, pp. 76-78, figs. 13, 15, 17-18).

Amuletic Keys

The idea of a key implies control, and for people in the Early Christian era this
could mean control of the spiritual world as much as of the physical. We have
seen that in the *Testament of Solomon* it was written that the king was given a seal
with which to "lock up all the demons" of the earth. On some amulets this magic
seal was depicted in the form of a key. A haematite amulet now in the collection
of the Kelsey Museum of Archaeology at the University of Michigan at Ann
Arbor, for example, depicts Solomon in the form of a mounted rider spearing a

female demon, Abyzou, or Gyllou, who was responsible for causing the deaths of infants during childbirth. On the reverse of the same amulet is depicted a key beneath the inscription "Seal of God" (fig. 7). Earlier Roman amulets gave the key a more specific meaning, by depicting it underneath a schematized engraving of the womb, indicating that the key could symbolically control the opening and shutting of that organ (Vikan, 1984, pp. 77-81, fig. 16).

Some pieces of jewelry incorporated miniature keys into their design in such a way that there is some doubt whether the keys were intended for the control of physical locks or for the control of unseen forces. The bronze ring illustrated in figure 8, from the collection of the Victoria and Albert Museum in London, has such a key attached to it. Because the complicated wards and barrel are positioned to lie along the length of the wearer's finger, the key would have been very awkward in practical use, but it may have given some intangible assurance of security to its owner (Ward, p. 39, no. 67). In the case of the silver ring and its attached key, number 87 in the exhibition, we may also wonder whether the key was intended to function in the physical world, in the spiritual, or perhaps in both.

Octagonal Designs

One other design, the octagon, must be considered under the heading of apotropaic designs. As we know from the therapeutic handbook written by the sixth-century Byzantine doctor Alexander of Tralles, a ring with an eight-sided hoop had the power to prevent colic (Puschmann, 8, 2). On some early Byzantine rings, an octagonal hoop accompanies an engraving of the Chnoubis on the bezel, suggesting that the octagon was also considered an effective talisman against problems with childbirth, since, as we have seen, the Chnoubis had the power of ensuring the tranquility of the womb (Vikan, 1984, pp. 76-77, fig. 13). An association of the octagon with fertility and healthy childbirth could explain why this shape was particularly favored among the early Christians for marriage rings. On such rings, an engraving of the couple shown flanking either Christ or a cross appears on the bezel, while the hoop is eight-sided; these rings were produced in gold (no. 82 in this exhibition) and in bronze (no. 83), indicating that the octagon could be equally effective in either material, protecting rich and poor alike (Vikan, 1987, p. 39, fig. 11).

Designs Invoking Prosperity

Creatures and Plants

Through the domestic arts of the Early Christian period runs a stream of life-bringing images, designs illustrating the riches of the earth and the water, such as fish, waterfowl, fruits, and game. Such subjects were more than mere illustrations of abundance and prosperity; in many cases they also took on the nature of charms, designed to *attract* the wealth that they depicted. The element of magic in these depictions of nature's abundance can be seen clearly on an object such as a gold phylactery of the fifth or sixth century preserved in the Frühchristliche-Byzantinischen Sammlung of Berlin. This amulet takes the form of a

9

Fig. 7. Ann Arbor, Kelsey Museum of Archaeology, Amulet. The Seal of Solomon.

Fig. 8. London, Victoria and Albert Museum, Bronze Ring with a Key.

hollow cylinder designed to be worn around the neck, and originally held some propitious object, such as an invocation or a relic. Portrayed in relief on the body of the cylinder are two fish, two birds, and two snakes, representing the creatures of water, air, and land, respectively. On the other side of the cylinder there is an inscription reading, in reversed letters, EP AGATHO, or "For good" (Elbern, pp. 67-73).

The natural life of the earth was depicted on virtually every kind of object used in the house. Fish, for example, can be found inlaid in bone into a wooden chest, or incised into the handle of an iron frying pan (no. 65). Dolphins leap over bronze lamps (no. 12), or form the tangs and loops of silver buckles (nos. 97 and 100). Ducks can be found drinking from a vase, in a vignette decorating a silver plate (no. 57). The duck was an especially popular motif, because in the Early Christian world it was a bird associated with game provided by the winter, even in a time of scarcity (Maguire, 1987a, p. 36, and p. 91, n. 36). The two boys proffering ducks in a weaving now in Toronto (no. 75) may signify this season.

Another creature appearing in domestic art, and like the duck associated with water, is the frog. This animal held a special meaning for the inhabitants of Egypt, where lamps depicting frogs were produced from the second century A.D. until the Early Christian period (no. 21). Frogs were significant for the Egyptians because the amphibians appeared after the annual summer rising of the Nile, an event upon which all life in Egypt depended. The sources of the Nile were unknown to the people who lived along its banks, and so it is small wonder that the rising of the river was regarded as a miracle, the gift, first of the pagan gods, and then of Christ. The frogs, which seemed to spring spontaneously from the wet mud when it was warmed by the sun, became a symbol of that miracle, and thus of creation and life. For the pagan Egyptians, the frog was the animal of Heqet, the goddess of childbirth. The philosopher Chairemon, in his work on the symbols of the ancient Egyptians which he wrote in the first century A.D., explained that the frog was a symbol of resurrection. There was also an association between frogs and the sun, because sun and water were the two elements indispensable to life, and because the rising of the river took place during high summer, the hottest time of year. The linking of the frog with the illumination of the sun might explain why this creature appeared particularly on lamps (Leclant, pp. 563-70).

When Christianity arrived in Egypt, the frog came to symbolize the life and resurrection assured by Christ. The frog lamps continued to be made, but now they were frequently marked with inscriptions such as "I am the Resurrection," or with symbols of the new faith (Cabrol and Leclercq, 1925, cols. 1810-14;Ćurčić and St. Clair, pp. 114-15, no. 137). In some examples a cross was depicted alongside the frog; in others, more inventively, the frog itself took the shape of a familiar Christian symbol, as shown in number 22, where the head, legs, and tail of the creature (which perhaps should be termed a tadpole rather than a frog) form the Chi Rho, the monogram of Christ. The reader should compare number 18 in the exhibition, a lamp on which the Chi Rho appears in inanimate form.

The beasts of the land, both large and small, were frequently portrayed on the domestic artifacts of Early Christian households. Thus we find

10

a rabbit and a deer on a pottery vase (no. 54), or a sitting lion on a weaver's comb (no. 80). On a magnificent silver ewer once used in a rich man's dining room, and now displayed in the Cleveland Museum of Art (fig. 9), we find deer pursued by a lioness, and also hares chased by dogs (Weitzmann, 1979, pp. 153-54, no. 131). The last motif underscores the meaning of much of this animal imagery in household art; it represents the wealth of game which, the owner hopes, will end up on the family table. The same ewer has a frieze around its base depicting a variety of sea creatures, all of them edible. Another favored motif portrays a mounted hunter with his quarry; it was especially popular on textiles, and can be seen in number 75. In these designs the horse itself conveyed the idea of wealth and prosperity, because only the rich and powerful could afford to keep these animals. Moreover, the rider was a talisman which could protect and defend, as will be seen below.

   In addition to ducks, other birds of various kinds appear on our objects, painted on vases (nos. 54 and 55), perched on bronze lamps (nos. 12 and 16), crowning hairpins (no. 117) and cosmetic applicators (no. 111), or woven into curtains (nos. 1 and 2). Some species can be readily recognized, such as the cock on the bone hairpin (no. 117).

   Among the birds, there was one, the peacock, which had a special value. Tame peacocks graced the gardens of wealthy houses, where they were kept both for their meat and their appearance (Justinian, *Digest*, XLVII, 2.37). They were considered to be one of the most beautiful ornaments of God's earth and were described as such by several Early Christian writers. The seventh-century writer George of Pisidia, in his account of the six days of the Creation, gives an especially vivid description of the peacocks's tail: "How could anyone who sees the peacock not be amazed at the gold interwoven with sapphire, at the purple and emerald green feathers, at the composition of the colors in many patterns, all mingled together but not confused with one another?" (*Hexaēmeron*, 1245-92). The peacock was not only the supreme ornament of creation, it also had symbolic meanings. For several reasons, this bird had been linked since the Roman period with immortality and eternal life. First, the peacock shed its splendid tail feathers annually in winter and renewed them in the spring. Second, there was a tradition that the flesh of the peacock was incorruptible: it was not subject to decay. St. Augustine himself verified the truth of this fact by keeping some of the bird's flesh in his larder over the period of a year and tasting it at intervals (*De civitate Dei*, XXI, 4). Finally, poets from Ovid to George of Pisidia compared the eyelike markings of the peacock's tail feathers to stars. The Romans associated the bird with Juno, and it became a symbol of the apotheosis of empresses. The Christians adopted the peacock as a symbol of the Resurrection in funerary art, in tomb paintings, on carved stone sarcophagi, and on floor mosaics over graves (Maguire, 1987a, pp. 39-40). The meanings of the peacock, therefore, were multifarious. The bird's rich associations could enhance both expensive objects, such as the bronze lamp in the shape of a peacock, number 14 in the exhibition, and also inexpensive artifacts, such as the simple terra-cotta lamp adorned with a peacock that is our number 20. The peacock also found a natural place on the jewelry of the early Christians, where its connotations of beauty and eternal life were elegantly combined (no. 95).

   On many objects of daily life the earth's abundance was expressed through its produce. A frequent theme on textiles was that of chil-

Fig. 9. Cleveland Museum of Art, Silver Ewer.
Game, Seafood, and Bacchic Scenes.

Fig. 10. Chicago, Field Museum,
Tapestry Weave.
Earth and the Waters.

Fig. 11. Cleveland Museum of Art,
Tapestry Weave.
Earth and the Waters.

12

dren holding out baskets or bowls filled with fruits or bread (see our nos. 74 and 75). On some containers the fruit portrayed may have been appropriate to the function of the vessel, as in the case of the grapes painted around the body of a jar (no. 55) possibly used for wine.

Women Who Bring Wealth

On many domestic artifacts, the fertility of the earth was conveyed not by portrayals of animals or plants, but by means of personifications. Foremost among these was the personification of *Ge*, or the Earth herself, who was shown sumptuously dressed as a sign of her ability to bring riches. This personification appears with some frequency in textiles in which weavers were able to condense the fruitfulness of all of nature into a design not more than a few inches across, which could be repeated several times over on a hanging, a cover, or a garment, like the reiteration of a charm. A typical example of this motif is a square panel of wool-and-linen tapestry weave which is preserved in the Field Museum of Chicago and which could have come either from a garment or from some other cloth, such as a curtain (fig. 10). The decoration consists of two squares enclosing two circles. In the innermost circle there is the frontal bust of a woman, richly dressed with a diadem, pendent earrings, a necklace or band around her neck, and a jeweled collar. Behind her head is a halo. The outer circle, which surrounds this figure, is filled with water creatures and plants: fish, dolphins, ducks, and papyrus. This design renders pictorially a common concept of late Roman cosmography, the notion that the inhabited earth was surrounded, like an island, by a continuous sea, which here, as in other Early Christian works of art, is signified not only by creatures of the oceans, but also by freshwater life. Another piece of tapestry weave, now preserved in the Cleveland Museum of Art, condenses the design and depicts it several times (fig. 11); the size and shape of this fragment indicates that it could possibly have been part of a tunic. The composition comprises a square ornament (*segmentum*) in wool and linen, which is framed on two sides by an L-shaped strip (*gammadion*). The motif in the central square is once again the bust of a woman, who wears a jeweled crown, pendent earrings, and a jeweled necklace or collar around her neck. Her head is framed by a large yellow halo, and the whole figure is set against a dark blue background. The bust is supported below by a pair of ducks with red and white bodies and green necks. The birds face each other in symmetrical poses, with their heads turning away over their backs. The same motif of the richly dressed female bust supported on a pair of ducks is repeated on a smaller scale five times in the *gammadion*. The woman may be identified as Earth on account of her rich costume, and because she rises above a pair of symmetrically confronted ducks, which in this, as in other textiles, signify the waters that surround the earth (Maguire, 1987b, pp. 223-24). Another portrait of Earth can be found in this exhibition; on our number 72, a sleeve cuff from a tunic woven in tapestry weave, the personification wears a diadem and necklace and is flanked on either side by fish set against a blue background representing the waters.

In some portrayals of Earth, in textiles and in floor mosaics (fig. 12), she holds in front of her body a crescent-shaped scarf full of fruits, as a sign of her bounty. This image may be echoed in certain bronze stamps, which

13

were probably used by merchants to stamp containers in the marketplace (Vikan and Nesbitt, p. 28). Some of these stamps are crescent-shaped, like the scarf held by Earth, and contain the word KARPOI, or "fruits" (fig. 13). The exhibition shows another stamp of this type containing the invocation HYGEIA, or "health," which, of course, was a consequence of good and plentiful produce (no. 40).

Besides Earth, there were other female personifications associated with health and wealth. For example, there was *Tychē kalē*, or Good Fortune, who appears with an inscription identifying her on a clay lamp from Egypt, now in the Frühchristliche-Byzantinischen Sammlung of Berlin (fig. 14). Like Earth, she is richly dressed, wearing a high headdress with a diadem, earrings, and a jeweled necklace and collar. Another such personification was *Hestia polyolbos*, or the Hearth Rich in Blessings, who is identified by an inscription on a famous hanging in the Dumbarton Oaks collection. She, too, is richly dressed (Friedlander, pp. 1-26, pl. 1). Very often, however, such female personifications appear on the household objects of the early Christians without any identifying features or inscriptions. A case in point is the square panel of tapestry weave from the Textile Museum in Washington with which we started our discussion of the imagery of Early Christian domestic art (fig. 1). It depicts a woman with costly jewelry, but without the flanking ducks or fishes that might identify her as Earth, and without any legend to inform the viewer what she represents. Number 138 in our exhibition, a bronze censer in the shape of a female head wearing a jeweled necklace and a high headdress, also cannot be associated with any particular personification. In such cases it was possible for the user or the wearer of the object to read into the richly attired woman the benificent associations of *all* of the wealth-bringing personifications whom she resembled.

The Blessings of the Nile

A subject closely connected with the themes of abundance and prosperity which occurs with some frequency in Early Christian art is the river Nile, portrayed either by means of its typical flora and fauna, or, more rarely, by personifications. Naturally, the fertility of the Nile was a subject especially favored by artists working in Egypt. It was also a sign of fruitfulness in other parts of the Mediterranean world. Thus, Egyptian weavers frequently incorporated Nilotic scenes into their textiles, as can be seen from figure 15, one of a pair of roundels depicting the personification of the Nile—a reclining god holding a cornucopia—together with two boys flanking a nilometer whose markings show that the inundation has reached a favorable level (du Bourguet, p. 132). A similar vocabulary is used in the relief decoration of the silver bowl shown in figure 16, which was made probably in Constantinople at the turn of the fifth and the sixth centuries; it, too, depicts a couple of boys who are marking the height of the river's waters on a nilometer, while around them runs a border teeming with water plants and creatures. In the case of the dish made in Constantinople, however, it is significant that the number which one of the boys is carving on the nilometer is considerably below the optimum watermark of the Nile's flood. This shows that the specific details of the inundation were not of interest in the capital of the Byzantine empire, seven hundred miles from the

Nile, but the general significance of the imagery, that is, wealth and prosperity appropriate to a rich man's dining room, was clearly understood (Bank, 1978, pp. 15, 279).

The rise of the Nile was too important an event to be left in the control of natural forces alone. In the Roman period, sacrifices were made to ensure the proper rising of the river, as we learn from the following letter of the second century, written by a pagan priest to a priestess in the region of Oxyrhynchus: "Marcus Aurelius Apollonius hierophant, to the priestess who bears

the basket in Nesmeimis, greeting. You will do well to go to Sinkepha to the temple of Demeter to perform the usual sacrifices on behalf of our lords the emperors and their victory and the rise of the Nile and the increase of the crops and the healthy balance of the climate" (Coles, p. 79). This letter, with its request for rites at the temple of Demeter, who was identified with Isis, can be compared with a sixth-century letter from a Christian, a landowner's agent at Oxyrhynchus, who attributes the control of the waters to a different source: "To the most honorable Calus, secretary of the noble house. I again bring the good news to your honor that the blessed fertilizing river of Egypt has risen by the power of Christ. From the 5th. of Mesore till the 7th. it rose 12 finger-breadths, so that there are 2 cubits, 20 finger-breadths of new water" (Grenfell, Hunt, and Bell, pp. 7-8).

The carved wooden frame that is number 6 in this exhibition represents a fine example of the association of the Nile's fertility with the Christian faith. At the center of one of the long sides of the frame, two angels hold up a cross enclosed in a wreath; flanking the angels are peacocks, symbols, as we have seen, of resurrection and eternal life. The rest of the frame is taken up by typical Nilotic motifs, such as boys fishing from boats, water creatures of various kinds, and aquatic plants.

Fig. 12. Khirbat al-Makhāyyat, Church of the Priest John, floor mosaic in the nave. Earth and Offerers.

Fig. 13. Houston, Menil Collection, Stamp inscribed with KARPOI ("Fruits").

Fig. 14. Berlin, Frühchristlich-Byzantinische Sammlung, Clay Lamp. Personification of Good Fortune.

Fig. 15. Paris, Louvre, Tapestry Weave. The Nile with the Nilometer.

Fig. 16. Leningrad, Hermitage, Silver Trulla (Handled Bowl). Nilometer.

Pagan Designs

The last category of designs we shall examine, before turning to the explicitly Christian motifs that appeared in Early Christian houses, is pagan myth. Initially it may appear surprising that Christians continued to harbor the old discredited gods, goddesses, and other pagan subjects on objects that they saw and used every day. Even in death, a Christian girl such as Theodosia, buried under the watchful eyes of painted saints in a tomb at Antinoe (fig. 41), was dressed in garments decorated with centaurs (Breccia, p. 303, fig. 11). But the continued popularity of such subjects was not necessarily evidence of a lingering paganism, though this may occasionally have been the case. It is more likely that pagan subjects continued to be acceptable in Christian households insofar as they served as symbols of the physical rather than of the spiritual world. Venus, for example, could evoke feminine beauty and physical love, even on a casket intended for a Christian; this is why that goddess appears on the lid of the silver casket of Projecta, looking into a mirror and so echoing the actions of the bride who is depicted below, on the front of the casket (color plate I). In a dining room, the pagan gods could stand for the elements from which an abundance of food and drink had been drawn (Schneider, pp. 124-57). Thus Neptune holding a trident, embossed onto the handle of the Constantinopolitan dish mentioned above (fig. 16), could appropriately signify seafood, in a household that at this date was almost certainly Christian. On some pieces of silverware, from both pagan and Christian contexts, Bacchus evoked the fruits of the earth, especially grapes and wine. On the great silver dish from the fourth-century Mildenhall treasure, for example, a central mask of Ocean with dolphins in his hair is surrounded by scenes depicting a Bacchic revel (fig. 17), suggesting the gifts of water and earth respectively (Schneider, p. 150). On the silver ewer illustrated in figure 9, which could have been used for wine, portrayals of fish and game are accompanied by the wine god's maenads and satyrs.

It is in this context that the square of tapestry weave exhibited as number 74 can be interpreted. In the center of the textile there is a depiction of Leda together with her lover Jupiter, shown in the form of a swan. This scene is encircled by a rich border containing, among other motifs, a piping shepherd, boys carrying game animals or bowls, lions, birds, and foliage. In short, everything around the central circle calls to mind the riches of the land, while the scene with the swan in the center signifies fertility and the element of water; as in the great dish from Mildenhall, a central medallion emblematic of water is surrounded by motifs associated with the land. The mythological scene on the textile takes its place as part of a composition invoking earthly prosperity, but not necessarily as evidence of pagan beliefs on the part of the owner or the weaver.

Christian Designs

The Power of Words

Among the finds from the excavation of the Early Christian sanctuary at Beišan, in Palestine, was a large bronze pendant bearing a long inscription beginning as

Fig. 17. London, British Museum,
Great Silver Dish from Mildenhall.
Ocean and Bacchic Scenes.

17

follows: "Holy names and symbols and dread characters protect from all dangers the man or woman who carries your august divine powers" (Bonner, p. 215). This invocation shows that letters and words (that is, "Holy names" and "dread characters") were equal partners with designs ("symbols") in providing safety from malevolent powers. Accordingly, the Early Christian house and its contents could be protected either by inscriptions alone, or by designs, or by both working together. The door lintel of a house from Herakêh in Syria shows how an inscription on its own could secure a dwelling; it reads: "Our Lord Jesus Christ, the son, the Logos of God, dwells here; let no evil enter" (Dölger, I, p. 244).

Protecting words could take the form of magical incantations, such as the formulae listed in the *Testament of Solomon* as specific defenses against specific demons. A householder plagued by domestic disputes, for example, could learn from the *Testament* that such quarrels were caused by a spirit named Katanikotael; he or she could send the demon packing by writing out these words: "Angel, Iae, Ieo, Sabaoth, shut up Katanikotael" (McCown, p. 54*).

Among the popular invocations on surviving amulets are IAŌ, for "Jehova" (nos. 132 and 135), SABAŌTH, for "Sabaoth" (nos. 134 and 135), and AGIE, for "Holy" (no. 132). A very common appeal, on all types of objects, is the formula KYRIE BOĒTHEI TON PHOROUNTA, or "Lord, help the wearer." Variants of this plea can be found on belt buckles, pins, rings in gold and in bronze, combs, and even woven into garments. Sometimes the request is directed to Michael, as in the amulet that is number 135 in the exhibition, or to the Theotokos (Mother of God), as in the case of the silver seal stamp, number 33. On other objects, it is not the source of the benefit but the benefit itself that is specified. We have seen above, for example, that a stamp used for sealing containers in the marketplace may be inscribed HYGEIA, or "Health" (no. 40).

The Cross

In a homily which was once attributed to the church father St. John Chrysostom there is the following triumphant paean to the sign of the cross:

> No imperial crown can adorn a head in such a manner as the cross, which is in all the world more prized. This thing had lately been cause of horror to all, but now its image is so much sought after by all, that it is found everwhere, among rulers, among subjects, among women and men, among virgins and matrons, among slaves and freemen. . . . One can see [the cross] celebrated everywhere, in houses, in marketplaces, in deserts, in streets, on mountains, in valleys, in hills, on the sea, in boats, on islands, on beds, on clothes, on weapons, in chambers, at banquets, on silverware, on objects in gold, in pearls, in wall paintings, on the bodies of much-burdened animals, on bodies besieged by demons, in war, in peace, by day, by night, in parties of luxurious livers, in brotherhoods of ascetics; so much do all now seek after

this miraculous gift, this ineffable grace. (*Contra Judaeos et Gentiles*, 9)

Although this passage may sound like rhetorical exaggeration, it was, in fact, nothing more than the truth; in the Early Christian period, the sign of the cross was indeed found everywhere, and especially at home. Crosses, for example, protected the structure of the house itself, particularly at doors and windows where evil might easily come in if these openings were left unguarded. As we know both from texts and from surviving buildings, such crosses often literally replaced images of pagan deities which had previously served the same purpose; the old protectors were hacked out of the stone, and the cross was carved in their place (Engemann, 1975, pp. 44-45, pl. 15a-b). John Chrysostom himself recommended the marking of entrances in this manner: "Therefore we depict it [the cross] with much zeal both on houses and on walls and windows, . . . for this is indeed the sign of our safety" (*In Matthaeum Homilia LIV*, 4). It should be noted that the church father says that the cross is merely the *sign* of our safety, not its cause; he does not impute any magical qualities to the cross itself. For many people in the Early Christian period, however, the cross acquired the supernatural powers associated with non-Christian designs, such as the knots, the much-suffering eye, and the dotted circles discussed above. The power of the cross to protect against evil forces is explicitly stated by inscriptions accompanying this sign on the door lintels of houses in Syria. For example, the following text was written on the lintel of a house at Sabbâ, dated 547: " + The Lord will protect the comings in and the goings out of this house; for as long as the cross is set in front of it the evil eye will not have power" (Dölger, p. 247). An inscription on another lintel, from El-Bardouné in Syria, states: "Where the cross is set in front, envy has no power" (Engemann, 1975, p. 42). These and similar inscriptions reveal clearly the apotropaic function of the crosses carved over the entrances of Early Christian buildings, such as an early seventh-century structure at Anasartha in Syria (fig. 20). In some cases crosses were attached to doors in the form of handles (Baltimore, p. 74, no. 316).

Public buildings as well as domestic structures were protected by crosses. One of the most telling examples of the faith put in this sign's powers to secure a building comes from the city of Kourion in Cyprus, after it had been devastated by earthquakes. In the fifth century a certain Eustolios restored the city's baths and their annexes, declaring in an inscription on a mosaic floor (fig. 18): "Not by big stones, not by firm iron and tawny bronze, and not even by steel are these buildings girded, but, by the much-invoked signs of Christ" (Engemann, 1975, p. 47). These words refer to the common practice of ancient builders to fasten masonry blocks with hidden metal clamps. Now a further, more effective means of stabilizing the building has been found: the floor that bears the inscription displays large crosses framed by interlace, the latter also being a protective device, if of a non-Christian kind.

Not only did the sign of the cross guard the houses of the early Christians, but it also defended their persons. Some people crossed themselves on their foreheads, a practice which was described as a protection from harm by Christian writers such as Cyril of Alexandria, who died in the fifth century, and James of Sarûg, who died in the sixth. Both authors related the

19

Fig. 18. Kourion, Baths of Eustolius,
Floor Mosaic.

custom to the signing of the Hebrews' doorposts with the blood of the lamb, to keep God's people safe (Reine, p. 189). John Chrysostom said that marking the sign of the cross on the face with one's finger would prevent any of the impure demons from coming near (*In Matthaeum homilia LIV*, 4). Saints, the holy doctors, would effect cures by means of the cross. Nicholas of Sion, for example, a holy man who lived in the sixth century, cured a blind man by anointing his eyes with the sign of the cross, using oil taken from the lamp that burned before the shrine of St. Theodore at Diolko in Egypt (Ševčenko, p. 58). To a hostile observer, such as the apostate Emperor Julian, such practices smacked of superstition. "The sum of their theology," he said of the Christians, "consists of these two things: whistling to keep away the demons, and making the sign of the cross on their foreheads" (*Epistula*, 79; Cochrane, p. 268).

Many people in the Early Christian period wore crosses, as they do today. This practice was not always to the liking of the church authorities, who, like the pagan Julian, were sensitive to superstition. St. Jerome complained of the "superstitious little women" who by wearing cross-relics showed more religious zeal than good sense (*Commentaria in Evangelium S. Matthaei*, XXIII, 6). Number 90 in this exhibition, a gold necklace hung with a jeweled cross as well as two hexagonal cases for relics or amulets, demonstrates how crosses in jewelry, like those on the entrances to houses, could have an apotropaic function. Such pectoral crosses could be in a variety of materials: gold, as in numbers 90 and 92; bronze, as in numbers 91 and 93; or, for the very impecunious, even plain wood, as in number 94. The cross also appeared on other items of jewelry, such as earrings (no. 95), buckles (no. 100), and rings (nos. 83 and 87). As John Chrysostom noted, the sign was woven into clothing (no. 76). It was also used as a protective device in the workplace. Traders, for example, stamped the stoppers of jars with crosses to protect the contents from harm (Badawy, pp. 345-46, fig. 5.52). Weavers used combs marked with crosses to beat down the wefts of their textiles (e.g., Newark Museum, inv. no. 84.41). Crosses ensured health and safety in the kitchen and dining room; bronze strainers used to remove impurities had a pattern of crosses marked in their perforations (e.g., Indiana University Art Museum, Bloomington, inv. no. 70.71.10), and spoons used for domestic dining had crosses marked upon them (M. M. Mango, pp. 216-18, figs. 49-55). Finally, as will be seen from several examples in this exhibition, this all-pervasive shining sign of safety and salvation frequently marked household lamps (nos. 12, 15, 16, and 19).

In some designs the power of the cross was combined with the power of words. A common device, for example, was a cross-shaped acrostic composed of the words PHŌS and ZŌE, or "Light" and "Life," after the saying of Jesus: "I am the light of the world: he who follows me will not walk in darkness, but will have the light of life" (John 8:12). This acrostic is one of the designs that protects the entrances to sixth-century houses in Syria (Dölger, pp. 247-48). In this exhibition, it can be seen on the bezel of a silver ring (no. 86). It was also engraved into other items of jewelry, such as belt buckles (Dalton, p. 115, no. 586), and was woven into textiles (Brooklyn Museum, inv. no. 15.440).

Another sign combining holy letters with the force of the cross was the Chi Rho (✼), the monogram formed of the first two letters of the name of Christ, which can be seen on the discus of the clay lamp shown as number 18 in this exhibition. Often the monogram took the form of a Latin cross, with the upright arm in the form of a Rho (similar to a Latin "P"), as can be seen in number 19, a clay lamp from North Africa. The Christian monogram appears not only on such domestic furnishings as lamps, but also on instruments used for personal hygiene, such as a remarkable silver object from the mid-fourth-century treasure found at Kaiseraugst in Switzerland (fig. 19), which was a combined toothpick and ear cleaner (Cahn and Kaufmann-Heinimann, pp. 122-32, pls. 27, 30). The function of the Christogram here was to be not only a sign of the owner's faith, but also, perhaps, a guarantee of good health.

Often in the domestic art of the Early Christians, the cross was associated with other, non-Christian devices. We have already seen how the powers of the knot and the cross were united in the so-called Solomonic knot. In addition, other forms of interlace were used as frames for crosses, as in the floor mosaic at Kourion referred to above, or woven into cross-shaped patterns, as can be seen in a roundel of tapestry weave in this exhibition (no. 76), which features a complicated pattern of interlace based upon a grid of seven crosses.

Dotted circles and concentric circles were frequently combined with crosses. On wooden combs, dotted circles were arranged in cruciform patterns (e.g., Rutschowscaya, p. 29, no. 15). Concentric circles often were incised into pectoral crosses, especially the cheaper varieties in wood and bronze. On some examples the circles surrounded jewels or glass inlays, which themselves were invested with apotropaic powers (e.g., no. 91 in this exhibition). On other pectoral crosses, the circles appear to take the place of jewels (e.g., no. 93), as we have seen. Occasionally the circles flank a cross, as on the lintel at Anasartha, Syria (fig. 20), mentioned earlier. Here the design is accompanied by the following inscription: "+ When we engrave your cross, O Christ the God . . . we escape every form of wickedness" (Engemann, 1975, pp. 42-43).

Fig. 19. Kaiseraugst, Römermuseum, Silver Toothpick and Ear Cleaner.

Fig. 20. Anasartha, Door Lintel.
Inscription, Cross, and Circles.

Since the two circles on the lintel are not inscribed within the cross but are engraved in the fields on either side of its upper arm, they cannot be cyphers for jewels, but are more likely to be independent apotropaic signs. A similar design, of a cross flanked by concentric or dotted circles, appears on certain pilgrims' flasks made of terra-cotta, which were originally filled with substances such as oil or dust taken from holy shrines and worn as amulets around the neck.

Christian Creatures

Some subjects drawn from the natural world, such as fish, lambs, and doves, had a special potential for Christian interpretation. Their Christian meanings overlaid their more general role as signifiers of wealth and prosperity, or, in some cases, as apotropaic devices.

We have seen that fish often represented water in compositions evoking the fertility of the earth. In some parts of the Roman world, especially North Africa, they also took on an apotropaic function, which continues in Tunisia to this day (Engemann, 1975, p. 33, figs, 11d., 14c; Maloney, pp. 70-71). For Christians, the image of the fish could have several, sometimes contradictory meanings. Fish, for example, could refer to the role of Christ and his apostles who rescued humanity from the abyss of mortality: "Follow me and I will make you become fishers of men" (Mark 1:17). According to this interpretation, the watery element inhabited by the Christian fish was without grace. A totally different interpretation, however, could be suggested by the image of the Living Water described in the ninth verse of Ezekiel 47: "wherever the river goes every living creature which swarms will live, and there will be very many fish . . . so everything will live where the river goes." Here the fish are able to prosper (Drewer, p. 534). But the most important signification of the fish for Christians was undoubtedly the Greek word for "fish," ICHTHYS, which the Early Christians took as an acronym for "Iēsous CHristos THeou Yios Sotēr," or "Jesus Christ Son of God, Savior." The word ICHTHYS, with its letters sometimes arranged in the form of a cross, was used as an apotropaic device to protect access to holy places in churches (Kitzinger, 1970, p. 645, figs. 2, 4), and was also frequently carved over the entrances of private houses. A stone lintel from the door of a house in Kerrātin in Syria, for example, has the following inscription: "One God. The building of Silvanus was erected through ICHTHYS" (Dölger, p. 249). Another door lintel from Syria implies that the sacred acronym had the power to restore health to the house's inhabitants. It states: "Doctor and Deliverer from ills, Jesus the Christ, the God over all. ICHTHYS" (Dölger, p. 253).

On these door lintels the fish is evoked only by means of letters; its actual form is not portrayed. However, fish were engraved as symbols on Christian jewelry, as we know from a famous passage in the writings of the early church father Clement of Alexandria who listed the fish among the motifs he sanctioned for engraving upon signet rings (*Paedagogus*, 3, 11). Like the word ICHTHYS inscribed on the lintels, the symbol of the fish seems to have been invested with the power to protect from illness, for on one surviving bronze ring it appears with the inscription "Solomon guard health" (Vikan, 1984, p. 80, fig. 21).

The potential for multiple meanings of fish imagery in the art of the Early Christian period raises difficult issues of interpretation. For example, how was the user of the iron frying-pan, number 65 in our exhibition, intended to interpret the fish engraved upon its handle? The most obvious answer would be to see the fish not as a Christian symbol, but more directly as an illustration of the dinner. "And for God's sake," wrote a starving Christian official from his post in Egypt to some anonymous correspondent, "please send me some fish, either to keep or for the frying pan, since I cannot get it here; for the fishermen of this place have sent everything to the Count in Antinoopolis" (Barns and Zilliacus, pp. 109-11). The fourth-century silver treasure from Kaiseraugst contained a pair of fish-shaped oval dishes, each engraved with a fish upon its bottom, and each evidently designed for seafood (Cahn and Kaufmann-Heinimann, pp. 165-74, pls. 71 and 73). In such cases there was no need to look for Christian meanings (Engemann, 1972, p. 167). On the other hand, there would be nothing to prevent a Christian who looked at the designs from being reminded of the well-known Christian symbolism of the fish; and since at least one of the objects from the Kaiseraugst burial was marked with an explicitly Christian motif (the Christogram on the toothpick illustrated in fig. 19), such a possibility of religious interpretation cannot be ruled out.

Besides the fish, other creatures depicted on domestic objects in this exhibition had a special potential for Christian significance. Images of sheep were impressed into the bottoms of pottery bowls and plates (nos. 61 and 62), and hanging lamps were fashioned in the shapes of doves (no. 13). Although we know that silver and even gold doves were suspended in churches, the dove-shaped lamps made in humbler materials such as clay were probably for domestic use. For Christians, the sheep could bring to mind the Lamb of God, as well as the flock of the Lamb (see no. 59, a bowl decorated with a shepherd and his flock of rams), while the dove could recall the Holy Spirit. However, not all Christians would necessarily wish to see these creatures as representing one or another person of the Trinity. There were those who objected to finding the Holy Ghost portrayed as a dove, even in churches. For example, John Diakrinomenos, a writer of the late fifth century, said that "it is an infantile act to represent the most-holy and venerable Ghost in the likeness of a dove, seeing that the text of the Gospel teaches not that the Holy Ghost became a dove, but that it was once seen in the form of a dove. . . ." (trans. C. Mango, p. 43). Another Christian who was uncomfortable with the idea of suspending doves as symbols of the Holy Ghost was Severus, the patriarch of Antioch between 512 and 518, who was accused by his opponents of melting down the gold and silver doves that hung above the fonts and altars, "saying that the Holy Ghost should not be designated in the form of a dove" (C. Mango, p. 44).

If it was controversial to see the dove as a Christian symbol, this can hardly be said of the vine, for the use of this image had been sanctioned by Christ himself. The vine also was a symbol that had been widespread in pre-Christian art, and that acquired new meanings with the advent of the new religion. First and foremost, the vine was associated, as we have seen, with wine and autumnal fruitfulness, whose pagan deity was Bacchus. When a grapevine appears upon a jar, such as number 55 in this exhibition, there is probably little need to search for further meanings. On other household objects, however, such as the clay lamp (no. 19) where we find a grapevine filling the arms of a cross, there can be little doubt of the plant's Christian significance. As in the case of the fish, the potential range of meanings provided by Christian scriptures was quite wide. Not only could the vine signify the Eucharist, but it was used by Christ as an image for his own person (John 15:1) and for his people (John 15:5), while the vineyard became the Kingdom of God (Matthew 21:33-43).

Saints

Portraits of saints are found with some frequency in Early Christian domestic art, in contexts showing that these images possessed the same kinds of powers as crosses and other protective designs. A passage from St. John Chrysostom's encomium of Meletios, the saintly Bishop of Antioch, reveals how widely such images of a holy man could be employed, and also how pictures could reinforce the effect of names. John Chrysostom declares that the citizens of Antioch were not satisfied with calling their children after their deceased bishop, but: ". . . what you have done in respect of names, you did also with regard to his image. Indeed, many persons have delineated that holy image on the bands of their rings and on the reliefs and on bowls and on the walls of their rooms and everywhere, so they might not only hear that holy name, but also see his bodily form everywhere, thus having a double consolation after his departure from this life" (*Homilia encomiastica in Meletium*, 1).

The church father terms the ubiquitous appearance of Meletios's portraits a "consolation," but for other Christians the purpose of such images was clearly apotropaic. We are told, for example, by the historian Theodoretus that depictions of St. Symeon the Elder, the fifth-century stylite saint who mortified himself by living for forty-two years on top of a column, were placed at the entrances to workshops in Rome in order to protect them (*Religiosa historia*, XXVI; Kitzinger, 1954, p. 94). Such portraits may have resembled the two tokens of St. Symeon the Younger exhibited here (nos. 126 and 127). St. Symeon the Younger was an ascetic of the sixth century who resided on top of a column on the "Miraculous Mountain," near Antioch in Syria, in imitation of St. Symeon the Elder. His tokens, which were made of earth taken from around the base of the column, depict the saint on top of the shaft, between angels and supplicants. These souvenirs were impressed with the image of the holy man to serve as *eulogiai*, or blessings, for the pilgrims to take away. Such *eulogiai* were endowed with the holy power of the saint himself, so that they could work cures and protect from harm, even when the beneficiaries were far away from the saint's person (Vikan, 1982, pp. 27-39). Some tokens from the Miraculous Mountain, such as our number 128, depict the Virgin Mary rather than St. Symeon; she was portrayed because she was invoked along with the stylite in appeals for miraculous healings. The purpose of the image in each case was to focus the prayers and desires of the supplicant (Vikan, 1984, p. 70).

The objects displayed in this exhibition help to bear out the truth of John Chrysostom's claim that images of saints were to be found on a wide variety of household objects. The Early Christian writer specifically mentions bowls, and in our exhibition there is a fine pottery bowl bearing the image of a standing saint holding a cross (no. 60).

Images of the saints also appeared on spoons. A remarkable example is a silver spoon in the Cleveland Museum of Art depicting St. Paul in the guise of an athlete standing naked and victorious in the arena, his palm of victory in his hand and his winner's wreath crowning his head (fig. 21). The imagery of this portrait of the Christian martyr as athlete of Christ was suggested by St. Paul himself: ". . . in a race all the runners compete, but only one receives the prize. . . . Every athlete exercises self-control in all things. They do it to receive a perishable wreath, but we an imperishable" (1 Corinthians 9:24-25; Salomonson, 1979, pp. 80-81).

As John Chrysostom stated, the early Christians often evoked the saints by their names, rather than by their portraits. An example of naming may be found on number 63 in our exhibition, a silver spoon which is inscribed PETROS on the stem of the handle. It is possible that this was originally one of a set of twelve spoons, each marked with the name of a different apostle (Milojčić, pp. 113-27; Engemann, 1972, p. 168). Such sets of spoons were used in domestic dining rooms, in memory of the Last Supper. On some surviving sets the name of each apostle is preceded by the formula "Blessing of . . . ," indicating that the blessing of the apostles was sought on the food (M. M. Mango, pp. 217-18, figs. 49-55).

Images of saints can also be found on *ampullae*, the little flasks that pilgrims took home with them from holy shrines, filled with dust, water, or oil. On these objects, the portrait served to remind the traveler of his or her journey and also to reinforce the efficacy of the contents to protect the bearer from sickness or harm. Number 130 in this exhibition is a flask that once contained dust from the tomb of St. John at Ephesus. On one side it depicts the seated Evangelist writing; on the other, a standing figure, probably representing the same saint, is shown holding a book. Number 131 originally contained a substance from the shrine of St. Menas in Egypt, either oil from the lamps that burned over his grave, or wonder-working water. The saint is shown standing in an attitude of prayer between two camels, a composition perhaps copied from a relief that could be seen by the pilgrims who visited his underground tomb (Weitzmann, 1979, pp. 567, 573-76). On some of the Menas ampullas, the saint is encircled by an inscription reading: "We receive the blessing of St. Menas" (Dalton, 1901, p. 154, pl. 32).

The ampullas were provided with holes so that they could be worn on a cord around the neck. Sometimes the clothes worn by the early Christians were embellished with figures of saints, either as single figures, or in compositions such as the "holy rider," which will be discussed below.

The Holy Rider

A motif found with great frequency in Early Christian art, especially on objects from Egypt, is that of a mounted horseman killing a foe (fig. 22). In a general sense, this image signified power and swiftness of succor, the horse being

Fig. 21. Cleveland Museum of Art,
Silver Spoon.
St. Paul as Athlete of Christ.

Fig. 22. Amulet from Smyrna.
Holy Rider and Female Demon.

25

associated with both wealth and speed (Perdrizet, 1922, p. 12). The motif of the victorious equestrian had appeared in pagan Egyptian art under various guises: the Thracian rider-god, Heron; the god Horus, who was portrayed on horseback spearing a crocodile, in a composition that seems to foreshadow medieval paintings of St. George killing the dragon; and the dwarf god Bes, guardian against evil spirits and protector of women in childbirth, who was sometimes shown mounted on a rearing horse (Parlasca, pp. 19-27, pls. 10, 13). The image of the conquering rider was also associated with rulers, such as Alexander the Great, who is depicted on a fragment of Egyptian weaving in the Textile Museum of Washington, D.C., as an armed warrior with two boys holding a wreath over his head (Vienna, p. 195, pl. 6). Some Roman coins of the second century depicted the emperor as a horseman spearing an enemy lying on the ground (Bonner, p. 210). A similar device appeared on Byzantine coins issued in the fifth and sixth centuries, on which an emperor was shown holding a shield embossed with a rider spearing a prostrate foe, indicating that the image had the power to protect both the ruler and his realms from danger (Wroth, pls. 1-19).

The rider could protect an individual as well as a whole empire, for the motif is often found on amulets during the Early Christian period. Frequently the equestrian is labeled "Solomon" in reference to the beliefs in that king's power over demons (Vikan, 1984, pp. 79-80, figs. 19-20). On several charms, the foe of the horseman is a bare-breasted woman, who may be identifed as Alabasdria or Abyzou. According to the *Testament of Solomon*, she was responsible for causing the death of infants during childbirth (McCown, p. 43*). Several of the amulets are cut in haematite, a black stone that, when powdered, becomes red; this material was associated with the healthy functioning of the womb, since it was invested with magical powers to stop hemorrhages (Vikan, 1984, p. 81).

Although several of the church fathers condemned the magic of Solomon (Viaud, p. 111), in the popular mind the Jewish king came to be associated with the Christian saints. The assimilation of Solomon to the saints is revealed clearly by the inscriptions on some of the rider amulets: "Flee O Detested One!" declares one, "Solomon, Sisinnios, Sisinnarios Pursue You." This legend appears beneath an image of a mounted warrior with a halo around his head: he pierces the head of a bare-breasted woman lying on the ground beneath the hooves of his galloping horse (fig. 22). The top of the rider's spear is marked with a cross (Perdrizet, 1922, p. 27, fig. 7). The stories about the two saints invoked on the amulet, Sisinnios and Sisinnarios, were similar in character to those attached to Solomon. According to one medieval text, St. Sisinnios and his two brothers succeeded in capturing the demon Gyllou and forcing her to restore to life their sister's seven infants, whom she had killed. The three saints, like Solomon, made the demon reveal her twelve-and-a-half names, which included Abyzou and Myia, or "fly." Any house, said the demon, where these twelve-and-a-half names were written, together with those of the saints, would be protected from her visits. As for the name Myia, this had been given to her because she had the ability to change herself into a fly in order to gain entry into houses. The Sisinnarios of the amulet's inscription can probably be identified with one of Sisinnios's brothers (Perdrizet, 1922, pp. 16-17).

Fig. 23. Bawit, Monastery of St. Apollo. St. Sisinnios and Alabasdria.

On other rider amulets, St. Sisinnios is invoked alone, as he was on a famous wall painting of the sixth or seventh century at the Monastery of St. Apollo at Bawit in Egypt (fig. 23). In this painting a horseman with a halo, identified by an inscription as Sisinnios, was shown piercing a bare-chested female demon labeled "Alabasdria" (Clédat, pp. 80-81, pl. 55-56). On many amulets, including all of those shown in this exhibition, the horseman is unidentified. For example, in the case of our number 135, a Syrian or Palestinian amulet with the "much-suffering eye" on one side and a rider on the other, the inscription above the horseman merely reads NIKŌN, or "Victorious." In such a case, the wearer could call any or all of the powerful riders to her aid. However, several of the images on other amulets have features which clearly identify them as Christian. Number 134, for example, a bronze medallion, shows the rider with a cross-tipped spear, which he uses to transfix a demon who has the body of a lioness and the head of a woman. A bronze amulet, number 136, also shows a rider with a cross-tipped spear. Here, the horseman's enemy is too indistinct to be recognized, but on number 133 in our exhibition the demon

27

under the horse's feet can be distinguished as a snake with a human head; she can possibly be identified with the "daughter of Alabasdria," who is shown in this form in the fresco at Bawit mentioned above.

The rider was not confined to amulets, for he appeared on many other objects of domestic apparel, such as rings or clothing (Schiemenz, p. 113). He may be seen, for example, engraved on the bezel of the bronze ring, number 84 in this exhibition, and he appears repeated in the medallions of a tunic, our number 68. Often the rider appears without a foe, as in the case of the design cut into the soapstone seal that is number 34 in the exhibition. Such images are not specific enough to be identified as any particular saint or hero. They are generalized to the extent that the user or the wearer could read into the design the positive connotations of all possible horsemen, including not only the holy riders who protected from evil, but also hunters who, as we have seen, were associated with plenty and prosperity.

Biblical Scenes

The last category of Christian designs, scenes that were derived from the Bible, might seem the furthest removed from the magic that permeated so much of the domestic imagery of the Early Christian home. But even the biblical subjects that appeared on items of apparel or jewelry often took on the nature of charms. For example, figure 24 illustrates one of a group of gold marriage rings of the seventh century. Each of these rings bears on its bezel portraits of the married couple with Christ and the Virgin, and on the seven remaining facets of its octagonal hoop a sequence of seven scenes from the life of Christ, as recorded in the Gospels (Vikan, 1984, pp. 83-84). On the ring illustrated here, these scenes are: the angel announcing Christ's birth to Mary, the visit of Mary to her cousin Elizabeth before Christ's birth, the nativity of Christ, his presentation in the temple, his baptism, his crucifixion, and his appearance to the women after the Resurrection. Each scene is, of necessity, depicted in a highly condensed form as a pictograph, reduced to the most essential figures. On the edge of the bezel there is an inscription reading "Lord help thy servants, Peter and Theodote" (Ross, 1965, pp. 58-59, pl. 43). This plea suggests that the life of the Savior is here invoked in order to protect the wearer of the ring (Kitzinger, 1980, pp. 151-52). The reader will recall how the octagonal shape itself was considered to be a guarantee of protection from harm, especially during childbirth (Vikan, 1987, p. 39).

Another piece of evidence which suggests that the Gospel imagery on the rings was intended to be apotropaic comes from a group of silver armbands, dating to the sixth and seventh centuries. They depict similarly condensed episodes from the life of Christ together with motifs of a frankly magical character, such as the Chnoubis. An armband in Cairo, for example, depicts the Annunciation, the Nativity, the Baptism, the Crucifixion, the women visiting the empty tomb, and the Ascension, as well as a rayed Chnoubis with the amuletic invocation "One God the Victorious One" (Vikan, 1984, p. 75, fig. 8). The Chnoubis, as a protector in childbirth, appropriately follows the Nativity in the sequence. Cycles of scenes from the life of Christ were also depicted on the metal ampullas which pilgrims brought home from the Holy Land and wore around their necks as amulets (fig. 25). On these ampullas the individual scenes

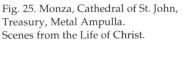

Fig. 25. Monza, Cathedral of St. John,
Treasury, Metal Ampulla.
Scenes from the Life of Christ.

Fig. 26. Toronto, Royal Ontario Museum,
Bronze Mirror.

were set within circles, and the circles were themselves arranged in a circle around the body of the flask—a circle of circles. The pattern has close parallels in some Roman and early Byzantine mirrors (e.g., Hayes, 1984, pp. 189-91, figs. 319-20; Colt, p. 61, pl. XXVI, 10-11). These mirrors were decorated not with concentric circles, like number 119 in this exhibition, but with a ring of circles (see fig. 26). The resemblance to the flasks may not be entirely fortuitous, given that the mirror, as we have seen, had apotropaic powers.

Fig. 27. Washington, D.C., Dumbarton Oaks
Collection, Gold Encolpium.
Virgin and Child between Angels;
Nativity; Adoration of the Magi.

On some domestic objects only one or two scenes from the life of Christ were depicted. A small gold locket of the seventh century in the British Museum, for example, which probably contained relics or a *eulogia* of the medical saints Cosmas and Damian, displays on its lid nielloed scenes of the birth of Christ and the three Magi adoring the Child, while on its back is inscribed: "The secure safety and averting of all the evils" (Dalton, 1901, pp. 46-47, no. 284). The nature of the evils is suggested by the saints' avocation as doctors, and by the locket's octagonal shape, a form associated, as we have seen, with healthy childbirth. The same two scenes, the Nativity and the Adoration of the Magi, appear beneath an image of the enthroned Virgin and Child on the front of a magnificent sixth-century gold encolpium, or pendant, from the highest level of society, now in the Dumbarton Oaks collection (fig. 27). Here, too, the scenes were accompanied by an invocation: "Christ, our God, help us." The reverse of this pendant shows Christ's baptism (Ross, 1965, pp. 33-35, pl. 28).

A bronze ring from a humbler social stratum, number 89 in our exhibition, is engraved with the visit of the two Marys to the tomb of Christ, a subject which also appeared on the amuletic armband described above. Although in this case the function of the imagery is not specified by an inscription, it was probably intended to serve both as a reminder of the wearer's faith in salvation and as a physical protection. Another scene from the life of Christ having an apotropaic function is the Entry into Jerusalem, for here Christ appeared in the guise of a triumphant holy rider. Psalm 118 was shouted by the crowd on that occasion to invoke the Lord as a helper and a savior. The subject

29

Fig. 28. Chicago, Field Museum,
Tunic Fragments with Panels of
Tapestry Weave.
Scenes from the Life of Christ.

appears on some earthen tokens, such as number 129 in the exhibition, which are of a type often used medicinally (see p. 200).

The early Christians also displayed scenes from the Bible on their clothes. We know that episodes from the life of Christ were woven into garments as early as the fourth century, because of a remarkable complaint made by Asterius, the Bishop of Amaseia in northern Turkey. He attacks those who

> . . . devise for themselves, their wives and children gay-colored dresses decorated with thousands of figures. . . . When they come out in public dressed in this fashion, they appear like painted walls to those they meet. . . . The more religious among rich men and women, having picked out the story of the Gospels, have handed it over to their weavers—I mean our Christ together with all His disciples, and each one of the miracles the way it is related. You may see the wedding of Galilee with the water jars, the paralytic carrying his bed on his shoulders, the blind man healed by means of clay, the woman with an issue of blood seizing [Christ's] hem, the sinful woman falling at the feet of Jesus, Lazarus coming back to life from his tomb. In doing this they consider themselves to be religious and to be wearing clothes that are agreeable to God. (*Homilia I;* trans. C. Mango, pp. 50-51)

The first point to note in this passage is the statement that clothes decorated in such a fashion were felt to be "agreeable to God"; that is, by wearing them, people hoped to win God's favor. Second, with only one exception, the scenes listed by Asterius are miracles. It is clear from his description, even though he does not say it specifically, that the purpose of the imagery on the clothing was similar to that of the scenes on the rings and the bracelets, to protect from sickness and misfortune and to win good health. Such a conclusion is confirmed by an examination of surviving tunics decorated with images of the life of Christ. The scenes are often highly condensed, like those on the jewelry, and the individual subjects are frequently repeated several times on the same garment. The reduction and the repetition of the imagery shows that the scenes did not serve to instruct, like the pictures in a book, but rather suggests that they were charms.

One of the best-preserved pieces of clothing with Gospel scenes is a tunic in the Field Museum in Chicago, dating to the seventh or eighth centuries (figs. 28 and 29). The individual scenes on the tunic are hard to read, but among them can be recognized the Annunciation, the Nativity (fig. 29; the scene, at the center of the *clavus* strip, is reduced to show only the Child lying in his crib flanked by the heads of the ox and the ass), the Adoration of the Magi (showing only one of the three wise men kneeling before the Virgin and Child), and the Baptism (in the roundels at the bottom of fig. 28). Of these scenes, both the Adoration of the Magi and the Baptism were repeated at least twice.

The selection of subjects on the tunic preserved in the Field Museum is similar to that which appears on the sixth- and seventh-century

jewelry described above. Another textile, a *clavus* strip from a tunic, now in the National Museum at Copenhagen (fig. 30), is interesting in that it preserves the subjects listed by Asterius of Amaseia, namely a series of miracle scenes. The cures are depicted one above the other on the narrow band, and are, as usual, hard to read on account of their reduction and lack of detail. In two of them we can recognize the haloed figure of Christ standing behind a pallet and gesturing to a prostrate figure who lies on the bed. In another scene Christ stands beside a figure who kneels before him with outstretched hands.

We should mention one other context in which biblical scenes occurred within the house, the decoration of bowls. In the fourth century, North African potters produced bowls embellished with impressed reliefs depicting scenes from the life of Christ and from the Old Testament, such as our number 58, which portrays Abraham sacrificing his son Isaac. The Sacrifice of Isaac, a foreshadowing of the Crucifixion, was considered to be a sign of the saving power of Christ. Often these scenes have the same reduced character as those on the later jewelry and textiles. These bowls, which were probably imitations of more precious vessels in silver, were produced in sets, with a different subject appearing on each piece in a series (Salomonson, 1979, pp. 26-41).

Conclusion

The most important conclusion to be drawn from the material presented above is that the word "decorative," in its twentieth-century sense, does not adequately describe many of the designs found on the domestic arts of the early Christians. Indeed, the aspects of these objects that may strike the modern viewer as completely unfunctional—the octagonal shape of the hoop of a ring, for example, or a composition of concentric circles incised into a comb—may have been intended to play an important role in the world of spirits and demons, a world which, to the early Christian, was ultimately more real and potentially more threatening than the material world.

This exhibition also suggests that the house and its contents present a very different view of art from the one conveyed by Early Christian churches. At home, the imagery was for the most part derived from popular culture, and at all levels of society there was a heavy infusion of magic (Russell, pp. 544-45). When Christian themes appear, the emphasis was not on instruction or dogma, as it often was in ecclesiastical buildings, but on protection and the ensuring of prosperity. That is not to say that there was no interchange of imagery between the official and unofficial spheres. Occasionally a domestic object displays a composition originating in the monumental art of churches, such as the scene of Christ in his majesty appearing at the top of the amuletic medallion that is number 134 in our exhibition. Here we see in miniature a scene better known from the apses of Early Christian churches, such as those of the Latomos monastery at Thessaloniki, or the Monastery of St. Apollo at Bawit, namely Christ sitting enthroned in an oval aureole surrounded by the four beasts of the apocalyptic vision, the angel, the eagle, the lion, and the ox (Grabar, 1967, figs. 141, 186). More frequently, however, the influence went the other

Fig. 29. Chicago, Field Museum, Tunic with Panels of Tapestry Weave, Detail. The Nativity and Other Scenes from the Life of Christ.

way, and we find a penetration of church art by the magical and apotropaic imagery of the household. We have seen that knots and crosses were used in churches, set in floor mosaics or carved into stone screens, to protect the entrances to sanctuaries or to revered shrines. The church also assimilated other non-Christian motifs that were popular in the home, such as the personification of Earth. She appears, for example, in the center of a sixth-century mosaic floor in the nave of a church at Khirbat al-Makhāyyat in Jordan (fig. 12). Here the personification in the church is clearly labeled as GĒ, or "Earth," and, as on the domestic textiles, she takes the form of a bust wearing a richly adorned headdress and holding before her a crescent-shaped fold of cloth brimming with fruits (Maguire, 1987b, p. 223). She receives offerings of fruit-filled baskets proffered by two boys approaching on either side.

Such assimilation of popular imagery by the church was evidently the cause of some discomfort to those in authority. There is, for example, a passage in John Chrysostom's ninth homily on Genesis where the church father discusses humanity's relationship to the earth. The preacher says that the earth has been made our nurse and our mother. We feed from it, in every other way we have the benefit of it, and we return to it. It is our fatherland and our tomb. However, he warns, we should not regard the earth with too much reverence on account of its necessity and utility to us; we should not ascribe all of its benefits to the nature of the earth itself, but rather to the power of the Creator who made it (*In Genesim, Homilia IX, 2*). The tension in John Chrysostom's sermon, between gratitude to the earth and gratitude to its creator, is also felt in the composition of mosaics in churches. At Khirbat al-Makhāyyat, boys extend their arms to give fruits directly to the richly dressed central figure of Ge. Here the two boys seem to make their offerings of produce to Earth herself, rather than to God. It is as if the church wanted to assimilate to itself the power of the vernacular image of Earth and her fertility. In this mosaic the official and the popular levels of Early Christian art can be seen coming together.

In the exhibition we have recreated two worlds. One world is concrete and tangible: the house and its contents. The other world is invisible, and accessible only through the mind: the world of competing powers, good and evil, whose activities could be controlled by designs marked on many of the objects on display. Both of these worlds, seen and unseen, belonged to the same Early Christian culture, a culture that can still be explored through the skill, creativity, and imagination exhibited in its domestic art.

Fig. 30. Copenhagen, National Museum, Strip of Tapestry Weave from a Tunic. Miracle Scenes.

I. London, British Museum, Silver Wedding Casket of Projecta. Venus and the Bride Adjust Their Hair with the Aid of Mirrors.

II. Florence, Biblioteca Laurenziana, Cod. Plut. I, 56 (Rabbula Gospels), folio 9v.
St. John Writes by the Light of a Floor Lamp.

III. Trier, Imperial Palace, Ceiling Fresco. Lady with a Box of Jewels.

IV. Trier, Imperial Palace, Ceiling Fresco. Lady with a Mirror.

V. Vatican Library, Cod. lat. 3867 (Poems of Vergil), fol. 100v. Dido and Aeneas Served at Table.

VI. Vienna, Nationalbibliothek, Cod. theol. gr. 31 (Vienna Genesis), pict. 31.
Temptation of Joseph; Women Spinning.

40

VII. Vienna, Nationalbibliothek, Cod. theol. gr. 31 (Vienna Genesis), pict. 34.
Pharoah's Feast with the Butler Reinstated and the Baker Hanged.

VIII. New York, Metropolitan Museum of Art.
Painted Plaster Statuette of a Woman from Egypt.

Fig. 31. Ravenna, San Apollinare Nuovo, Mosaic, Detail.
The Palace of Theoderic.

44

Soft furnishings in this exhibition are represented by curtains and covers, none of them complete. Cushion covers, and fragments of what may have been coverlets or blankets, have been found in burials, where the head was sometimes supported with a cushion borrowed from domestic use. Curtains and wall hangings also have been at least partially preserved by being used to wrap the dead. In houses of the Early Christian period, curtains were used in doorways and other openings. As depicted in mosaics, curtains were hung by rings sewn along the top edge (fig. 31). The rings either fitted over rods, or were suspended from hooks above the openings. Bronze curtain hooks in the form of human fingers still survive (see no. 3). Luxurious houses may have had gilt-bronze curtain rods, or even silver ones, such as those recorded among the fittings of a small Egyptian church (Hardy, p. 173). Curtains were an important enough feature of life in the Early Christian period to be one of the items carried across the wilderness on camel and donkey back, by traders from Nessana in the Negev desert (Kraemer, pp. 253-58).

It is well to remember the ambivalent role of curtains: they were veils permeable by air and light, and at the same time they could provide welcome screening and concealment. A house with its curtained openings was a refuge from the crowds that town-dwellers must have had to brave in narrow streets and marketplaces every day. But although one of the curtain's functions was to provide protection, too dense a patterning of the fabric would have blocked the light. Doorway curtains had to be adaptable to the need for more or less daylight in the house, and more or less outdoor air. Often hung in pairs, they would have been used as screen doors are, when the outer door was open. Pictorial evidence suggests that they were also used instead of solid valves to close internal doorways or arches, and they probably partitioned the rooms of smaller houses (Gervers, pp. 70-73). The fashion for curtains in doorways reached even to the throne room of the imperial palace, where the doors were covered by hangings, and where the curtain before the throne was drawn back when a visitor was admitted (Corippus, *In laudem Iustini Augusti minoris*, III, 207, 255).

It was customary to knot the curtains when drawing back one or both sides to let in light and air (see fig. 31). Because the frequent handling of curtains made it desirable for them to be easily laundered, they were woven of linen, and were usually fairly lightweight, with ornamental repeat patterns tapestry-woven into them by means of a woolen weft (see nos. 1 and 2). In this respect, as in others, curtains should not be confused with wall hangings, which differ from them both in function and in design.

Wall hangings often portray tapestry-woven allegorical images across the whole surface, with scenes directed inward, to glorify the interior of the house. Curtains, on the other hand, with their plain linen weave providing most of the surface area, commonly carry outdoor or garden images structured in a different way. They refer to freedom from confinement, and to the sweetness of flowers and birdsong (see nos. 1 and 2), inviting the inhabitants of houses, even in crowded towns, to take pleasure in imagining these things year round, at the openings of the indoor space. The patterning of curtains with reminders of air and sunshine is a natural association with the role of open doorways in admitting more light than windows could. Even in wealthy households where glass panes might be used, the window embrasures were fitted with a heavy grid of rectangles, circles, or other shapes into which the small panes were inserted. House interiors must have been dark. The birds and flowers and outdoor themes on curtains released the viewer from confinement; "when the cage is opened, the birds fly out," wrote John Climacus, a monk at Mount Sinai (*Heavenly Ladder,* step 27). The small, discrete units of curtain patterns and their overall repeated design allowed the weavers to adapt their model to different dimensions, and the users to loop the whole curtain, or knot it, or hang it in various ways without disturbing the general effect of the visible parts of the textile design. A large-scale image unified by a pictorial framework would not be suitable for this kind of use, nor would the stiffer fabric of wall hangings.

On curtains, songbirds and colorful little parrots appear more often than the peacocks, eagles, game birds (such as ducks), or ibis and other long-legged water birds known elsewhere in the visual vocabulary of the time. On some curtains, the birds are distributed inside a simple rectangular grid (e.g., Royal Ontario Museum, inv. no. 910.125.2). This design recalls the gridded illustrations of birds which can be found in some natural history texts (Weitzmann, 1977, p. 71, pl. 20). The same pattern has another affinity: with ceiling decoration, when actual or painted rectangular coffers are filled with individual birds, as on the vault of a chapel inside the walls of Justinian's monastery at Mount Sinai (Forsyth and Weitzmann, pl. 135). Birds in a coffered grid on the ceiling refer to the sky, just as birds in a grid on a curtain refer to the open air.

On many curtains, blossoms are dispersed between the birds in one way or another. Usually pink or red with a green stem and calyx and white accents, they may take the form of short-stemmed buds, or of open blossoms seen from above. The sprigged blossoms on number 2 in our exhibit conflate the bud-shape with petals borrowed from the conventional five lobes of a vine leaf. As in nature, the color at the base of the bud is different from the color at the tip. The buds elsewhere may be only one lobe or two, like a schematic heart. Four heart-shaped petals similarly zoned with color make up the standard design for an open flower. This design has been varied, in our number 1, by the addition of lily-shaped fillers between the petals, to naturalize the flower with a deceptive asymmetry.

In Christian thought, the role of curtains to cover what is most precious is expressed in a sacred sense, where the veil of the Tabernacle is equated with the flesh of Christ (Hebrews 10:19-22; Cosmas Indicopleustes, *Topographia christiana,* V, 29), and Mary spins its wool at the moment his human body is conceived, an event commemorated as a domestic scene in visual representations. In daily life, the sense of exclusion created by curtains lent dignity and excitement. Even outdoors, the street decorations for state occasions in Constantinople reflected the social psychology of the use of curtains.

Arcades were closed with curtains to impress the crowds, and "covered
. . . over so that they might marvel the more." Corippus spells out the principle:
"that which is common is worthless: what is hidden stands out in honour. And
the more a thing is hidden, the more valuable it is considered. Then no one was
allowed to go beneath the closed arches, but the wide path in the middle was
open to all" (*In laudem Iustini Augusti minoris*, IV, 83-88; trans. Cameron, p. 112).

Inside the house, floor coverings varied from the mats
woven of rushes or palm fronds used to cover the dirt or stone floors of poorer
houses, to the multiple carpets covering the patterned pavement of a palace
floor (Corippus, *In laudem Iustini Augusti minoris*, III, 204). The basketwork mats
woven and sold by monks provided a humble source of labor and income for
the monasteries where they were made. Examples were found in the excavation
of the monastery of Epiphanius at Thebes, and are currently on view at the
Metropolitan Museum of Art (Crum and Evelyn White, vol. I, pp. 72, 155).
However, the principal evidence of carpets comes from their reflection in the
design of certain floor mosaics, like the one from a house near Antioch and now
at Dumbarton Oaks (Richter, 1956, no. 43).

In addition to floor coverings, curtains, and wall hangings,
covers and cushions for chairs, couches, and beds were important soft furnishings in the Early Christian house. Paradoxically, they have survived better than
the hard furniture (see color plates V-VII) that they once covered or padded, and
thus can be exhibited today. Such covers are often richly tapestried and were
considered to add to the splendor of a room, as may be learned from Corippus's
description of an audience hall in the imperial palace at Constantinople (*In
laudem Iustini Augusti minoris*, III, 205-6). Beds appear to have had wooden
frames, strung with webbing to support the mattresses; a comprehensible
example of a simple type is the bed carried on the back of the paralytic whom
Christ heals in the mosaic scene at San Apollinare Nuovo, in Ravenna (Deichmann, pl. 179). Funerary sculpture gives us some details of the soft fittings of
couches (Matz, no. 11). We also know that bolsters were sometimes carried
outdoors for luxurious picnics (see fig. 37).

A cover fragment of striking design, from the collection of
the Museum of Fine Arts in Boston, is number 5 in our exhibition. In a medallion
framed by a square is the image of a centaur. He trots blithely along, turning his
torso to face the viewer, and carrying a club, the weapon of Hercules, in playful
defense of domestic repose. Around the square, bright baskets brimming with
large flowers adorn the border. The looped pile on this piece is more than a
reference to the shagginess of a centaur. It is the effect of a weaving technique
used to make a warm, well-insulated fabric for winter clothing (see p. 140). The
softness of the fabric's pile is its appeal, giving extra comfort to the user of the
cover, an added layer of resilience, a tactile invitation to fingers in repose, and a
sharpness of contrast in texture to the panel's tapestry weave.

1
Curtain

Egypt, 5th century

Linen and wool

L. 120, W. 64

Toronto

Royal Ontario Museum, 910.125.29

This fragment of a fine-textured linen curtain is decorated with blossoms, birds, and buds arranged into two identical designs, one on each side of the fragment. Each design consists of a large blossom in the center, two pairs of the birds placed one below and one above the blossom, and the flower buds filling the spaces in between the birds. All these motifs are woven individually into the linen cloth of the curtain in a tapestry weave in red, green, yellow, and pink woolen yarns, their shapes clearly defined. A comparison with better-preserved textiles such as a curtain in the Vatican Museum (Renner, 1982, no. 15, pls. 14-15) suggests that the Toronto fragment came from either the top or the bottom portion of a similar curtain, which would also have been decorated in its corners with the tapestry-woven designs and finished with a fringe. Similarly arranged motifs—obviously fragments from other curtains—decorate fragmentary textiles in other collections; see Kendrick, no. 61; du Bourguet, D 163-64 and E 120; Renner, nos. 16-18.

The overall appearance and the decorative effect of these curtains is captured in their representations in floor and wall mosaics, for example in the tholos mosaic from a floor in Carthage (Dunbabin, pl. 139) and in the wall mosaic showing the Palace of Theodoric from San Apollinare Nuovo in Ravenna.

Unpublished

2
Curtain?

Egypt, 6th century

Linen and wool

L. 66, W. 65

Toronto

Royal Ontario Museum , 910.128.27

This large textile is decorated with two vertical
bands filled with blue and green birds and red-
and-white blossoms. Two large red-and-white
blossoms with green stems have also been
woven on the outer sides of the bands, one on
each side. The textile is made of an undyed
plain linen cloth textured along the vertical
bands with self-bands. The vertical bird-and-
blossom bands and the large lateral blossoms
are executed in a tapestry weave in colorfully
dyed wool. They were inserted into the ground
fabric of the textile, which may be a central
portion of a linen curtain.

Vertical bands and panels occur frequently in
Early Christian curtain decoration, although it
is also possible that this piece came from a tunic.
In this case, the vertical direction of the
decoration is accentuated by the upright stance
of the large-bodied, long-legged birds and the
upright position of the blossoms. The birds are
turned alternately to the left and to the right.
They all have neckbands, and their tail and
wing feathers are distinctly indicated by color
patches and stripes.

Birds, blossoms, and flower buds were
employed frequently among curtain ornaments
(see also no. 1 and p. 46). For example, very
similar floral buds and standing birds fill two
vertical bands on a fragment in Lyons (Musée
historique des Tissus, inv. no. 35559/927.1.7;
unpublished); see also Kybalová, pl. 28; du
Bourguet, E 59 and E 117-21, and an unpublished fragment in Boston (Museum of Fine
Arts, inv. no. 10.126a).

Unpublished

3
Curtain hook

Byzantine, 6th century or later

Bronze

H. 12, L. 17, W. 2.5

University of Toronto

Malcove Collection, M82.416

This L-shaped bronze hook takes the form of a finger to which is attached a small cross at its base. The finger is realistically modeled, with the nail and upper knuckle clearly indicated. The hook may originally have been embedded in the lintel above an entrance door, as a fitting for a curtain. In the narthex of the Hagia Sophia in Constantinople, rows of finger-shaped metal hooks may still be seen projecting from the lintels above the entrance doors (Mainstone, pp. 30-34; Kähler and Mango, ill. 20-23).

Unlike the rod-and-ring method of suspending curtains, which is frequently represented in art—for example, in the mosaic image of Theodoric's palace in San Apollinare Nuovo in Ravenna (C. Smith, p. 51)—the hook method is seldom shown, perhaps due to the problem of foreshortening. A rare image of its use may be seen in the mosaic of Theodora and her retinue in the presbytery of San Vitale, Ravenna, where the curtain in the doorway leading to the gallery is securely fastened to the architrave with metal fittings, presumably hooks (C. Smith, pp. 86-88).

Bibliography: Campbell, 1985, p. 75, no. 97.

4
Fragment of a tapestry band

6th century

Wool

L. 25, W. 20.5

University of Toronto

Malcove Collection, M82.44

This fragment of an all-wool textile shows a band with a haloed female bust flanked by stylized acanthus plants. The apricot-colored plain cloth weave of this textile's ground fabric is now preserved only along the bottom border of the tapestry-woven band with the bust. The characterization of the woman is robust, with a wide face framed by dark hair falling in large curls to either side. The face is dominated by large eyes with dark pupils and blue irises further stressed by clearly drawn eyebrows. The sharp leftward glance of the large eyes almost gives the face a three-quarter-view appearance. Other facial features, the small mouth, barely visible nose, and a dotted chin, are less prominent. The female is richly bejeweled: besides double-pendant earrings with drop pearls, she also wears a pearl headband and a pearl collar covering the neckline of her robe. A halo, in apricot wool with lighter beige border, isolates the dark-haired head from the dark blue ground of the band. The bust is placed between the arrangements of paired acanthus leaves with shoots and abstract blossoms and buds in green, red, pink, and beige.

The Malcove Collection textile comes from a border of a woolen cloth used either as a hanging, or more likely a couch cover. A complete design of the border consisted of a row of busts alternating with acanthus and other floral arrangements. Fragments of several such borders are known (Museum of Fine Arts, Boston, inv. no. 30.685, unpublished; Brooklyn Museum in Thompson, no. 5, pp. 20-21; Montreal Museum of Fine Arts, inv. no. 52.Dt.38, unpublished; related but not belonging to the same group is a band in the Fogg Art Museum, Harvard University, inv. no. 1975.41.23, published before its restoration in Brooklyn, no. 62). The bust and acanthus motifs of all these fragments are very similar, although not identical in every detail. The Brooklyn, Boston, Malcove, and Montreal pieces had to be made in the same workshop; the first three may even come from the same textile or set of related textiles, since such design variations are common to the weavings and other arts of the Early Byzantine period.

Although the bust motifs were used frequently in Late Antique and Early Christian art, the jeweled busts of the Malcove band and other related textiles particularly resemble similarly bejeweled portrayals of female personifications of seasons and benevolent powers such as *Ananeosis* (Renewal), *Apolausis* (Enjoyment) or *Megalopsychia* (Magnanimity), very popular in late-fifth- and sixth-century art. For the use of similarly arranged stylized acanthus leaves, this time on a sixth-century silver lamp, see Dodd, 1973, no. 3, pp. 7-8.

Bibliography: Campbell, 1985, no. 199, pp. 138-139.

5
Looped cover with a tapestry panel

Egypt, early 6th century

Linen and wool

L. 63, W. 46.5

Boston

Museum of Fine Arts, 51.566

This large fragment of a loop-pile cloth comes from a blanket or another kind of covering. As was customary for this type of household textile, the piece is decorated with a panel woven in a tapestry weave directly into the loop-pile cloth of the ground fabric. The panel is framed by a simple fillet. A narrow fillet also outlines the medallion design of the panel, with the largest medallion in the center and four smaller ones in the corners. The central medallion contains a centaur wearing a spotted cloak and holding a club in one hand; a shield lies underneath his hooves. Fish-tailed monsters, two with leonine and two with jackal-like foreparts, fill diagonally the four corner roundels. Rows of squarish dots inside the roundels represent abstract versions of stylized vegetal sprays used often in textiles as an indication of a landscape setting and as ground fillers. The lunette fields between the roundels contain foliate shoots and large baskets with heart-shaped petals. The design is woven mainly in dark purple wool and undyed linen, although the baskets are executed in orange, yellow, and red wool; touches of yellow and red are found throughout the panel. Much of the inner detailing of the centaur and the four creatures is carried out in a flying shuttle technique (actually a supplementary light-colored weft yarn placed over the dark woven surfaces of the main design elements). Although the weaving of the Boston panel is quite coarse, its bold forms create a very effective decorative design.

The large number of fragments, many of which are also stylistically related to the Boston piece, indicate that such loop-pile tapestry-decorated textiles were very common. Complete pieces were decorated with two or four panels as well as broad end-stripes in the width of the finished piece. As in this case, the decoration includes centaurs, hunters, and warriors, but also hybrid creatures, playing putti, and baskets with fruit and flowers. Especially closely related textiles include pieces in Paris (du Bourguet, D132 and D133, pp. 169-70); in New York (Metropolitan Museum of Art, inv. no. 89.18.123, 89.18.315, and 89.18.333, all unpublished); and in London (Victoria and Albert Museum; see Kendrick, nos. 68-70, pp. 67-68, pls. 16-17, and no. 168, p. 95, pl. 25; also inv. no. 842.1886, unpublished).

Unpublished

53

6
Frame and panel

Egypt, 6th century (frame), 8th century (panel)

Wood

L. 144.3, W. 70.5

Cleveland

The Cleveland Museum of Art, John L. Severance Fund, 54.799

This wooden panel and its wooden frame came originally from different contexts and are probably of different dates. The rectangular panel has been cut down from its former dimensions on all four sides. In its present state, it displays two large bosses in the form of six-petaled rosettes in broad circular frames which are set at either end of the rectangle. Surrounding each circular frame in the outer field is a lobed frame formed of a triple strand, the lobes being filled with flat-surfaced lacy sprigs. In the spandrels between the lobes, the triple strands separate into loops of an interlace, which continues to fill the entire field of the panel with irregularly shaped compartments enclosing mostly flat elements: smaller rosettes, florets, and leaves, as well as bulbous fruits resembling pears. The outer frame, like the panel, has been cut down from its original dimensions, but only on its short sides. The images in each of the four panels are oriented to face a viewer positioned on that side of the frame. In one of the long sides there is a cross at the center, with four equal arms; it is enclosed in a wreath held by two flying angels who turn their heads to look back over their shoulders. Flanking the angels is a pair of columns with capitals and with curtains knotted around their shafts. Beyond each column is a peacock standing in profile to face the cross. The two ends of the panel are taken up by sprigs of scrolling foliage, inclining toward the cross. The remaining imagery of the frame is devoted to water life, especially that of the river Nile and its banks. Centered on the other long side is a bisected twelve-petaled rosette, with pointed tips like a lotus flower, displayed in a medallion and flanked on the right by a lowing cow or an ox, followed by a figure in a boat who bends forward while holding an oar, and by a large fish. On the left of the central rosette there is an octopus, a seated fisherman holding a long line with a fish on the end of it, and behind him his jar-shaped basket. One of the short sides shows water creatures with a hippocamp, a fantastic sea-beast from the Roman repertory; the other side also features sea life, including a swimming boy and a dolphin. The tail of the hippocamp and one foot of the swimmer were amputated when the panel was cut down. Both the frame

and the central panel are covered with the same paint, which is presumably modern.

It is difficult to determine the original functions of both the panel and its present frame, because they no longer preserve their original proportions. On account of their scale, it is probable that they formed part of an architectural element, such as a carved ceiling.

Parallels for the design of the central panel can be found in stucco sculptures from Umayyad palaces of the eighth century. A similar two- or three-strand interlace enclosing small rosettes and other flowers was found, for example, at Khirbat al Mafjar (Hamilton, pl. XXIV, nos. P3-P5, and pl. XXIX, nos. 28-29). Large rosettes framed by circles were featured on the exterior facade of Qasr el-Heir (D. Schlumberger, pl. XLVI, no. 4). Umayyad floor mosaics also provide parallels for the design of our panel; one of the pavements at Khirbat al Mafjar is a composition of encircled rosettes set in a field of interlace enclosing small flowers (Hamilton, pl. LXXIX, no. 25).

The four narrow panels of the frame share qualities with other works that suggest these carvings are of an earlier date than the central panel, probably in the sixth century. The central composition of one side of the frame—two flying angels holding a wreath and flanked by columns with knotted curtains—is echoed in several other surviving wood carvings, including two panels from a set of doors from the Sitt Barbara Church in Old Cairo, which may date from the sixth century (Badawy, fig. 3.34). A similar composition can be found on a wooden panel preserved in the Louvre (Rutschowscaya, p. 103, no. 342). A wooden frame showing two peacocks flanking a cross is preserved in the Coptic Museum in Cairo (Simiaka Pacha, p. 28, no. 3532, pl. LXVIII). Many parallels for the Nilotic images on the other three sides of our frame can be found on the wooden cladding for the ceiling beams of St. Catherine's church at Mount Sinai, which were carved between A.D. 548 and 565. Comparable motifs on the beams include the lowing ox (Forsyth and Weitzmann, pl. LXXVII,

B), the half rosettes (ibid., pls. LXVI, 5, and LXVII, 13), the pair of peacocks flanking an equal-armed cross (ibid., pls. LXVI, 5, and LXVII, 13), the fish (ibid., pl. LXVII, 11), and the fisherman in his boat (ibid., pl. LXVIII, A). For other parallels to the Nilotic images, see the panels published in the 1941 Brooklyn Museum catalogue *Pagan and Christian Egypt*, figures 66 (swimming boy and fish) and 95 (a fisherman in a boat holding an oar). The parallels with Mount Sinai extend beyond the imagery to the format of the composition, with the central unit in our piece anchoring an undulating, bi-directional stream of separate elements. A pair of scrolling stems behind the angels, and the leaves used as fillers elsewhere, suggest a rinceau which controls the design, even though its continuing stem, seen on some of the Sinai beams, has here been omitted. In every detail, the rhythm of alternating curves has been repeated to create a unifying flow, as if the stem were there. This skillful patterning indicates the sureness of an artist working in a well-established tradition. Keeping consistently to low relief within this pattern, the carver of the

border strips used an illustrative vocabulary entirely different in its aims from that of the central panel with the nervous intricacy of its meshwork, its emulation of openwork in the play of figure and ground, and its variation in levels of relief. The framing strips were probably originally painted in colors like the traces of red, blue, green, and black pigment found on the Sinai beam claddings.

For the significance of the Nilotic imagery in conjunction with the cross, see p. 15.

Bibliography: Driston, no. 197; *Bulletin of the Cleveland Museum of Art* 45 (1958), plate following p. 41.

Fig. 32. Rome, Catacomb of SS. Marcellinus and Peter, Wall Painting.
Excavator Working by Lamplight.

The technology of lighting in the Early Christian house was simple, but the artistic forms associated with the provision of light were rich and complex. The commonest source of illumination was the oil lamp, which consisted of a wick, usually of flax, placed in a reservoir of oil. Lighting devices of this type had been in use since as early as the third or fourth millennium B.C. (Sussman, p. 43). By the Early Christian period there were two varieties of oil lamps, those with closed reservoirs, which were easily portable, and those with open reservoirs, which were more difficult to move.

The open reservoirs were commonly made of glass, and, like our numbers 7 and 8, were often conical in shape. The wick either floated freely on top of the oil filling the cone, or it was secured by means of a strip of bronze attached to the reservoir's rim (Crowfoot and Harden, pp. 206-7). Some of the glass reservoirs were cylindrical, with a glass tube attached vertically to the base for the purpose of holding the wick in place (no. 9). The open reservoirs themselves were held in a variety of fixtures whose materials and decoration were as varied as the lamps made to hold the light bulbs of today. At their cheapest and simplest, the fixtures could be no more than a simple wooden tripod designed to hold a single glass cone (no. 10). Wealthier households would have been able to afford the magnificent *polycandela,* great wheels of silver or bronze hanging on chains from the ceiling and holding as many as sixteen glass reservoirs in one cluster of lights (Bouras, 1982, p. 480).

The closed lamps of the Early Christian period generally took the form of a reservoir flanked on one side by a handle and on the other by a nozzle containing the hole for the wick. In the center of the cover to the reservoir there was usually a little hole, or in some cases two holes, through which the lamp could be filled. In the exhibition is a glass flask, number 11, provided with a long narrow spout; it is possible that this curiously shaped vessel was designed for pouring oil into the small openings in the tops of lamps. As in the case of the fixtures for the glass reservoirs, the closed lamps were made in a variety of materials, to suit every budget. Clay lamps were the most widespread, but bronze lamps were relatively common. For the luxury market, there were also lamps in silver (Cleveland, p. 35).

The metal lamps were frequently cast in the form of birds and beasts, such as a griffin (no. 12), a dove (no. 13), or a peacock (no. 14). Some bronze lamps, such as our number 15, were shaped like shod feet, a motif still used as a good-luck charm in parts of the Mediterranean world today.

Bronze lamps were often provided with lugs, so that they could be suspended from chains. Figure 32, a painting from the Early Christian catacomb of SS. Marcellinus and Peter at Rome, shows a workman excavating an underground chamber by the light of a lamp hanging from a hook attached to a spike driven into the face of the rock (Ferrua, p. 54). As today, there were stands, made of bronze, for supplying lamplight from a variety of heights.

57

Bronze lamps could also be made with sockets in their bases to fit over prickets on the tops of the lampstands. Such stands could vary in height between not much more than a foot (no. 16), for resting on a table or other raised surface, to over four feet (no. 17), for standing on the floor. A tall lampstand is shown in use in color plate II, a miniature from a Syriac Gospel book written at the monastery of St. John at Zagba in 586. In this portrayal St. John the Evangelist writes by the light of an elevated lamp placed beside his chair. Although this painting shows a lampstand being used in a religious context, we know from archaeological excavations that such stands were commonly used in private houses during the Early Christian period. At one house, in the ancient town of Kourion on the island of Cyprus, which was probably destroyed by an earthquake in A.D. 365, a short lampstand was discovered together with the marble table on which it had been placed (Soren, p. 58).

Most bronze lamps were designed so that they could also be stood on flat surfaces, such as pieces of furniture, or wherever else they were needed. At Karanis, in Egypt, lamps were placed in small niches set into the walls of the houses, as shown by the carbon deposits left by their smoking flames (Husselman, p. 47).

Clay lamps were produced in great numbers, from molds of plaster, clay, or stone. Their figural decoration was for the most part confined to the discus, the circular area covering the reservoir of oil. A great variety of motifs—pagan, profane, and Christian—could appear on the discus during the Early Christian period (Lyon-Caen and Hoff, pp. 79-83). Among the Christian designs, some were explicit, such as the cross-shaped Chi Rho monograms appearing on numbers 18 and 19. Other designs were subject to both Christian and secular interpretations, such as the peacock of number 20 or the grapes of number 23. The domestic use of clay lamps bearing crosses is known from the excavation of private houses (for example, at Carthage: Wells and Wightman, p. 52; Wells, Freed, and Gallagher, pp. 248-49).

Only occasionally is the whole body of a clay lamp fashioned in the shape of an animal, as in the case of number 24, which represents a mouse nibbling at the wick. This lamp, which probably copies a prototype in bronze, illustrates a presumably common problem in Early Christian households, for it was used as an image in a didactic text attributed to the sixth-century patriarch John the Faster: "If the lamp of your soul is wholly alight and ardently burning with the love of God, in no way will any work of darkness be able to reach you; but if that light should be put out, without delay the demon of voluptuousness will come and, like a mouse, will drink the oil and carry off the wick, or often even upset the lamp itself and break it" (*Asceticae regulae*, XXVI; Pitra, p. 426).

Occasionally clay lamps, such as our number 25, were provided with rings so that they could be hung on chains, but usually they were designed either to be held in the hand or to be set on a flat surface. For use outdoors, or for suspension indoors, they could be placed in clay lanterns such as number 28, which would protect the flame from drafts (Forbes, VI, pp. 166-68).

Lamps, for the early Christians, had a more than utilitarian significance. In the hands of a preacher, a clay lamp could be an image of the incarnation. One anonymous homilist wrote: "[The wisdom of God] came from heaven; it takes the earthen lamp of the body, lights it with the light of divinity, and sets it upon the lampstand of the cross" (Migne, col. 781). Metaphors of this kind match a group of clay lamps from Syria and Palestine which bear such inscriptions as "The light of Christ," or "The light of Christ shines for all" (Lyon-Caen and Hoff, pp. 81, 132, nos. 172-73).

7
Conical lamp

Egypt (Karanis), 4th-5th century

Glass

H. 12.5, Rim D. 6.3

University of Michigan

Kelsey Museum of Archaeology, 5922

This free-blown conical glass lamp is in excellent condition with no evidence of weathering. The glass is colorless with a greenish tint, and bubbly, with some impurities. The plain, unworked rim, molded outward just below the top, tapers down with slight convexity to a solid pointed base, somewhat flattened by pressure. The decoration is simple and consists of three groups of horizontal wheel-cut incisions near the rim, and four groups around the center of the body.

The beaker would be filled with oil, or with a layer of oil floated on water, and lit by means of a wick floating freely on the surface of the oil, or held in place by an S-shaped strip of bronze, one end bent over the rim of the glass, the other crimped to hold the wick (Crowfoot and Harden, pp. 206-7). Such lamps were placed in tripod lampstands, or set into horizontal rings, singly or in a polycandelon, suspended from chains.

Glass lamps emerged as lighting devices during the Early Christian period. Representations in mosaic decoration, and references to such lamps by ancient writers begin in the fourth century (Crowfoot and Harden, p. 196; Trowbridge, pp. 190-91; Forbes, V, 1966, p. 191). The conical type is well known in Egypt. Twenty complete examples and many fragments found at Karanis suggest that they rivaled terra-cotta lamps in popularity (Harden, pp. 155-58). Similar lamps have been found at many sites in the eastern Mediterranean, and generally date from the fourth to the sixth century. For comparative examples, see Matheson, pp. 98-99, no. 263; Hayes, 1975, p. 121, no. 477, fig. 11, pl. 31; Berger, 126, grave 262.2, fig. 115, pl. CIII, 7; Harden, p. 159, nos. 436, 449, pls. V and XVI.

Bibliography: Root, p. 43, vitrine XIX, no. 7; Harden, p. 160, no. 438, pls. V and XVI.

8
Conical lamp

Egypt (Karanis), 4th-5th century

Glass

H. 9.2, Rim D. 6.8

University of Michigan

Kelsey Museum of Archaeology, 5545

Like the preceding example, this cone-shaped glass lamp shows no signs of weathering; it is in good condition, aside from a small chip in the rim. The glass is a dark greenish-yellow with bubbly blobs. The sides taper upward with gentle convexity from a solid pointed base, flattened slightly by pressure, to a widely flared rim, plain and unworked. Two types of decorative motifs are used on this lamp: a narrow band of horizontal wheel-cut incisions near the rim, and just below, a zone of blue blobs consisting of a series of three small ones in a group, alternating with one large one.

Similar examples may be found in Auth, p. 153, no. 201; Hayes, 1975, p. 104, no. 380, fig. 11, pl. 31 (from Antioch); and Harden, p. 162, no. 457, p. 165, no. 460, pls. V and XVI (both similar in form and decoration, but with hollow bases).

Bibliography: Root, p. 42, vitrine XIX, no. 3; Harden, p. 160, no. 440; pls. V and XVI.

9
Lamp with wick holder

5th-6th century

Glass

H. 13.7, Rim D. 12.9, Base D. 7

University of Illinois

World Heritage Museum, 17.2.47

This green, beaker-shaped glass lamp was free-blown of "colorless" glass. Aside from the partially broken wick holder, and incrustation and iridescent weathering, the lamp is in good condition. The wall of the lamp is tapered upward to form a wide mouth. The rim is folded outward. The base of the vessel is flattened and pushed in, creating a convex protrusion of the interior floor to which was fused, in a separate process, a glass cylinder designed to hold the wick.

Lamps of this type could be used either standing on a flat surface or hanging in a polycandelon. A similar example may be seen in Auth, p. 152, no. 198. For a detailed discussion of glass lamps and wick holders, see Crowfoot and Harden, pp. 196-208.

Unpublished

61

10
Tripod stand

Egypt (Karanis), 3rd-5th century

Wood

H. 18.6, W. 14

University of Michigan

Kelsey Museum of Archaeology, 3633

Wooden tripod stands such as this one may
have supported conical glass lamps (Crowfoot
and Harden, p. 206; Gazda l983a, p. 25, fig. 41).
The three legs, planed smooth on the outer
surfaces, are joined by means of wooden pegs to
two crosspieces on each side (one crosspiece is
missing). All outer surfaces of the stand are
decorated with concentric circles. Randomly
placed gouges and drill holes suggest that the
wood was reused.

Bibliography: Gazda, 1983a, p. 28, fig 41.

11
Lamp filler

Syria or Palestine, late 3rd century

Glass

H. 10.9, Rim D. 6.3

University of Illinois

World Heritage Museum, 17.2.5

This small yellow-green feeder-vase of "colorless" glass is similar in shape to dropper flasks of the third century (cf. Hayes, p. 78, no. 282, pl. 22). Once thought to be a baby bottle, this type of vessel is now considered to be a filler for terra-cotta oil lamps (Auth, p. 152). The ribbed globular body has a rounded, pushed-in base, a tall, tapering neck, and a wide, flaring mouth with a rounded rim. A small tapered filling spout with a small orifice projects from the side of the body. Incrustation and iridescent weathering are evident.

A close Syro-Palestinian parallel may be seen in Hayes, 1975, p. 81, no. 299, pl. 21. For earlier examples where the body is pulled distinctly to one side to form the spout, see Hayes, 1975, p. 77, no. 279, pl. 20 (Syrian), and p. 131, no. 539, pl. 33 (Cypriot). More developed types of the fifth and sixth century are illustrated in Auth, p. 152, no. 199, and p. 227, no. 503.

Unpublished

12
Lamp with griffin's-head handle

Byzantine, 4th-5th century

Bronze

L. 17.8

Richmond

Virginia Museum of Fine Arts, Glasgow Fund, 66.10

This handsomely detailed bronze lamp with a griffin's-head handle is a type popular throughout Byzantium in the early period. While many equipped with lugs were meant to be suspended, this example with a stemmed base was also made to rest on a pricket stand or table. The opening for the oil on top of the body is covered with a domed lid terminating in a knob finial. Directly below the filling hole, a Christogram appears in relief. A collar of leaves with a molded base ring envelops the body at the back and around part of the long nozzle. On the upper surface of the nozzle, resting on an up-turned leaf, is a dolphin with her offspring on her back. A griffin's head with a curved, spiny neck emerges from the collar of leaves at the back of the lamp to form the handle. The sharply down-turned beak holds a small sphere. Rising out of the griffin's head is a cross, on which is perched a dove.

The popularity of the griffin's-head motif for the handles of bronze lamps may be due to the ancient association of this mythical animal with Apollo and with the light of the sun (Simon, pp. 763-67; Brandenburg, pp. 959, 972). In addition, the powerful and exotic creature probably had an apotropaic function, for it also appeared on magical gems and amulets (Brandenburg, pp. 972, 978). This particular lamp suggests another possible level of significance, for here the griffin's head serves as the support for a cross. The griffin, since it combined the body of a lion and the wings and beak of an eagle, could be seen as emblematic of the elements of land and air, while the dolphin, on the other side of the lamp's filling hole, could signify the sea. Thus the two animals together may have been intended to represent terrestrial creation, subject to the saving sign of Christ.

The several examples of lamps featuring the griffin motif found in Turkey may point to their production in the region around Constantinople. The greatest concentration of finds, however, has been in Italy, suggesting their manufacture in the west, possibly Rome (Ross, 1970, p. 32). For other examples of lamps with griffin's-head handles, see Hayes, 1984, pp. 138-39, no. 215; Bank, 1966, p. 335, pl. 19; Weitzmann, 1979, pp. 624-25, nos. 560 and 561; Volbach, 1958, p. 49, pl. 13; Wulff, no. 764; Dalton, 1901, p. 101, nos. 502 and 503, pl. XXVII.

Bibliography: Gonosová and Kondoleon, 1985, p. 437, fig. 6; Ross, 1970, p. 34, no. 6.

13
Lamp in the form of a dove

4th-5th century

Bronze

H. 4.1, L. 12.1, W. 7

Richmond

*Virginia Museum of Fine Arts,
Gift of Dr. Richard H. Howland, 68.14*

This small lamp was cast in the form of a bird, a favored motif in bronze lamps produced in the Late Roman and Early Byzantine periods. The small head, elongated body, and wings folded over the back suggest a dove and present a delicate, contained profile. The legs folded under the body form the base of the lamp. A lid, now missing, once covered the filling hole located on the back of the bird, behind the head. Two lugs on the raised rim around the filling hole were possibly attachments for suspension chains. A double source of light was provided by two wick spouts projecting from the shoulders.

Among the zoomorphic lamps produced in late antiquity, bird lamps in many variations represent the largest group, and date between the fourth and sixth centuries. The organic form and naturalistic detailing of the Virginia lamp suggest a fourth- or fifth-century date.

For other examples of the general type, see Campbell, 1985, p. 53, no. 48; Hayes 1984, pp. 137-38, no. 213; Badawy, p. 325, fig. 5.8 (Museo Egizio, Turin) and 5.9 (Museo Archaeologico, Florence); Mitten, pp. 196-98; Beckwith, 1972-74, pp. 463-65 (Victoria and Albert Museum); Coche de la Ferté, 1958, p. 37, no. 28; and Dalton, 1901, p. 102, nos. 508 and 512, pl. XXVII.

For the significance of the shape, see p. 23.

Bibliography: Ross, 1970, p. 34, no. 2.

14

Lamp in the form of a peacock

Egypt, 6th century

Bronze

H. 12, L. 14, W. 5

University of Toronto

Malcove Collection, M82.398

This elegantly styled bronze lamp takes the shape of a peacock perched upon a conical base. A square socket in the base served as a fitting for the pricket of a lampstand. The body of the bird forms a deep, rounded reservoir. The wings, folded against the sides of the body, are incised with overlapping feathers, schematically rendered as herringbones terminated with a circle. The filling hole in the back of the bird is covered by a hinged lid detailed with a herringbone pattern. The nozzle and wick hole at the end of the tail are balanced by the high, gracefully arched neck and head. A crest of feathers projects from the crown of the head.

Peacock lamps made in Egypt, where bronze-casters had perfected production methods, were exported throughout the Byzantine empire (Ross, 1960, pp. 134-36). Similar examples may be seen in Menzel, pp. 112-13, figs. 93, 94; Coche de la Ferté, 1957, pp. 63-64, pl. VI, no. 64; Ross, 1962, p. 39, pl. XXVIII, no. 41; Ross, 1960, p. 134 (three lamps in the British Museum, two from Tell-el-Yehudiyeh, Egypt, and one of unknown provenance), and p. 135 (National Museum, Athens; Nelson Gallery, Kansas City); Wulff, no. 768; Stryzgowski, pl. XXXIII, no. 9142; Dalton, 1901, p. 102, pl. XXVII, no. 509 (illustrated by Ross, 1960, p. 134).

The significance of the peacock is discussed on p. 11.

Bibliography: Campbell, 1985, p. 52, no. 47.

15
Lamp in the form of a foot

5th-6th century

Bronze

H. 14, L. 18, W. 5.5

University of Toronto

Malcove Collection, M82.433

The realistic rendering of a right foot bound in a
sandal represents a class of bronze lamps commonly found in the Late Antique household.
Fine detailing of the leather sandal enhances the
appearance of the foot. The sole is accented with
a series of horizontal fillets on the outer edge,
and is treaded on the bottom. A panel, tooled
with vertical fillets and a molded edge, cradles
the heel of the foot. The sandal is tied on top of
the foot with thongs terminating in an ivy-leaf
motif. From the position of the large toe
emerges a large circular wick hole with
scalloped edges. The smaller toes are articulated with creases in the skin, and nails. Above
the ankle, the filling hole with a flanged rim is
covered with a hinged conical lid, flared around
the base. The lid is decorated with three sets of
three round holes in a triangular arrangement,
and engraved with a cross and palm branch.
The lid terminates in a bird finial, possibly a
dove, resting on a knob-like element. This lamp,
like many of the bronze lamps, was meant to be
suspended. Three short chains attached to lugs,
two above the ankle and one behind the wick
hole, converge into one chain terminated with a
hook.

Images of feet were commonly employed by
both pagans and Christians as a type of good-
luck charm, expressing a desire for health,
safety, or protection from malevolent unseen
forces. In the Early Christian home, the bronze
foot-lamp served not only as a source of
material light, but also as a reminder of the
spiritual light that illuminated the path to
salvation (Psalm 119:105).

For comparative examples, see Campbell, 1985,
p. 47, no. 40; Weitzmann, 1979, pp. 337-38, no.
317 (Metropolitan Museum of Art, New York).

Bibliography: Campbell, 1985, p. 51, no. 45; Ostrogorsky, p. 32, fig. 10.

69

16

Lamp with branching handle
and stand
Byzantine, 5th-6th century

Bronze

H. 48, L. 20, W. 11.5

University of Toronto

Malcove Collection, M82.437 a, b.

This lamp with open-work handles dividing
into two antler-like projections is representative
of a large class of Late Antique bronze lamps
found chiefly in Egypt. The bulbous, somewhat
squat body is linked to the circular wick hole by
a long tubular nozzle. A domical lid with a knob
finial covers the filling hole. The lid is attached
to a circular collar which in turn is hinged to the
back of the opening. A curved armature rises
from the back of the collar to which is attached a
disc incised with concentric circles. Surmount-
ing the disc is a small bird with outstretched
wings sitting on a cross. The elaborately
designed handle is composed of two inward-
curving tendrils branching from a thick, square
stem. At the point where the tendrils divide, a
leaf rises up, curving outward. The lamp rests
upon a high, flanged foot enclosing a square
depression for the pricket of the lampstand.

The bronze stand was cast in several pieces. A
tapering pricket rises from a thick-walled
saucer with a flat rim. It is supported on a short
baluster shaft which, in turn, rests upon a tripod
base in the form of three lion's paws on flat
round pads.

Parallels, especially with respect to the style of
the handles, may be seen in Hayes, 1984, p. 140,
no. 217; W. Rudolph, p. 36, no. 38; Weitzmann,
1979, p. 340, no. 321 (Metropolitan Museum of
Art, New York); Ross, 1962, pp. 36-37, no. 38, pl.
XXVIII; Coche de la Ferté, 1958, pp. 36, 99, no.
29; Wulff, p. 209, no. 997, pl. L; Dalton, 1901, p.
100, nos. 495, 496, pl. XXVI.

For the significance of the disc decorated with
concentric circles, see. p. 5.

Bibliography: Campbell, 1985, p. 49, no. 43; Ostrogorsky, p. 84.

17
Lampstand

6th-7th century

Bronze

H. 127, W. 25.4

Richmond

Virginia Museum of Fine Arts, Glasgow Fund, 73.26

This tall, elegantly proportioned bronze stand, cast in four sections, served as the support for an oil lamp or candle in the Late Antique home. The lamp or candle was secured to the stand at the top by a four-faceted tapering pricket attached to a shallow, flanged saucer. The hexagonal shaft, swelling at the center, is flanged at the ends where it joins the saucer and the baluster section above the tripod base. The base, in the form of an inverted lily with six lobes, is supported on three splayed feet on flat discs. Between the feet, the leaves of the flower are weighted with knobs.

Lampstands or candlesticks of this height were placed on the floor. A stand, similar to the Virginia example, is illustrated in the late-sixth-century Rabbula Gospels (see color plate II).

Stands of this type were common throughout the eastern Mediterranean. Sixth-century bronze parallels from Syria in the Dumbarton Oaks Collection may be seen in Ross, 1962, pp. 37-38, no. 39, pl. XXXIX. Similar examples in silver are illustrated in M. M. Mango, 1986, pp. 96-101 (from the region of Hama, Syria, in the Walters Art Gallery in Baltimore).

Unpublished

18
Lamp with Chi Rho monogram

North Africa, 5th century

Earthenware

H. 5, L. 12.7, W. 7.7

University of Illinois

World Heritage Museum, 44.3.89

The lamp, made of a fine-grained red clay covered with a thin red-orange slip, belongs to a group of mold-made lamps produced in the workshops of North Africa, especially Tunisia, and exported throughout the Mediterranean. Related to the fine African Red Slip Ware popular in the Late Roman world, they share a similar clay fabric and many of the same motifs (Hayes, 1972, pp. 310-14). On this lamp, which corresponds to Fulford and Peacock, Form 2B, the shoulders of the reservoir are rounded and rest on a flattened base with a molded ring joined to the stump handle at the back of the lamp by a ridge. A palm motif incised in the center of the base may have served as the potter's mark. The upper surface of the reservoir is relatively flat, having a slightly depressed circular discus pierced by two small filling holes, and a broad, somewhat convex rim. A ridge separating the discus from the rim extends down the projecting nozzle to form a broad channel terminated by a large wick hole, a feature devised to contain and direct the flow of oil spilled in the process of filling or transporting the lamp.

The stock of motifs used to decorate lamps of this type includes geometric forms, animals, birds, kantharoi (handled vases), crosses, and holy persons from the Old and New Testament. The relief decoration on the World Heritage Museum lamp consists of two simple elements, a Christogram surrounded by a wreath in the center of the discus, and a herringbone pattern on the rim.

Similar lamps may be seen in Graziani Abbiani, pp. 121-23, no. 383, pl. XVIII, fig. 70 (Museo Civico, Turin), and pp. 125-26, no. 395, pl. XIX, figs. 73, 74 (Museo Civico, Tortona).

For the significance of the Christogram motif, see p. 21.

Unpublished

19
Lamp with Chi Rho monogram

North Africa, 5th-6th century

Earthenware

H. 3.2, L. 14.4, W. 8

Private collection

Although this well-preserved lamp, a product of North African lampmakers, is similar to number 18, it is distinguished by a crisper, more refined relief decoration. The fine-grained red clay fabric is covered with a thin red-orange slip, characteristic of African Red Slip Ware. The shoulders of the circular body curve down to a flattened base that rests on a molded ring. A ridge connects the base ring with the stump handle at the back of the lamp. The profile of the upper surface of the reservoir is flat, consisting of a broad rim, a slightly depressed discus pierced by two filling holes, and a long channeled nozzle terminated by a large wick hole.

The finely detailed Chi Rho monogram in the center of the discus represents a common motif on lamps of this type. A delicate rinceau of vines and grapes fills the arms of the cross, complemented by a small cross in the center, where the arms meet. The rim around the discus is decorated with a series of concentric horseshoe-shaped forms filled with hatching and dots, separated by larger dots at their base. Three small circular impressions in a triangular arrangement appear on the nozzle.

Similar cross-monogram lamps with geometric motifs on the rim are classified by Hayes as Type II and by Fulford and Peacock as Form 1. They date from the second quarter of the fifth century to the mid-sixth century (Hayes, 1972, pp. 310-11). The many variations of this type are well documented. For close parallels see Ennabli, pp. 192-93, pl. LII, nos. 951, 952, 959; and Hayes, 1972, pl. XXI, fig. a.

For the significance of the Chi Rho monogram, see p. 21, and for the meanings of the vine, p. 23.

Unpublished

20

Lamp with peacock

North Africa (Hippo), 5th-6th century

Earthenware

H. 3.4, L. 11.5, W. 7.9

University of Michigan

Kelsey Museum of Archaeology, 202

Like catalogue numbers 18 and 19, the form and fabric of this partially damaged lamp are characteristic of the Red Ware produced in North Africa during the fifth century (Fulford and Peacock, Form 1). Made of a coarse red clay with a red-orange slip, the lamp has a circular reservoir that curves down from the shoulders to a flattened base raised on a molded ring. On the lamp's underside the area within the ring is incised with a palm motif. From the base ring, a ridge extends toward the back of the lamp. The surface of the discus is slightly depressed, and pierced with two small filling holes. A peacock in low relief appears in the center, facing away from the nozzle. The discus is set off from the rim by a ridge that extends along the nozzle to the large wick hole, blackened from use. The rim around the discus contains a series of four-petalled rosettes, and heart-shapes nearest the nozzle.

The peacock, among other birds, is a common motif on the lamps produced in North African workshops during the Early Christian period.

Comparative examples may be seen in Ennabli, pp. 142-43, no. 637 and 643, pl. XXXIV; and Broneer, p. 285, no. 1454, pl. XXI.

The significance of the peacock is discussed on p. 11.

Unpublished

21

Lamp with frog motif

Egypt, late 3rd to early 4th century

Earthenware

H. 3.8, L. 7.3, W. 5.4

University of Illinois

World Heritage Museum 44.3.65

A small, buff-colored ovoid lamp, this piece belongs to a large group indigenous to Egypt known as "frog" lamps. The reservoir has deep, rounded sides, and a nozzle fully merged with the body. The base is flat, and marked with a palm motif. A molded band forms the discus around the filling hole. The small wick hole at the narrow end of the nozzle is set off by a single curved incised line. The upper surface of the lamp is decorated with a naturalistic-looking frog modeled in low relief. The anatomical details are articulated with incised lines and prick marks.

Lamps such as this example were popular over a long period of time in Egypt. Production began as early as the second century, or earlier, and continued throughout the Early Christian period (Shier, 1978, pp. 24-30). Comparable lamps are illustrated in Shier, 1978, p. 102, no. 246, pl. 29; Menzel, pp. 88-89, nos. 584-86; Hölscher, p. 68, fig. 88a, pl. 40, no. 7; Dalton, 1901, p. 150, pl. XXXII, no. 819.

For the significance of the frog motif, see p. 10.

Unpublished

22
Lamp with frog and cross monogram

Egypt (Medinet-el Fayoum), 3rd-4th century

Earthenware

H. 3.7, L. 7.6, W. 6.4

University of Michigan

Kelsey Museum of Archaeology, 22432

A coarse, pinkish micaceous clay was used to manufacture this pear-shaped lamp, which was covered with a thin buff slip. The lamp is in good condition, except for a long crack along the joint where the upper and lower sections of the body were fused during manufacture. The body is double convex with an integrated nozzle and plain, flat base incised with a potter's mark (Petrie, Type F). A single curved groove sets off the wick hole at the narrow end. Behind the nozzle, a deep groove near the shoulder of the reservoir surrounds a highly stylized relief that combines the frog motif, commonly seen on lamps indigenous to Egypt, with the cross monogram. A frog's head placed at the base of the nozzle is followed by five grooved bands radiating from the filling hole in the center. Between the bands, the surface of the lamp is incised with the palm branch or herringbone motif.

Frog lamps with images of the cross are a late type, dating from the late third and fourth centuries. For a discussion of these lamps and their chronological development, see Shier, 1972, pp. 349-58; 1978, pp. 24-30.

On the significance of the frog as the Chi Rho, see p. 10.

Unpublished

23

Lamp with stylized grapes

Syria, 7th-8th century

Earthenware

H. 3.2, L. 9, W. 7.1

University of Illinois

World Heritage Museum, XX.9.13

This pear-shaped lamp was made of a fine pinkish orange clay. The shoulders of the reservoir slope sharply to meet the flared sides of the lower half, creating a low, angular profile. The shoulders are decorated with stylized grape clusters, consisting of groups of raised dots set within a zigzag design. A small, narrow molded ring forms a discus around the fill hole. The nozzle, subsumed into the body of the lamp, is channeled to the wick hole, and decorated with a palm-branch motif. The base ring is oval, following the outline of the lamp. At the back of the reservoir, the handle is broken off, leaving a triangular mark characteristic of a tongue-like handle design.

This lamp belongs to a group from Syria known as "slipper lamps." Those found at Antioch are described by Waage as "the sixth-century lamps par excellence" (Waage, p. 67, Type 56).

Evidence from other sites in Syria-Palestine suggests that lamps of this type were produced over a long period of time, extending from the sixth to the ninth century. A lamp with a grape motif and two birds found in the excavation of a church at Khirbat 'Asida is dated by Baramki to the early Islamic period (Baramki and Avi-Yonah, 1933, p. 19, Pl. XII, 2). The excavation of a church at 'Ein Hanniya yielded a tongue-handled lamp along with three Umayyad coins (Baramki, 1933, p. 166, pl. XL, 1.) A lamp from Khirbat al-Mafjar dates to the occupation after the earthquake of 746 (Baramki, 1940-42, pl. XVII, no. 7).

Similar examples may be seen in Menzel, p. 132, no. 754; Kennedy, pp. 90-91, pl. XXIX, no. 785, Type 23 (Abu Shusa); Day, pp. 71-74, pl. XII, fig. 2 (Mersin in Cilicia); and Fitzgerald, pl. XXXVI, nos. 22-24 (Beth-shan).

Unpublished

24
Lamp with mouse

Egypt (Fayoum)

Earthenware

H. 4.3, L. 5.6, W. 3.5

University of Michigan

Kelsey Museum of Archaeology, 4964

This unusual lamp takes the form of a mouse sitting on top of a pear-shaped bowl raised on a triangular base. It is made of a brown micaceous clay with a red glossy slip, and is in good condition, except for the handle, broken off at the top. Unlike most small clay lamps, the filling hole is a small spout projecting from the right side of the reservoir. The mouse, naturalistically modeled in high relief, faces the wick hole located at the narrow end of the reservoir, and appears to be nibbling at the wick.

Examples of the related type are found in bronze. A first-century lamp from Armant, Egypt, formed as a mouse nibbling the wick, may be seen in the British Museum (inv. no. GR 1922.7-12.10). Another lamp in the British Museum, dated to the sixth century, shows a mouse sitting on the filler-lid with its mouth just at the wick (inv. no. l964.4-2.1) On the significance of the motif, see p. 58.

Unpublished

25
Lamp with chain

Rome, 3rd-5th century (?)

Earthenware

H. 4.8, L. 9, W. 6

University of Michigan

Kelsey Museum of Archaeology, 426

A reddish brown glossy slip seals the reddish buff clay used to make this small oval lamp. The double convex body has, near the center on the upper surface, a ring handle with a single groove. A bronze suspension chain with a large ring at each end is attached to the handle. The base ring is marked by a grooved band that runs up the back of the lamp. A short channel leads from the handle to a large wick hole at one end. The filling hole is located directly behind the handle. Two decorative motifs are employed on this lamp, an incised double ladder pattern behind the filling hole, and a raised reticulated pattern on either side of the rim.

Unpublished

26

Lamp with two boys

Egypt, early 2nd to mid-3rd century

Earthenware

H. 2.9, L. 8, W. 7.5

Private collection

This well-preserved lamp made of creamish tan clay is a type related to lamps with the frog motif (Shier, A 5.2b) The triangular reservoir has a double-convex profile, and rests on a plain, flat base incised with an alpha mark. The nozzle, short and tapered, is not entirely merged with the body of the lamp, and has a small molded circle at its base. A single, incised curved groove emphasizes the wick hole at the narrow end of the nozzle. Two fetus-like figures in relief with large heads, referred to by Petrie as "two boys," are symmetrically disposed around the simple molded rim of the filling hole. The figures face each other across the base of the nozzle with their outer arms raised. Anatomical features are crudely indicated with incised lines.

The specific meaning of the "two boys" motif is obscure, but its general significance must be an invocation of fertility and prosperity. The two figures can be associated with the pairs of boys who appear frequently in Early Christian art as offerers of game, fruits, or other produce, as may be seen, for example, on our number 75, a weaving from Egypt.

Discovery of similar lamps at sites in the Fayoum, Memphis, and Medinet Habu suggest a wide distribution in Egypt during the second and third centuries. For comparable examples see Shier, 1978, pp. 77-78, pl. 20, nos. 120-24; Menzel, p. 130, no. 135; Hölscher, p. 69, fig. 90c, pl. 40, no. 12; and Petrie, 1905, pl. LXVI.

Unpublished

27
Lamp with orans figure

Egypt (Karanis), late 3rd-early 4th century

Earthenware

H. 4.1, L. 9.9, W. 7.2

University of Michigan

Kelsey Museum of Archaeology, 22399

This lamp was made of buff-to-pinkish clay, covered with a fine smooth slip of the same color. The ovoid reservoir has an integrated nozzle, similar to the "frog" lamps to which it is related, and a small knob handle (cf. Petrie, Type Y). The top of the lamp is almost flat. The sides curve down to a flat base, incised with a potter's mark. A curved incised groove sets off the wick hole. Extending from the handle to the base of the nozzle near the shoulder, a molded rim incised with horizontal grooves forms a series of rectangular boxes, each with an incised circle in the center. Within the rim, a stylized figure with raised arms is shown standing in a pedimented facade. The figure is flanked by two sets of columns: the outer, twisted, the inner, plain with bases and capitals that rest on a molded band decorated with six incised circles. The columns are surmounted by a curved triangular pediment that is decorated with circular impressions at the left and right corners, and at the left of the knob handle at the apex of the pediment. The filling hole occupies the center of the pediment.

Among the lamps indigenous to Egypt, the orans figure, characterized by arms raised in prayer, is unusual. For comparative examples in other media, mainly Coptic textiles and funerary stelae, see Volbach, 1969, p. 29, fig. 11 (fragment of curtain from Schech Sayet in the Institute of Arts, Detroit); Badawy, p. 213, fig. 3.198 (stela from Bultya in the Staatliche Museen, Berlin), and p. 216, fig. 3.200 (stela in the Museo Egizio, Turin); and Hooper, pl. XVI, c (stela from Terenouthis in the Kelsey Museum).

Bibliography: Shier, 1978, p. 110, no. 286, pl. 4, 33.

28
Lantern

Egypt (Karanis), late 3rd-early 4th century

Earthenware with painted decoration

H. 21.4, D. 15.5

University of Michigan

Kelsey Museum of Archaeology, 8144

This lantern, or "lamp house," was designed to hold a small clay lamp. The chamber is cylindrical with a square opening, and is covered with a conical roof from which rises a thick ring handle for suspension. A band of thumbprints surrounds the entrance to the chamber. The base is plain and slightly convex. The lantern is made of a coarse red clay, and covered with a pinkish white slip. Thick brush strokes in red and dark red decorate the exterior surface. On the upper half, a range of vertical lines is framed by two horizontal bands. On the chamber below, groups of short horizontal strokes, hooked at one end, are superimposed on four loosely formed swags.

Lanterns of this type allowed lamps to be carried outdoors, or used indoors, suspended from the ceiling or from a bracket mounted in the wall (see Forbes, VI, 1966, p. 166-68, for further discussion of the use of lanterns in antiquity). Smaller, more elaborate versions made of finer clay were used as lantern shrines, and often included a head, bust, or complete figure on top of the lantern (Shier, 1978, p. 8).

A similar example from Karanis may be found in Shier, 1978, no. 7716, pl. 55. For the general type, see Johnson, p. 36, nos. 132, 133, pl. 76; Hayes, 1980, p. 144, nos. 566-68, pl. 68; Rosenthal and Silvan, nos. 623-25; Forbes, VI, 1966, p. 168, fig. 36 (Rijksmuseum van Oudheden, Leiden); Perdrizet, 1921, no. 318, pl. CXXVI; Loeschcke, pl. XXXVI; and Petrie, 1905, pl. LII A, nos. 155-57.

Bibliography: Johnson, p. 36, no. 131, pl. 76.

Fig. 33. Florence, Biblioteca Laurenziana, Codex Amiatinus I, fol. V.
The Scribe Ezra with a Cupboard Containing the Bible in Nine Volumes.

"I find not how to go and leave my house, lest I be robbed." So complains an anonymous Egyptian of the late sixth or early seventh century to his correspondent (Crum and Evelyn White, ostracum 222, vol. II, p. 212). The safekeeping of treasured possessions was as much a concern at that time as it is today, but, unlike modern homeowners, the early Christians protected their homes by invoking supernatural forces, invisible defenses provided by potent signs such as the mirror and the cross, which have been discussed in this book's introduction (see p. 19). Yet householders did not neglect physical protection: doors were secured by bolts which could be fastened by locks operating with sliding keys (nos. 29 and 32), and windows were frequently closed by bars (Husselman, pp. 40-46, pls. 45-67).

 Inside the house, possessions were stored in a variety of ways. Some things were simply kept on windowsills, such as the miscellaneous assemblage of glass vessels, baskets, and wooden combs which excavators discovered on a window ledge in a second-century house at Karanis in Egypt (Gazda, 1983a, p. 26, fig. 43). At Karanis, many of the houses were fitted with square niches set into the walls, which were used as cupboards for keeping small objects (Husselman, p. 47, pls. 69-70). Some of these niches were provided with wooden shelves. Wealthier houses would have contained free-standing cupboards, such as the splendid example decorated with ivory inlays that serves as a bookcase for the scribe Ezra in a painting prefixed to a northern English Bible of the late seventh or early eighth century (fig. 33).

 Early Christian homes also contained a number of chests and boxes of various sizes and materials, depending on the types of objects stored and the wealth of their owners. For example, at the upper end of the social spectrum there is the large silver casket of the aristocratic Roman Projecta, almost two feet in length (color plate I). A relief on the front of the casket shows how it might have been used, for here we see a large box of similar dimensions held by a maid who attends Projecta while her mistress is fixing her hair. Presumably the casket contained items that this fashionable lady required for her toilet. At humbler levels of society people used wooden chests, but often these were beautifully decorated, as can be seen in the case of our number 30, from Karanis.

 There were also smaller wooden boxes, some of these richly adorned with inlaid panels of carved ivory or bone (Randall, p. 90, no. 135). Others, such as our number 31, were decorated more simply with such motifs as punched circles. Besides being used for toiletry articles, these containers could have held jewelry. Color plate III illustrates an early-fourth-century ceiling fresco from an imperial palace at Trier, in which a handsome woman, either a personification or a member of the imperial family, is seen drawing a pearl necklace from a box filled with jewels.

 Boxes and doors were frequently equipped with locks, operated either by sliding or by turning keys. The locks and their keys exhibited

85

varying degrees of mechanical sophistication and were of various materials. Number 32 in the exhibition is a simple wooden sliding key, designed to unlock the sliding bolt which secured a door, such as number 29. Number 87, on the other hand, is a small silver key attached to a finger ring, which may have been used to open a small box or casket, or alternatively, may have been purely amuletic. Upon the circular panel, or "bit," of this key there is an engraved cross. The cross would have added its supernatural security to the relatively insecure mechanism of the lock, since the shape of the bit is very simple. In the Middle Ages it was a common practice to mark the bits of keys with crosses which, although they were non-functional in a physical sense, acted as powerful guarantees of safekeeping (e.g., Vikan and Nesbitt, figs. 6, 8).

A necessary supplement to the primitive locks of the time was the practice of sealing, which provided the owner of a container with assurance that its contents had not been disturbed. Seals were made of wax, pitch, or clay, and were impressed with a variety of stamping implements (Vikan and Nesbitt, pp. 10-23). The most common of the sealing devices was the engraved ring. In the first century A.D. the Roman author Pliny the Elder said that there was so much dishonesty and pilfering in his day that even the food and drink in the larder had to be sealed from theft by means of a ring (*Naturalis historia*, XXXIII, 26-27). "Most of the organization of our lives has begun to revolve around this instrument," he complained. Standards of honesty had evidently not greatly improved by the end of the second century, for the church father Clement of Alexandria, in spite of his disapproval of jewelry, was forced to concede that the possession of a gold sealing ring was necessary for women, so that they could protect their valuables around the house. He remarked that such measures would not be needed if both masters and their servants were honest Christians. He also said that men who were away from home on business would need to use signet rings "for safety's sake" (*Paedagogus*, III, 57-58). Many legal transactions, such as drawing up wills, required the use of seals, as they were a guarantee that the documents would not be tampered with. In addition, in a society that was largely illiterate, private seals could serve as signatures (Vikan and Nesbitt, p. 10). In view of their many uses, it is small wonder that sealing rings have survived in great numbers, and in a range of materials for all price-brackets: gold, silver, and bronze.

A less common type of sealing device was the cone seal, a cone-shaped stamp of stone or metal, which was usually provided with a hole or a loop at its top so that it could be hung around one's neck. These seals also were made in a range of materials, including rock crystal and steatite, in addition to gold, silver, and bronze (Vikan and Nesbitt, pp. 21-22).

The devices engraved into signet rings and cone seals were extremely varied. Often they were personalized, showing the owner's monogram, or an invocation containing his or her name. The silver cone-seal that is our number 33, for example, is inscribed "Mother of God, help Theophila," a common formula on both cones and rings (Vikan and Nesbitt, pp. 16-19). Another favored design was the Holy Rider, a potent apotropaic sign (see p. 25), which can be seen on both a bronze ring, number 84, and a steatite cone seal, number 34, in our exhibit. Most of the other sealing rings in this exhibition bear designs whose supernatural ability to turn away harm reinforced the physical security provided by the seals. The bronze ring number 85 bears the amuletic invocation AGIOS AGIOS AGIOS ("Holy Holy Holy") (cf. Vikan, 1984, p. 75, note 53, fig. 10), while number 86, a silver ring, is engraved with the cross-shaped acrostic of PHŌS and ZŌĒ ("Light" and "Life"). The bronze ring number 88 depicts an angel holding a cross, perhaps the archangel Michael, who was invoked in inscriptions on magical amulets (cf. no. 135). Finally, the intaglio design cut into the bezel of the bronze ring number 89, depicting the two Marys at the tomb of Christ, can be compared with a design appearing on amuletic armbands (Vikan, 1984, fig. 10).

In spite of all these protective measures, material and immaterial, there was no doubt that the best way to secure one's valuables was to bury them underneath the house. This method proved so successful for one third-century citizen of Karanis that his hoard of coins lay undisturbed until it was unearthed from its hiding place by archaeologists seventeen centuries later (Husselman, p. 26, pl. 4b).

The storage of food and drink was another concern for the Early Christian householder. Then, as now, it was necessary to keep food from spoiling and to protect it from insects and vermin. Flies were a perennial problem; in the popular imagination they were associated with demons such as Gyllou (see p. 26), and in the imagery of Christian ascetics they were compared to the impure thoughts which cluster around the heart that neglects the spirit (Budge, p. 911). One type of storage container used in Early Christian houses is represented by number 35, a tall, painted pottery jar from Egypt, with a narrow base and four small handles under its wide rim. It is similar in shape to the jars shown on an ivory panel from the throne of Maximian, a sixth-century arch-bishop of Ravenna (fig. 34). The jars on the ivory, which illustrates the Wedding at Cana, contain the water that Christ turns into wine.

The commonest type of storage vessel was the pottery amphora, which was the standard shipping-container of the ancient world. The name of this large vessel came from the two handles by which it could be lifted, the word *amphoros* in Greek meaning "that which is carried on two sides." Amphoras usually contained wine or olive oil, but they could also hold such produce as milk, honey, vinegar, olives, beans, figs, and dates (Martin, pp. 21-22). In addition, they could function as water jars. They were designed to be carried on the shoulder in the manner illustrated in figure 35, an early fifth-century ivory carving which shows a servant pouring out the water that Christ will turn into wine. The two handles were provided primarily for lifting the amphora and for setting it down. The boy on the left of figure 36, a detail from a floor mosaic in the Great Palace of the Byzantine emperors at Constantinople, is presumably about to lift the amphora in front of him by its two handles; to judge from the scene on the right, the vessel contains goat's milk. The amphora in the mosaic, with its surface covered by horizontal grooves, can be compared to the amphoras numbers 36 and 37 in the exhibition. The purpose of the grooves was evidently to prevent the heavy container from slipping when it was being handled. Some amphoras, such as our number 36, have indentations in their sides which were created when the vessels were carried on the shoulders of the potters before being placed in the kiln; after the firing, the same indentations made it easier for porters to carry the amphoras when they were loaded.

Fig. 34 (right). Ravenna, Archiepiscopal Museum,
Ivory Throne of Archbishop Maximian, Detail.
Christ Turns the Water into Wine.

Fig. 35 (above). Berlin, Staatliche Museen,
Ivory Carving, Detail.
Christ Turns the Water into Wine.

In the house, amphoras could be stored in a variety of ways.
They could be simply set on the ground and stacked leaning against a wall, or
they could be placed in racks. When they were used in the dining room, they
were placed in special holders designed to keep them upright.

The large amphoras had miniature relatives, under a foot in
height, which were made of pottery (no. 38) or glass (no. 39). Like the full-sized
amphoras, these *amphoriskoi* had narrow necks flanked by two handles, and
would have needed stands when they were used at the table. In an early fourth-
century floor mosaic from the aristocratic villa at Piazza Armerina in Sicily,
small amphoras of glass are shown in use at a picnic (fig. 37). Here we see a
party of diners reclining in the shade of trees after a hunt; they are served wine

Fig. 36. Constantinople, Great Palace, Floor Mosaic, Detail.

in glass goblets by a servant, who has just poured their drinks from two glass amphoras standing in a wicker basket in the foreground.

Amphoras were closed by various materials, wood, terracotta, pitch, plaster, or mud (Martin, p. 21). The seals of the vessels were frequently stamped, either by the producers or the shippers of the produce (Vikan and Nesbitt, p. 28). Sometimes a colored dye was used to enhance the impression of the stamp (Badawy, p. 345).

A number of bronze stamps which have survived from the Early Christian period were probably used commercially, as in sealing amphoras and grain sacks. Some of these stamps are marked with names, as can be seen in the case of number 41 ("Thomas"). These may have been names of producers or shippers of goods (Vikan and Nesbitt, pp. 25-28). Other stamps contain words invoking quality and prosperity, such as "Good Fruits," "Good Fortune," or "Beautiful Goods" (Vikan and Nesbitt, p. 26). Another group of stamps contains formulae possibly designed to ensure the safekeeping of produce and of those who consumed it, such as "Life," or the apotropaic invocation "One God!" (Vikan and Nesbitt, p. 26). Several stamps, such as number 40 in the exhibition, read "Health." Frequently, jar stamps are in the shape of a cross, to add a further protection to the container's contents (Badawy, p. 346, fig. 5.52).

Some householders resorted to spells to avoid spoilage of their food and drink. For example, a Byzantine recipe for preventing wine from turning reads: "Write on an apple these divine words from the 34th. Psalm: 'Taste and see how sweet is the Lord.' Then throw the apple into the wine" (G. Schlumberger, p. 140).

The last category of household containers to be considered here is baskets, of which this exhibition presents two beautifully preserved specimens (nos. 42 and 43). Baskets were used to hold such produce as bread, sweets, cheeses, fruits, and vegetables. Papyri from Egypt reveal that baskets were often used by separated family members for sending food to one another. Thus, in the third century, we read of one man sending a "basket full of sweetmeats" to his wife (Hunt, pp. 228-29), and another sending to his son "a palm-leaf basket of bread and a basket in which were cheeses and parsley-root" (Winter, pp. 271-72). In both the secular and the sacred art of the early Christians, baskets of produce connoted prosperity. A frequent theme on textiles,

89

such as number 75 in the exhibition, is that of children holding out baskets of fruits or bread. Brimming baskets were also depicted in the mosaics of Early Christian churches. In the mid-sixth-century mosaics of the choir of the church of San Vitale at Ravenna, for example, there are fruit baskets with flared tops and central bands, similar in form to the basket number 42, from Karanis (Deichmann, pl. 305).

Baskets served many other functions in the house. We have already seen that specially shaped wicker baskets served as portable containers for glass vessels such as the *amphoriskoi.* In color plate VI, a miniature from an illustrated Genesis of the sixth century, a basket at the bottom of the page serves as a container for flax or wool. It rests on the ground beside a seated woman who is preparing fibers for spinning by winding them onto a distaff. One of the stranger applications of baskets was discovered by the excavators at Karanis. In that town, some of the householders stuffed soft-sided baskets between the bars of their windows in order to close them, for the windows were provided neither with shutters, wood being expensive, nor with glass, which was even more costly. The baskets may have provided efficient insulation from cold, but only at the expense of light.

Fig. 37. Piazza Armerina, Villa, Floor Mosaic , Detail.
The Picnic after the Hunt.

29
Door

Egypt (Karanis), late 3rd-4th century

Wood

H. 164, W. 66

University of Michigan

Kelsey Museum of Archaeology, 8151

This well-preserved door made of palm wood was found in a house at Karanis. It is constructed of three boards held in place by battens fastened to the boards with iron nails and wooden pegs. The door opened on a pair of pivots, made of acacia wood, fitted into sockets in the lintel and threshold of the door frame. The pivots are fastened to the surface of the door with pegs, nails, and palm-fiber ropes. The ropes were tightened by being twisted and secured with small wooden pegs on each side of the door. A rope was also passed around the entire door and tightened in a similar manner, in order to bind the three boards more closely to one another.

The door still preserves its cased wooden bolt. The lock was manipulated by means of a simple wooden key, which was inserted into the rectangular slot on the outside of the door so that it could be engaged into the bolt.

The doors and windows of the multilevel, mud-brick houses of Karanis were made of wood, and highly valued. Lease agreements of the period often contained a clause stipulating that the rented house be returned to the owner with the doors and window frames intact (Shier, 1949, p. 62).

A set of paneled doors from Karanis may be seen in Husselman, pl. 56. For two handsome examples with finely carved detail from Bawit, see Rutschowscaya, 1986, pp. 155-56, nos. 539, 540.

Bibliography: Husselman, pp. 42-43, pl. 53.

30
Storage box

Egypt (Karanis)

Wood and bronze

H. 38, L. 41.5, W. 38

University of Michigan

Kelsey Museum of Archaeology, 24932, 7477 (lock plate)

This large wooden storage box rests on stretcher feet, formed from two boards running front to back, placed near the side ends. Fragments of a bronze circular lock plate indicate that a lid was once attached to the box. The interior is partitioned into three sections, one large and two small, to help organize the articles being stored. In its present state, only the front of the box displays decoration. Vertical bands of hatching, dots, and circles on the right and left frame a square panel. Around the edges of the panel are rows of dotted circles. The focus of the design is a large ring of concentric circles with another set of concentric circles at its center. Four bands, composed of dotted and plain circles, radiate diagonally from the medallion to the corners of the panel.

A box of similar proportions may be seen on the fourth-century Projecta casket, where an attendant holds a large box while her mistress completes her toilet (color plate I). It may have contained cosmetics and toiletries, or perhaps jewelry. In a panel from the fourth-century ceiling frescoes in the imperial palace at Trier, a well-to-do Roman matron is shown holding a box full of jewels in one arm, as she pulls out a necklace for display with the other (color plate III).

A fragmentary wooden box from Egypt may be seen in Petrie, 1927, p. 46, no. 33, pl. XL.

Unpublished

31
Box

Egypt (Karanis)

Wood

H. 8.5, L. 8.3, W. 7.5

University of Michigan

Kelsey Museum of Archaeology, 24760

This small rectangular box of dark wood rests on two stretcher feet that project beyond the front edge of the box. The lid is hinged at the back with two dowel pins. A simple design of rows of dotted concentric circles decorates the lid and front panel of the box. Vertical incised lines separate the three rows of circles on the front panel.

Small boxes of this type were used for jewelry or toiletry articles. In a fresco in Herculaneum, a maid is shown bringing a little box with a lid to her mistress (Richter, 1926, fig. 338).

Unpublished

32
Key

Egypt (Karanis), 1st-5th century

Wood

L. 17, W. 10

University of Michigan

Kelsey Museum of Archaeology, 3866

Found at Karanis, this is one of several examples of the "sliding" key used in a locking system developed in Egypt to secure homes from unwanted entry. It consists of a wooden L-shaped rectangular shaft with two long pegs inserted at right angles into the short section. A hole in the end of the handle was used for a loop cord. The key was inserted into the door through a slot, and the teeth manipulated into the bolt in order to release the tumblers of the lock. The bolt could then be drawn out of its channel.

The sliding-key system was utilized extensively by the Romans. Evidence from Pompeii indicates that it was in use as early as the first century A.D. (Vikan and Nesbitt, 1980, p. 2).

Comparative examples in wood from Karanis may be seen in Husselman, pl. 54a. For examples in bronze, see Strzygowski, pl. XXXVI, nos. 9196-98, 9200.

Unpublished

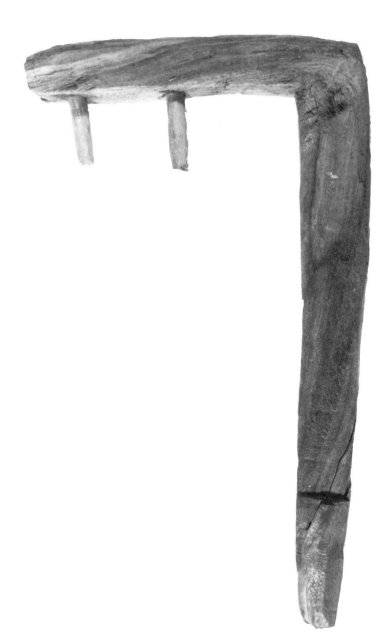

96

33
Cone seal

Eastern Mediterranean, 8th-10th century

Silver

H. 2.18, D. 1.34

Toronto

Royal Ontario Museum, 986.181.65

A collar and a tang surmount this cone-shaped seal with ribbed sides. There are surface scratches, but the seal is otherwise intact. On the base, enclosed within a circle, is the inscription in reversed characters that would imprint the following plea:

ΘΕΩ
ΤΟΚΕΒ
ΩΗΘΗΘΕ
ΩΦΗΛ
ΑC+

("Mother of God, help Theophila").

For the functions of this type of sealing implement, see p. 86.

Unpublished

34
Cone seal

Eastern Mediterranean, 9th-12th century

Steatite

H. 1.77, L. 1.05, W. .94

Toronto

Royal Ontario Museum, 986.181.69

This cone-shaped seal carved in steatite is octagonal in section, with alternating wide and narrow sides. Apart from minor surface scratches and chips, the object is intact. At the top there is a drilled hole, allowing the seal to be suspended by a cord. The base is engraved with a nimbed rider.

For the functions of this type of seal, see p. 86. For the significance of the rider motif, see p. 25.

Unpublished

35
Pithos

Egypt (Karanis), late 3rd–mid 4th century

Earthenware

H. 62.5, Rim D. 23.7, Base D. 15

University of Michigan

Kelsey Museum of Archaeology, 8146

This tall storage jar was made of a coarse red clay with a pinkish white slip applied to the upper exterior. The elongated, oval body has a wide mouth surrounded by a thick rim, molded outward, and four small, vertical handles attached to the shoulder and neck. It rests on a recessed base. Typical of Coptic Painted Ware, the surface of the vessel is enlivened with a bold design consisting of a horizontal band around the center of the body with a looped band beneath, and high arching concentric bands above. The bands alternate in pinkish white and dark red outlined in grey, with the red painted solid, and the pinkish white filled with the circled dot or dotted twist motif. In each of the arches is a stylized plant motif. Each spandrel area between arches is occupied by a medallion with a lattice pattern inside, and a series of loops around the circumference. A twisted band with a line running through it surrounds the neck.

Bibliography: Johnson, p. 38, no. 145, pl. 20.

36
Amphora

Palestine, 6th century

Earthenware

H. 101.3, Inner mouth D. 10.5, Max D. 51.3

University of Illinois

Krannert Art Museum, 87-20-1

This storage and shipping amphora was especially designed for olive oil, with a capacious bell-shaped body, and a convex base made to rest in a stand. Aside from some minor chips around the mouth, and soil and mineral incrustation on the body, the overall condition of the vessel is good. The neck is short with a narrow raised band at the base, and a slightly projecting rim. Two small, round, vertical handles with a wide groove in the center of each project from the slope of the shoulder. Horizontal tooled grooves, somewhat marred by numerous irregularities, begin at the top of the shoulder and continue down the body to the base. The grooves are narrow and tight over the shoulder, become broad as the body flares out, and then narrow again slightly at the base.

Amphoras of the type were produced in Palestine, a major supplier of cereal, oil, and wine to the Byzantine market. Widely distributed throughout the Mediterranean, these vessels have been found in Samos, Constantinople, Istria, Egypt, and Carthage. Fragments found at sites in Britain and Ireland attest to the extensive sea trade of the late fifth and sixth centuries.

Two amphoras from Egypt very similar to the Krannert example may be seen in the British Museum (1983, 10-1, 10-11). For a close parallel found in the Athenian Agora, see Delivorrias, p. 250, no. 157.

Unpublished

37
Amphora

Egypt (Karanis), 4th-5th century

Earthenware

H. 54, Rim D. 11.5, Max D. 31

University of Michigan

Kelsey Museum of Archaeology, 8023

The wide, vertical body of this large amphora tapers slightly downward to a convex base. The vessel is intact, including the clay stopper, except for some holes in the body, and chips around the mouth. The opening is narrow, finished with a thick, projecting rim. At the top of the neck, just under the rim, is a smooth, impressed band interrupted by two vertical handles attached to the neck and shoulder. Irregularly spaced horizontal tooled grooves cover the surface, beginning at the handle line, and continuing to the base.

Numerous storage and shipping amphoras were found at Karanis. Like catalogue number 36, this type was widespread throughout the eastern Mediterranean from the fourth to the seventh century. Recent theories place the center of production in Syria and Egypt (see Poulou-Papadimitriou, 1985, 286ff., pl. 143; Robinson, 1959, 115, no. M 333, pl. 32).

A comparable example from the Athenian Agora may be seen in Delivorrias p. 250, fig. 158.

Bibliography: Gazda, 1983a, p. 13, fig. 21.

38
Amphoriskos

Egypt (Karanis), 4th–mid-5th century

Earthenware

H. 23.6, Rim D. 4.5, Max. D. 8.5

University of Michigan

Kelsey Museum of Archaeology, 7866

This is a miniature amphora with an elongated ovoid form, tapered downward to a pointed base. The long, narrow neck flares outward at the top to form a small opening, surrounded by a tall rim, slightly carinated on the sides and molded inward along the edge. Two thick, heavy handles are attached to the neck just under the rim, and to the top of the shoulder. Turning marks are faintly visible on the surface of the vessel, with more pronounced impressed rings at the base of the handles and on the shoulder. The fine-grained yellowish red clay fabric is covered with a red slip on the exterior surface, which is extended to the area just inside the mouth. A simple painted decoration in dusty red and pinkish white is still apparent on the shoulder and body. It consists of two series of short, downward-sloping lateral brushstrokes placed on either side of a vertical line of white dots.

Bibliography: Johnson, p. 24, no. 44, pl. 5.

102

39
Amphoriskos

Eastern Mediterranean, 3rd-4th century

Glass

H. 20.5

University of Illinois

World Heritage Museum, 17.2.30

A pale green free-blown *amphoriskos* of "colorless" glass, this piece is related in shape to the large terra-cotta amphoras. The vessel is intact, but cracked near the handles and down the body. The surface reveals evidence of incrustation. Meant to rest in a stand, the slightly convex body tapers downward to a solid pinched and pointed base nib. The short neck is flared near the mouth, and finished with a rounded rim. Two short, looping, trailed handles in a darker green, with a ridge running down the center, are attached to the neck and shoulders.

Related types may be seen in Sotheby, p. 134, no. 241; Matheson, pp. 86-87, no. 234; Hayes, 1975, p. 110, no. 411, pl. 25; Harden, p. 264, no. 793, pls. X, XX.

Unpublished

40
Stamp in crescent shape

Eastern Mediterranean, 5th-6th century

Bronze

H. 2.8, W. 6

University of Toronto

Malcove Collection, M82.421

The boldly formed letters of the legend V ΓIA ("health") are enclosed in a crescent, one of a variety of shapes found in bronze stamps of the fifth and sixth centuries. The edges of the crescent are folded over to form the sides of the stamp.

Bronze stamps of this type were used in commercial contexts such as the marking of jar stoppers, and the sealing of sacks (Vikan and Nesbitt, 1980, pp. 25-28).

For comparable examples, see Campbell, 1985, p. 65, nos. 75, 76, 77; Weitzmann, 1979, pp. 627-28, no. 565; Galavaris, p. 39, fig. 20, p. 47, fig. 21, p. 50, fig. 23.

Bibliography: Campbell, 1985, p. 66, no. 78.

41
Triangular stamp

Eastern Mediterranean, 5th-6th century

Bronze

H.9, W. 5.8, Handle H. 2.6

University of Toronto

Malcove Collection, M82.422

This bronze stamp takes the form of a triangle with folded sides enclosing the letters θΩMA ("Thomas"). This example has a handle attached to the back. Three tiny crosses, in a punched technique, appear at each corner of the triangle.

Since such stamps were used in commerce (see the entry on no. 40), it is possible that Thomas was the name of a tradesman, either the producer or the shipper of the goods marked with his seal.

Similar bronze stamps may be seen in Campbell, 1985, pp. 65-66, nos. 75, 76, 78; Weitzmann, 1979, pp. 627-28, no. 565; Galavaris, p. 39, fig. 20, p. 47, fig. 21, p. 50, fig. 23.

Bibliography: Campbell, 1985, p. 65, no. 77.

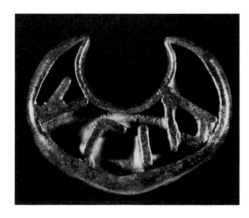

42
Basket

Egypt (Karanis), 1st-5th century

Reed

H. 20.2, D. 29.3

University of Michigan

Kelsey Museum of Archaeology, 3442

This handsome woven reed basket is in
excellent condition. The sides are woven in an
open lattice-work pattern, divided into two
zones by a horizontal band with a series of x's.
The lower section is cylindrical, the upper
flared outward. Four high looping, twisted
handles are attached to the rim.

Baskets of all types were indispensable in the
home, fulfilling a variety of needs from storage
containers for dry goods and household
accessories to sifters of granular material, and
sieves for beer.

For comparative examples from Egypt, see
Petrie, 1927, pl. XLII.

Bibliography: Gazda, 1983a, p. 27, fig. 45

43
Basket

Egypt (Karanis), 1st-5th century

Reed

H. 21.6, D. 32.5

University of Michigan

Kelsey Museum of Archaeology, 3443

This sturdy, well-preserved reed basket, unlike catalogue no. 42, is densely woven with groups of five or six reeds interwoven to form a close herringbone pattern. The form is cylindrical, rising from a circular base and flaring slightly at the rim.

Examples of baskets in a variety of shapes found in Egypt may be seen in Petrie, 1927, pls. XLI, XLII.

Unpublished

Fig. 38. Rome, Catacomb of SS. Marcellinus and Peter, Wall Painting.
Banqueters.

In the Early Christian period, no less than today, eating and drinking were social activities. In wealthy houses the dining room was often the principal reception room, and was accorded the richest decor; the furniture, vessels, and implements used there were the most ostentatious in the home. At the end of the second century, Clement of Alexandria, advising Christians to live moderately, tells them to use simple furniture when they eat—to shun tables with carved ivory legs, and silver couches (*Paedagogus*, II, 35-37). Paintings and mosaics of the Early Christian period help us to visualize such furnishings for banquets in the houses of the rich. A miniature in a fifth-century Italian copy of the poems of Vergil shows Queen Dido entertaining Aeneas in a dining room of her palace (color plate V). The guests recline around a dish containing a fish, which is set upon a small table with a circular or oval top, somewhat resembling the wooden table that is number 44 in our exhibit, from Karanis in Egypt. But the table portrayed in the painting, being in a palace, is of a more precious material, bronze, or perhaps even gilt silver. Silver tripod tables and stands have been discovered in first- and fourth-century hoards (Strong, pp. 159, 208-9, pl. 41A). The three diners in the painting have disposed themselves upon a *stibadium*, a semicircular couch which in late Roman times replaced the old *triclinium* arrangement of couches placed around three sides of a rectangle (Duval, pp. 292-94). Dining rooms in the grandest houses were designed to accommodate several groups of guests at one time, who reclined on *stibadia* placed in three or more curved apses (Ellis, p. 570).

Color plate VII, a painting of Pharoah's feast from a sixth-century manuscript of the book of Genesis in Vienna, shows diners reclining on a *stibadium* around a semicircular *sigma*-shaped table. This table has a bluish white top, which is similar in form to actual marble table tops found by archaeologists excavating sixth-century dining rooms in the private houses of the wealthy (Balty, 1984, pl. 52).

Food was commonly accompanied by wine, but it was usual to mix the wine with water. Clement recommended that Christians drink wine, but he warned that it should be consumed in moderation. "It is best to mix the wine with as much water as possible," he explained. "Both are creations of God, and thus the mixture of both contributes to our health" (*Paedagogus*, II, 23). The mixing of water with wine took place in the dining room, and required a variety of different serving vessels, as can be seen from figure 38, which reproduces a third-century painting of banqueters from the Christian catacomb of SS. Marcellinus and Peter in Rome (Ferrua, pp. 32-35). Here the feasters recline on a semicircular *stibadium* around a circular tripod table, on which is set their food. One of them, on the right, holds a glass wine goblet, similar to number 45 in the exhibition. On the ground, to the left of the table, is a container holding two *amphoriskoi*, or jars, of the type represented by numbers 38 and 39 (the necks of the *amphoriskoi* can be seen protruding from the top of the container). On the right of the table is a glass jug with a handle, resembling number 47, and an overturned glass flask without handles, whose shape can be compared to that of our number 49. A servant girl approaches the diners from the left, holding a glass goblet in her left hand and a handled jug in her right. Behind her is a tripod stand supporting a large metal vessel whose cover has an elaborate handle fashioned in the form of a bird in flight. The diner on the left gestures towards the girl, giving the command which is written above them: "Sabina misce," or "Mix it, Sabina!" While it is not possible to be certain of the functions of the different vessels that the artist has portrayed, a reasonable hypothesis is that the large vase on the left contains water, while the two small *amphoriskoi* contain un-mixed wine. The jug that Sabina is carrying, then, would contain water that she is bringing from the large vessel, in order to mix it with wine in the goblets of the diners.

Glass vessels, like the ones shown in the catacomb painting, were also used at picnics which took place out-of-doors. Figure 37 is a detail from a mosaic floor of the early fourth-century aristocratic villa at Piazza Armerina in Sicily, which shows hunters relaxing in the shade of an awning hung between two trees (Daltrop, p. 14). They recline around a *stibadium* while their servants serve them food and wine. In the foreground is set a basket containing two pale green glass *amphoriskoi*. This basket has the same shape as the container of the twin wine jars illustrated in the catacomb painting (fig. 38); a similar basket, holding three glass *amphoriskoi*, is preserved in the Metropolitan Museum of Art in New York (inv. no. 12.182.79 a-e). In the mosaic, a boy prof-fers to the diners a stemmed wine glass, which can be compared with number 45 in the exhibition, while one of the men drinks from a cylindrical beaker of clear glass (compare numbers 52 and 53). The use of so much glass in such a rough and rustic setting recalls Clement of Alexandria's complaints about the imprac-ticality of glassware because its "overdelicate artistry makes it more easily broken, and us ever-fearful as we drink" (*Paedagogus*, II, 35).

Silver was a more durable material, widely used among the wealthy for the serving of wine. In the banqueting scene of the fifth-century Vergil manuscript (color plate V), the guest at the right is drinking wine from a silver beaker, evidently handed to him by the servant boy at the lower left, who holds another beaker and a jug brimming with crimson liquid. On the other hand, the silver jug held by the boy on the right probably contains water, which the slave is bringing to wash the hands of the guests, who would rinse them over the little silver basin held in his left hand; in Early Christian art a similar jug and basin are seen in use by Pilate, when he washes his hands before condemn-ing Christ (Schiller, figs. 206, 208). Silverware of the type illustrated in the Roman Vergil has been discovered in hoards and in private houses (for beakers, see Kaufmann-Heinimann, nos. 43-46; for a handled jug, see M. M. Mango, pp. 270-71). Needless to say, the silver cups pleased Clement of Alexandria no more than the glass. If the drink is hot, he complains, silver cups are too hot to handle; if it is cold, the drinker is poisoned by the metal. In his eyes, gold and silver wine-coolers, wine pourers, and drinking cups, as well as silver dishes, saucers, and bowls are all "vulgar luxuries" (*Paedagogus*, II, 35). The church father also scorns the armies of slaves engaged to satisfy the appetites of the rich, whose presence is attested by our figure 37 and color plate V:

Men resort to servants to escape work and waiting on themselves. They hire a great host of bakers and cooks and waiters and men who can carve meat skillfully into slices. They portion out this service into many different duties: some are engaged to minister to their gluttony, carvers and cooks of rich blood puddings, others to prepare and to make the pastries, others to make the honey cakes, and still others to prepare the porridges; . . . others keep watch over their gold like griffins, others guard their silver and keep their goblets clean and get the dishes ready for the banquets. . . . There are a host of wine pourers in constant attendance upon them. (*Paedagogus*, III, 26; trans. Wood, p. 221)

In a similar vein, St. John Chrysostom, at the end of the fourth century, said that Christians should keep at the most one or two slaves, instead of one or two thousand (Grant, pp. 94-95).

There were many people, however, who made do without armies of servants, and whose needs had to be satisfied by pottery vessels rather than silver. Nevertheless, as the examples in this exhibition demonstrate, poverty of material did not mean a lack of artistic value. Number 56, for example, is an elegant thin-walled carafe from North Africa which, to judge from its relief decoration of river gods, was intended to hold water. The reliefs were an imitation of the repoussé work on more expensive jugs in silver, such as the magnificent piece illustrated in figure 9. Carafes of a similar shape are shown in use in a banquet depicted in a third-century floor mosaic from El Djem, in Tunisia (Salomonson, 1960, fig. 1; New York, 1987, no. 47, pp. 182-83).

When it came to eating, as with drinking, Clement of Alexandria was once again ready with advice for Christians. Their food should be moderate and frugal: "roots, olives, some green vegetables, milk, cheese, fruits and boiled vegetables of all kinds, but without the sauces" (*Paedagogus*, II, 15). The sumptuousness of the meals enjoyed by the wealthy is evidenced by the great variety of surviving silver dishes for different types of food. There are the great *lanxes*, round serving dishes as much as two feet in diameter (see fig. 17), and large rectangular platters. There are smaller side plates, sometimes in sets of twelve. There are special fish-shaped dishes, and bowls with lids to keep the food warm. There are bowls with handles for serving the sauces, and ladles to scoop them out (Strong, pp. 192-204; Cahn and Kaufmann-Heinimann, nos. 47-63). Some of this silverware has been found in houses (M. M. Mango, 1986, pp. 268-71), some in buried hoards. The variety of the shapes was matched by the variety of the decoration, with the more elaborately adorned pieces presumably kept for display rather than for use. Even in Christian houses there was silver decorated with pagan mythology (see the handle of the bowl illustrated in fig. 16), as well as pastoral scenes (Dodd, no. 9), Nilotic scenes (see the bowl in fig. 16), and the creatures of land and sea (see the silver plate in the exhibition, no. 57, with its relief of two ducks). There were also plates with Christian scenes, and portraits of saints (Dodd, no. 78). Sometimes the plates with Christian subjects were made in sets, like the famous seventh-century plates from Cyprus depicting a series of episodes from the life of David (Dodd, nos. 58-66).

111

Among the less affluent, pottery dishes imitated the forms and decoration associated with silver. Thus there were rectangular pottery *lanxes,* whose shape, unsuited to production on the potters wheel, evidently copied prototypes in metal. Especially in North Africa, plates and bowls were decorated with reliefs similar in effect to the repoussé work of silver, and depicting as wide a variety of subjects (Salomonson, 1962, pp. 53-95; 1979, pp. 21-90). There were pagan myths, sometimes appearing in sets, such as twelve plates depicting the twelve labors of Hercules. There were dishes commemorating games in the circus or the amphitheater, the chariot races and the wild-beast hunts; these dishes may have been offered to the spectators, somewhat as T-shirts are distributed at rock concerts today. There were plates and bowls decorated with Christian subjects, both from the Old Testament (see the bowl no. 58, with Abraham's sacrifice of Isaac), and from the Gospels. Some dishes showed martyrs in the amphitheater, confronted by lions and other savage beasts; these scenes, which in the flesh had delighted pagans with their cruelty, now in clay delighted Christians with their message of eternal life (Salomonson, 1979, p. 89). Other plates and bowls were decorated with saints (see no. 60), or with Christian symbols such as crosses and lambs (see nos. 61 and 62). As in the case of the dishes with mythological subjects, the pieces showing Christian scenes seem often to have been made in sets (Salomonson, 1979, pp. 35-38).

These pottery dishes were cheap and mass-produced, but in less wealthy houses they appear to have been treasured articles nevertheless, for some bear traces of ancient repairs (Salomonson, 1962, p. 89). The fact that the relief decoration is mainly on the insides of the bowls, rather than on their outsides, suggests that they may have served as the poor households' substitutes for the silver showpieces of the rich. As can be seen from the reclining youth, the second from the right in figure 38, people during the Early Christian period ate for the most part with their fingers, putting out the right hand to the common dish that was set on the table before the diners. Clement of Alexandria advises on the correct etiquette: "we should put our hand out only in turn, from time to time. . . . We must . . . partake of what is set before us politely, keeping our hands, as well as our chin and our couch, clean" (*Paedagogus*, II, 13; trans. Wood, p. 104). However neat the eater, however, the hands needed frequent washing; for this reason, the servant at the lower left of the miniature in the Roman Vergil (color plate V) stands in readiness with his jug of water and his silver bowl. Several late Roman silver treasures have preserved shallow fluted basins, which were filled with perfumed water so that the diners could rinse food from their fingers (Painter, pp. 19, 29, figs. 31-32; Cahn and Kaufmann-Heinimann, no. 41). Such silver wash-basins were, of course, condemned by Clement, who said that clay ones were just as good (*Paedagogus*, II, 37).

Eating implements consisted of knives and spoons; forks were not used. The knives, with their iron blades, have not been well preserved; Clement describes luxurious silver-studded table knives with ivory handles (*Paedagogus*, II, 37). By contrast, many spoons have survived, in bronze and in silver (see nos. 63 and 64). Spoons were used not only for eating liquids such as sauces, but also for fruits such as berries; in figure 39, a fourth-century mosaic from Carthage, a woman personifying the month of July can be seen spooning mulberries from a glass bowl. As was the case with the silver dishes, there were different shapes of spoons adapted to different functions. Some had handles with pointed ends, which could be used for spearing shellfish in their shells; others had looped handles and wider, deeper bowls, suitable for sauces and puddings (Cahn and Kaufmann-Heinimann, nos. 1-35).

Every household, whether rich or poor, needed cooking equipment. Clement, while he condemned the legions of cooks of the wealthy, felt that it was appropriate for a Christian housewife to be a good cook: "Nor is it a reproach to a wife—as housekeeper and helpmate—to busy herself in cooking, so that it may be well pleasing to her husband" (*Paedagogus*, III, 49). Some of the cooking ware that has survived from the Early Christian period would do credit to a modern kitchen, such as the sturdy and ingenious hinged frying pan from Luxor in Egypt, with its incised decoration of a fish (no. 65). The handsome pottery cooking pot, number 67, can be compared to the deep widemouthed pot shown at the lower left of the picnic scene from the mosaic at Piazza Armerina (fig. 37). However, the pot in the mosaic is set directly upon a fire (at which a crouching servant is blowing), while the pot in the exhibition was provided with four handles so that it could be suspended over the flames. In the kitchen, as in the dining room, the vessels and utensils were designed to meet the demands of both utility and aesthetics.

Fig. 39. London, British Museum, Calendar Mosaic from Carthage, Detail. July Eating Berries from a Bowl.

44
Tripod table

Egypt (Karanis), 1st-5th century

Wood

H. 44.1, Top D. 25

University of Michigan

Kelsey Museum of Archaeology, 10220

Small, wooden, round-topped tables of this type, with their sturdy three-legged design, were among the most versatile pieces of furniture in the Roman household. Although the horizontal supports are missing, and the top is warped, the piece as a whole is in good condition. The form with cabriole legs derives from more elaborate Roman prototypes.

Lightweight and easily transportable, the table could be moved to different rooms of the home to serve a variety of needs. It was most commonly used as a dining table. Similar examples are represented in the banqueting frescoes of Pompeii and Herculaneum, standing near dining couches, laden with dishes and wine containers.

Bibliography: Gazda, l983a, p. 24, fig. 39.

45
Stemmed cup

Egypt or Syria, 5th-6th century

Glass

H. 10.5, Rim D. 7.4, Base D. 4.3

University of Illinois

World Heritage Museum, 17.2.46

This stemmed drinking cup was made of a pale green "colorless" glass (cf. no. 46). The exterior surface shows evidence of iridescent weathering. The wall of the cup tapers upward and flares slightly at the rim, which was rounded off by reheating in a flame. A short, solid stem attached to a small, round base with an irregular profile supports the cup.

Other examples of related cups with varying profiles may be seen in Matheson, p. 113, no. 295; Auth, p. 150, no. 194; Hayes, 1975, p. 109, nos. 405-8, pl. 26; Harden, pp. 171-72, nos. 479, 482, 484, pls. VI, XVI.

Unpublished

46
Stemmed cup

Egypt or Syria, 5th-6th century

Glass

H. 9.5, Rim D. 10.5, Base D. 6.5

University of Illinois

World Heritage Museum, 16.3.4

A free-blown, blue-green, stemmed cup of "colorless" glass, this piece is in good condition, although some iridescent and milky weathering is evident. It is a characteristic example of a type found in Egypt and Syria used for drinking wine. The bell-shaped cup is supported on a tall, solid stem and round, concave base with an irregular edge. Marks of the tool used to flatten the base are faintly visible on its upper side. The cup flares sharply at the rim, which is broad and folded to the outside.

For other examples of the general type, see Matheson, p. 113, no. 295; Auth, p. 150, no. 194; Hayes, 1975, p. 109, nos. 405, 406 (decorated), 407, 408 (undecorated), pl. 26; Harden, pp. 171-72, nos. 479 (undecorated), 482, 484 (decorated), pl. VI, XVI.

Unpublished

47
Jug with handle

Eastern Mediterranean, 4th century

Glass

H. 12.8, Rim D. 4.1, Base D. 4.5

University of Illinois

World Heritage Museum, 17.2.36

This vessel is a free-blown flask made of a "colorless" purplish glass. Although broken and repaired near the neck, the object is in good condition. The body, spherical with a series of five depressions, rests on a low, thick pad foot. The neck is tall and slender, flaring outward near the top into a trefoil mouth with a rounded rim. A pale purplish trailed thread following the contour of the rim on the outside adds complexity to the design of the mouth, while a thick trailed thread of the same color at the base of the neck emphasizes the juncture between body and neck. The trailed handle, also purplish in hue, joined to the body and rim, is cylindrical in section, but flattened at the top where it connects with the rim.

For a comparative example, see Sotheby, p. 170, no. 304

Unpublished

48
Jug with handle

Eastern Mediterranean, 4th century

Glass

H. 19.5, Rim D. 5.5

University of Illinois

World Heritage Museum, 17.2.9

This free-blown, olive-green jug of "colorless" glass has a slightly squat, globular body. Although there appears to be some iridescent weathering, the vessel is in good condition. Like catalogue number 47, the division of upper and lower sections of the vessel is emphasized by a thick trailed thread of similar hue around the base of the neck. The tapered neck, splayed outward at the top, is pinched to form a trefoil spout. The rim was folded to the outside. The body, which has a concave depression at its base, is attached to a high foot encircled by a thick molded ring around the edge, and deeply cut out underneath. A flat strap handle is attached to the spout and body.

A similar jug, though without the ring at the base of the neck, is illustrated in Sotheby, p. 164-65, no. 290. Other closely related jugs with circular mouths may be seen in Matheson, p. 90-91, nos. 243, 244; Hayes, l975, p. 61, no. 158, pl. 8, pp. 107-8, no. 397, pl. 19; and Harden, p. 243, no. 722, pl. XIX.

Unpublished

117

49
Flask with funnel mouth

Eastern Mediterranean, 6th-7th century

Glass

H. 15.5, Rim. D. 3.1

University of Illinois

World Heritage Museum, 17.2.16

The body of this free-blown, blue-green flask of "colorless" glass is a well-formed globe. The flask has a tall, tapering neck and a funnel mouth. It rests on a simple pushed-in base. The rim is rounded and somewhat irregular. Characteristic of early Byzantine flasks, the surface decoration consists of spiral threading around the neck under the rim, and a wave pattern of trailed threads around the body.

A close parallel may be seen in Auth, p. 149. Similar fifth- and sixth-century flasks may be seen in Sotheby, p. 133, no. 239; Matheson, pp. 125-27, nos. 335-37; Hayes, 1975, pp. 108-9, pl. 26, no. 403, p. 131, pl. 33, no. 541.

Unpublished

50
Bottle flask without handles

Egypt, 4th century or later

Glass

H. 21, Rim D. 5.9, Base D. 5.5

University of Illinois

World Heritage Museum, 17.2.33

This free-blown, green bottle-flask of "color-less" glass belongs to a small class having a carinated body resting on a relatively high, circular concave base. The neck flares outward at the top to form a wide mouth. The rim is rounded. The base, with an irregular edge, was blown separately and joined to the vessel. Tool marks are visible where it was flattened on the upper surface. Thin lines faintly visible on the surface of the flask suggest that it may have been decorated with trailed threads.

A similar example may be seen in Harden, p. 223, fig. 4, e.

Unpublished

51
Lekythos flask

Eastern Mediterranean, 3rd-5th century

Glass

H. 24, Rim D. 5.3, Base D. 4.5

University of Illinois

World Heritage Museum, 17.2.10

The shape of this tall, pale blue-green flask is related to the lekythos. The vessel shows evidence of incrustation and iridescent weathering. The body tapers downward from steeply sloped shoulders to a small dark-green pad foot which is deeply indented at the center of its underside. The tapering neck is flared out at the top to form a wide mouth. The rim is rounded. Two high, looping, dark-green trailed handles connect with the neck and shoulders. The vessel is simply decorated with a single trailed coil of dark green around the neck and just below the rim.

Unpublished

120

52
Beaker

Syro-Palestinian, 4th-5th century

Glass

H. 10.3, Rim D. 6.5, Base D. 5.5

University of Illinois

World Heritage Museum, 17.2.48

The thick pad foot on which this bluish green beaker of "colorless" glass rests is formed in one piece with the rest of the vessel. On the inside of the beaker, a convex protrusion rises from its bottom, corresponding to the depression in the center of the foot. The wall is slightly concave, accentuated by an encircling trailed coil of similar color near the center. The rim, slightly flared, is rounded off.

Similar examples may be seen in Sotheby, 1979, p. 130, no. 231; Hayes, 1975, pp. 103-4, nos. 374-77, pl. 24.

Unpublished

53
Beaker

Gaul, 5th-6th century

Glass

H. 11.4, Rim D. 6.3

University of Illinois

Krannert Art Museum, 80-9-2

This translucent, green cylindrical beaker with straight, slightly flared sides rests on a flat base. Aside from overall soil incrustation, irides-cence, and a hairline crack near the top, the condition is good. The mouth is finished with a simple, polished rim. The upper portion of the beaker is handsomely decorated with a pattern of applied threads consisting of an arcade with the lowest thread allowed to drip and thicken at evenly spaced intervals. Immediately below, the surface is incised with a band of horizontal lines.

For related examples, see Paris, pp. 98-99, no. 19c; Mainz, p. 133, no. 184d.

Unpublished

54
Krater

Egypt (Karanis), late 3rd-4th century

Earthenware

H. 24, Rim D. 14.5, Base D. 9.1

University of Michigan

Kelsey Museum of Archaeology, 7967

One of the most common shapes in Coptic Painted Ware is exhibited by this large krater with a spherical body resting on a high flared base, and a short, broad, nearly vertical neck. The clay fabric, a coarse red-orange, is covered with a pinkish white slip. The entire surface of the pot is covered with an elaborate painted design consisting of a series of white and light red bands filled with vegetal, geometric, and figurative motifs. A vine with ivy leaves sets off the neck, while the shoulder is emphasized by a boldly painted twist. Especially attractive is the broad band around the body occupied by lively, well-drawn birds, deer, rabbits, and floral elements.

For similar examples from Karanis, see Johnson, pp. 33-34, nos. 106-10, pls. 13-14.

Unpublished

55
Handleless jug with tall neck

Egypt (Karanis), 3rd to mid-4th century

Earthenware

H. 24, Rim D. 11.5, Base D. 8

University of Michigan

Kelsey Museum of Archaeology, 7913

This handleless red-ware jug has a spherical body supported on a high, slightly flared base, and a tall, wide neck, flared at the top. The rim is molded outward. A groove marks the transition from the neck to the shoulder. The vessel is made of a coarse reddish brown clay with a pale red core to which was applied, on the exterior, a slip of similar color that was allowed to trickle down in streaks near the base. A series of horizontal bands of varying widths painted with designs in pinkish white slip or other pigment cover the surface. Around the neck, the design consists of two bands, the upper filled with lozenges, the lower with a series of short vertical lines. The shoulder decoration is a simple line with a row of small dots directly beneath it. A bold pattern, incorporating a vine with stylized grape clusters, birds, and pomegranates, floats across the surface of the body. A worn inscription in Greek placed just below the grapes reads: NEIATO (Johnson, p. 92, note 46).

Similar jugs from Karanis may be seen in Johnson, p. 42, nos. 177-78, 180-84, pls. 28-29.

Bibliography: Johnson, p. 42, no. 139, pl. 28.

56
Flask with relief decoration

North Africa (Tunisia), 3rd century

Earthenware

H. 14, Rim D. 3.8, Base D. 4.6

Private collection

This is one of a series of fine, thin-walled North African flasks with handles, produced during the third century, especially between c. A.D. 200 and c. 250 (African Red Slip Ware: Salomonson, 1968, table II, form I; Hayes, 1972, pp. 193-99, form 171). The flask, which is intact except for a small chip under the rim, has a small mouth, with a narrow projecting rim, and a pear-shaped body that rests on a high, slightly splayed foot-ring. At the junction of the foot with the body there is a finely turned molding. A horizontal molding three centimeters below the rim divides the decoration of the body into two zones. The handle was made in a mold, and features a relief decoration of two vertical framed bands containing laurel fillets. It was pressed into the body of the vessel at the top and applied at the bottom. The base of the handle is incised with vertical reeding.

The body of the flask is decorated with appliqué reliefs: a frieze of three rabbits in the upper zone, and in the lower zone two half-nude bearded male personifications of rivers, who recline each holding a tipped vessel with his left hand supporting its open mouth. The personifications are framed by tall vertical acanthus leaves with turned tips, rising from cupped bases. A garland-like canopy arches over each figure.

The motifs chosen to decorate this particular vessel suggest that one of its functions could have been to hold water, perhaps for mixing with wine. Similar jugs are shown in use at a drinking party of professional *venatores*, or wild-beast hunters who performed in the amphitheater, in a third-century floor mosaic from El Jem (Thysdrus) in Tunisia (New York, 1987, pp. 182-83, no. 47; Salomonson, 1960, pp. 25-55, figs. 1-2).

Other examples of this type of flask are listed by Hayes, 1972, pp. 193-95.

Unpublished

125

57
Dish with two ducks perched on a kantharos

Ravenna, 6th century

Silver

D. 21.6

Richmond

Virginia Museum of Fine Arts, Williams Fund, 66.30.1

The inner surface of this handsome silver plate displays a central medallion, formed by a band of concentric fillets, in which two plump, well-formed ducks are shown drinking from a tall, ribbed kantharos. The charming naturalism of the birds' forms, executed in a delicate chasing and repoussé, is achieved by sinuous, closely set lines articulating the bodies of the ducks. Surrounding the medallion are large, elegantly engraved acanthus leaves.

Sumptuously decorated silver dishes, vessels, and utensils were collected by the elite of Late Roman society as symbols of personal prosperity and as repositories of wealth. Many have been discovered in hoards of domestic treasures buried for safekeeping during the period of barbarian invasions.

The Virginia plate is assigned to the sixth century (Gonosová and Kondoleon, 1985, p. 35).

For the significance of the ducks, see p. 10.

Bibliography: Gonosová and Kondoleon, 1985, p. 34-35, fig. 2; Ross, 1967-68, pp. 56-55; Volbach, 1964, p. 173.

58
Bowl with appliqué of the Sacrifice of Abraham

North Africa (Tunisia), mid-4th to early 5th century

Earthenware

H. 4.7, Rim D. 16.7, Base D. 6

University of Toronto

Malcove Collection, M82.359

A fine-grained, hard-fired orange clay was used to make the bowl, which belongs to a group of African Red Slip Ware (Salomonson, Sigillata chiara C, form A; Hayes, Form 53 A) distinguished by a flat base, plain rim, and thin, curving wall decorated with grooves and stamped relief appliqués. The red slip, applied thinly over the entire surface, forms a matte finish with occasional glossy patches. This bowl, broken and repaired, is complete except for a few chips on the rim.

The decoration consists of two carefully incised circular grooves just below the rim, and two on the floor at center. Four stamped reliefs, in a vigorous but unrefined style, representing the Sacrifice of Abraham accompanied by a ram, lion, and bear are placed around the walls. With no indication of background, the forms seem to float in space. The muscular Abraham, dressed in a loincloth and boots, steps forward, raising a sword in his right hand as he pushes the head of Isaac toward a rectangular altar. Isaac is shown with his hands tied behind his back, kneeling over the altar. At the same time, Abraham turns his head back over his shoulder, as if noticing the fat-tailed ram moving toward him. The bear and the lion, both with open mouths and turning to the right, are drawn from the repertory of animal images depicted in pagan hunting and circus scenes. They have nothing to do with the central scene.

Red slip-ware bowls, like this example, were inexpensive substitutes for metal vessels with relief decoration. Similar examples may be seen in Weitzmann, 1979, p. 426, no. 384; Hayes, 1972, pp. 78-82; Salomonson, 1969, pp. 18-25, pls. 24-26.

Bibliography: Campbell, 1985, p. 41, no. 34; Weitzmann, 1979, p. 422, no. 379.

59
Bowl with shepherd-and-ram appliqué

North Africa, mid-4th to early 5th century

Earthenware

H. 4.5, Rim D. 18, Base D. 6.5

University of Toronto

Malcove Collection, M82.360

A red earthenware bowl of African Red Slip Ware with stamped decoration, this piece is similar to catalogue number 58 (Hayes, Form 53 A), but less carefully crafted. It is complete, except for some chips along the rim, and a piece restored in plaster. The thin, curving wall is finished with a simple, tapered rim. The bowl rests on a slightly hollowed base with a small molding around the outside edge. There is a series of roughly incised grooves under the rim on the interior, and one circular groove on the floor. The stamped decoration applied to the inner surface of the wall consists in part of a beardless young man carrying a ram stretched across his shoulder. He is dressed in a tunic with two tiers of soft folds, a long cloak fastened at the shoulder, and a Phrygian cap. He is flanked by two well-characterized rams with fat tails. Opposite the figure of the youth there is a palmette with pronounced trunk and branches.

The theme, unique to this piece in its class of vessels, is drawn from pagan art, but it was adapted for Christian use as the Good Shepherd.

Bibliography: Campbell, 1985, p. 42, no. 35.

60
Bowl with saint

Egypt (Karanis), 5th century

Earthenware

H. 7.4, Rim D. 26, Base D. 11

University of Michigan

Kelsey Museum of Archaeology, 20024

This African Red Slip Ware bowl from Karanis (Hayes, Form 93, Type A; Fulford and Peacock, Type 49) has a wide, shallow, curving wall, a high, slightly flared base ring, and a wide rim with a thickening at the lip. In a medallion at the center of the floor there is a worn, impressed design of a male figure with large round eyes, prominent ears, and curly hair. The man, who can be identified as a saint, is dressed in a tunic decorated with two vertical rows of circles. His right arm is raised in a gesture of speech, and in his left hand he holds a cross-headed staff diagonally across his body (see Hayes, Style E 232a).

For the significance of saints on domestic objects, see p. 24.

Bibliography: Johnson, p. 48, no. 239, pl. 37; Haeckel, p. 97, no. 98; Hayes, 1972, p. 147, no. 12.

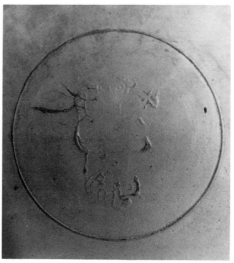

129

61
Bowl with lamb

Egypt (Karanis), 6th century

Earthenware

H. 7.6, Rim D. 35.6, Base D. 18.5

University of Michigan

Kelsey Museum of Archaeology, 7167

This large bowl is made of coarse red clay covered with a thick, semilustrous red slip on the interior and rim. It is representative of the African Red Slip Ware imported to Karanis for use in households where vessels finer than the local ware could be afforded. The pieces excavated there all have open shapes, and are decorated with grooves, feather rouletting, or grooves with stamped designs. The bowl (conforming to Hayes, Form 103, Type B, and Fulford and Peacock, Type 64) is characterized by a heavy ring base, a broad shallow offset floor, flaring wall, and heavy rolled rim. In the center of the bowl, a medallion formed by two concentric grooves inscribes a stamped design of a lamb (Hayes, Style Eii, Type 171)

For the significance of the lamb, see p. 23.

Bibliography: Gazda, 1983a, p. 17, fig. 28; Johnson, p. 49, no. 245, pl. 39; Hayes, l972, pl. 59, no. 6.

62
Plate decorated with a lamb (fragment)

North Africa, 6th century

Earthenware

L. 14.9, W. 10

Private collection

This fragment of Red Slip Ware, made from
fine-grained red-orange clay, was once part of a
plate produced in a North African workshop. It
is decorated with a lamb in double outline,
similar to the type represented in catalogue
number 61 (Hayes, Style Eii), with the fleece
indicated clearly, the tail long and heavy, and
the ears erect on the top of the head. The
position of the lamb near the rim suggests that it
was a subsidiary motif in a larger composition,
such as two lambs flanking a cross.

Unpublished

63
Spoon

Eastern Mediterranean, 6th century

Silver with niello inlay

L. 17.9

Toronto

Royal Ontario Museum, 986.181.94

This is a silver spoon, missing the rounded end of its bowl. Joining the bowl to the handle is a solid disc engraved with an incised cross monogram, which was originally inlaid with niello. The lower portion of the handle has the name ΠΕΤΡΟC (Peter) engraved upon its upper edge, preceded by a cross. The cross and the letter "C" still contain traces of niello. The upper part of the handle is divided into two fluted segments by three sets of moldings and is terminated by a baluster-like finial.

For the possible significance of the name "Peter" in the context of sets of Apostle spoons, see p. 25.

Unpublished

64
Spoon

4th-7th century

Silver

L. 17.8

Toronto

Royal Ontario Museum, 986.181.50

The spoon is intact, apart from slight surface corrosion and a hairline crack on the edge of the bowl. The pear-shaped bowl is attached to the spiral-fluted handle by a small solid disc. There is an animal-head terminal at each end of the handle.

Unpublished

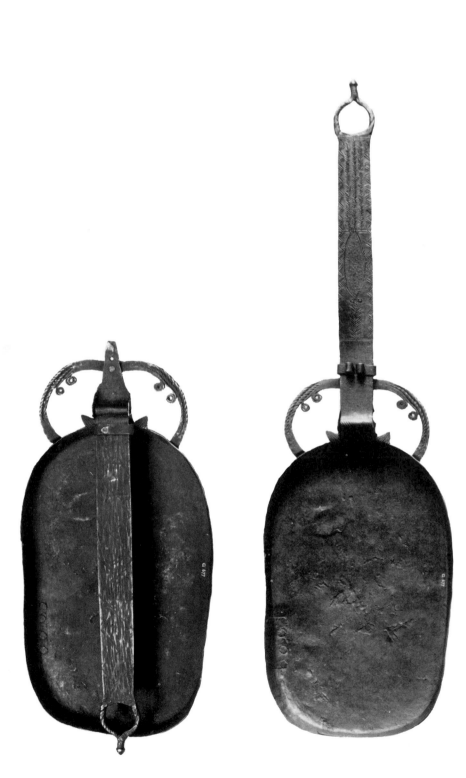

65
Frying pan with folding handle

Egypt, 4th-5th century

Iron

*H. 2.2-3.8, L. 30.6, (with handle extended)
65.6, W. 18.9*

Toronto

Royal Ontario Museum, 910.238.5

The handle of this rectangular, flat-bottomed
frying pan can be folded over the pan when not
in use. The low, steep sides are rounded at the
corners, modifying the rectangular shape.
Projecting from the back of the pan at the hinge is
a tapered tang, flanked by two triangular points.
The handle, a long, flat bar with a twisted ring at
the end, is hinged to the upturned sides of the
tang. Around the handle is a flat, mobile bracket
which, when the handle is extended, is used to
secure it to the tang. Two looped side ornaments,
composed of twisted spiral rods, are attached to
the underside of the tang and the outer wall of
the pan with rivets, forming arcs on either side.

The upper surface of the handle in the extended
position is decorated with three panels of
punched and incised decoration separated by
double grooves, and two opposed sets of diagonal lines on the hinge tube. The panel adjacent to
the tube is incised with an X and punched with
dotted circles. At the opposite end of the handle,
the panel decoration is composed of three
parallel lines of herringbone, flanked by double-
line zigzags and by notching along the edges.
The central panel features a schematic fish with a
stippled body. The fins are indicated with short
incised lines, the eye with a dotted circle.

This well-preserved pan, dated to the fourth or
fifth century, is one of several found among a
hoard of ironwork in the region of Thebes/
Luxor in Egypt. For similar examples, see
Wheeler, cat. no. 3, l930, pp. 118-19, figs. 41.1,
41.2; Harcum, 1921, 44-47 passim, figs. 5-7;
Hayes, l984, pp. 160-63, figs. 251, 252, 254.

On the significance of the fish, see p. 23.

Bibliography: Hayes, 1984, p. 162, fig. 253;
Harcum, l921, pp. 44-47, figs. 6, 7.

66
Ladle

Egypt, 4th-5th century

Iron

H. of bowl 5.8, L. 44.1, D. of bowl 14.7-15.3

Toronto

Royal Ontario Museum, 910.238.9

This ladle, like catalogue number 65, is from the ironwork hoard discovered at Thebes/Luxor in Egypt. The bowl is circular in shape with an almost conical section, and undecorated. Hammer marks cover the exterior surface. The handle, attached horizontally to the rim of the bowl, is composed of a shaft taking the form of a stylized column, with rectangular panels making an abstract capital and base. The panel at the end of the handle is terminated in a ring, finely notched around the edge. Notching also appears on the edges of the panels, and parallel incised lines cross their faces. Similar incised lines across the shaft mark off three stylized astragals.

Similar examples may be seen in Hayes, l984, pp. 163-65, figs. 255, 256, 258-61.

Bibliography: Hayes, 1984, p. 163-64, fig. 257; Harcum, l92l, p. 48.

135

67
Cooking pot

Egypt (Karanis), late 3rd-early 4th century

Earthenware

H. 28, Rim D. 17.3

University of Michigan

Kelsey Museum of Archaeology, 7799

Coarse reddish brown clay with a black core was the material used to form this cooking pot. The exterior surface is considerably blackened from use over the fire. The vessel has no neck, and is broad and capacious at the shoulder where two vertical and two horizontal handles are attached. Just below the handles, the body begins to taper sharply downward to a wide, rounded base. The mouth is finished with a simple molded rim. Shallow horizontal ribbing extends down the surface of the entire vessel, becoming broader and more faint below the shoulders, and then more pronounced again around the base.

While no painted decoration is preserved, this example belongs to a group of cooking pots from Karanis that were characterized by light painted decoration on the shoulder. The designs consist of loops, dots, and undulating horizontal lines (see Johnson, p. 83, nos. 563-67, pl. 71). Other examples of cooking pots may be seen in Petrie, 1905, pl. XXXI.

Bibliography: Johnson, p. 83, no. 568, pl. 71

137

Fig. 40. Piazza Armerina, Villa, Floor Mosaic, Detail.
Aristocrat with Two Retainers.

138

Even more than today, in the Early Christian period textiles were an important part of the fabric of life, both for practical reasons and for display. Articles of clothing were valued possessions, to be cared for and protected from damage and decay. Justinian's sixth-century digest of Roman law is full of references to clothes: legal actions against careless people who stained them, against borrowers who tore them, against cleaners who lost them, and against owners of the slaves who stole them (*Digest*, IX, 2, 27; IX, 2, 11; XLVII, 2, 48-52; XLVII, 2, 57). There are intimate glimpses in Egyptian papyri of the concern ordinary people had for their apparel. In a letter of the late third century, for example, a daughter writes to her mother asking her to "shake out my other dress without fail, so that it does not get moldy" (Lobel, pp. 153-54).

One reason for the high value people placed on their clothes may have been the fashion throughout the Early Christian period for elaborately patterned garments decorated with colorful squares, circles, and bands woven with a wide variety of designs, both abstract and figural. As we know from representations in works of art, such clothes were worn throughout the Mediterranean world and at all levels of society. Figure 40 is a detail from a floor mosaic of the early fourth century, in a villa at Piazza Armerina, in Sicily. It depicts an aristocrat accompanied by two armed members of his retinue watching the progess of a wild-beast hunt. The aristocrat is distinguished by means of his decorated cloak and his cylindrical hat, but both master and servants wear white tunics adorned with ornamental roundels at the shoulders and with colored cuff-bands at the sleeves. At the highest levels of society, and for the most formal occasions, men and women wore clothes of patterned silk. The silk costumes of the imperial court are sumptuously illustrated in the sixth-century mosaics of San Vitale at Ravenna (Deichmann, pls. X, 352, 360-61, 366-67). More commonly, however, polychrome textiles were woven of wool or of wool and linen.

Although ornamented textiles were worn throughout the empire, by far the majority of surviving examples come from the dry soil of Egypt, which is particularly conducive to the preservation of textiles. The Egyptians buried the dead dressed in their best clothes; in addition, they frequently wrapped the bodies in other textiles, such as hangings or curtains, and stuffed smaller cloths into hollows around the corpses. For this reason, many other domestic cloths besides garments have been preserved. These burial practices were not confined to Egypt. Epiphanius, a fourth-century bishop of Salamis in Cyprus, advised a church to donate a curtain for the burial of a pauper (C. Mango, p. 43), whereas both St. Jerome in Syria and St. Ambrose in Milan protested against the wasteful practice of burying people in their finery (Kybalová, p. 34).

The most frequently preserved item of apparel from Egyptian burials is the tunic, which was worn by men, women, and children. Number 68 in the exhibition is a well-preserved tunic worn by an adult; number 69 is

139

an example belonging to a child. The shape of this garment might be said to resemble the old-fashioned nightshirt. It came with long or short sleeves, and sometimes, as in the case of number 69, a hood. It was often worn beneath an outer garment such as a cloak or mantle. Most of the earlier tunics were woven in linen, but the decorative squares, roundels, and bands were woven in wool tapestry weave, since linen could not easily be dyed. Often the whole tunic was made on the loom in one piece of linen cloth, with the wool pattern wefts being inserted in the weaving of the garment at the appropriate places for decoration. Sometimes, however, small sections of tapestry weave were woven separately and sewn onto the linen tunics, or the decorations were cut off discarded garments and sewn onto new ones from one generation to another. The recycling of patches is especially obvious in the case of some surviving children's tunics which are adorned with incongruously large weavings cut out of adult garments (Thompson, 1971, p. 64, pl. 13). When a heavier cloth was required, linen was woven in the shaggy "looped pile" technique. Some tunics, like the child's garment number 69, were woven of wool throughout; woolen tunics were not only warmer, but they could be dyed in their entirety with solid colors such as red or green.

Occasionally robes were decorated with overall repeating patterns, similar to those found on curtains (e.g., du Bourguet, no. F198, p. 320). More commonly, however, the woolen tapestry weaves were restricted to specific areas of the garment. The typical scheme of decoration is shown by the tunic number 68: a woven band around the neck, vertical strips (*clavi*) descending from the shoulders, cuff bands and sleeve bands, a band around the hem, and circles (*segmenta*) at the shoulders and above the hem. A similar but somewhat more elaborately decorated tunic can be seen in figure 41, which reproduces a painting discovered in the tomb of a fifteen-year-old Egyptian girl named Theodosia, who died during childbirth, possibly in the sixth century (Breccia, pp. 285-306). Theodosia is shown between two saints, with her arms raised in prayer. Her tunic is decorated with a neck band, *clavi*, and cuff bands. The principal difference between her costume and the tunic number 68 is that it is decorated with square ornaments at the shoulders and above the hem, rather than with the circles. Similar squares are preserved on many surviving tunics.

Squares and circles of tapestry weave decorated other articles of apparel, such as shawls and cloaks (see Theodosia in fig. 41), and they also adorned textiles which were not used for clothing at all, such as blankets or cushion covers (see no. 5). For this reason, it is often difficult to determine the original contexts of patches when they have been cut out of the textiles to which they once belonged. It is probable that number 70, a set of decorations consisting of a *clavus* band and two circles, decorated a tunic; numbers 71 and 72 were probably sleeve bands. We can be less certain, however, about the original functions of the isolated squares, numbers 73, 74, and 75, and of the circle number 76. While it is possible that they came from tunics or shawls, which is the reason for their inclusion in the clothing section of the exhibition, they could equally well have decorated some other type of domestic textile.

Although there were large state factories that specialized in the production of woolen and linen textiles, much of the work was done at home or in small family workshops (Jones, pp. 187-90; Wipszycka, p. 56). The procedures involved in spinning thread, whether wool or linen, are well illustrated in

Fig. 41. Antinoe, Tomb of Theodosia,
Wall Painting.
Theodosia between Two Saints.

a miniature from the sixth-century Genesis manuscript in Vienna (color plate
VI), where vignettes of women spinning accompany an illustration of the
temptation of Joseph by Potiphar's wife. The miniature demonstrates clearly
that spinning was a domestic task performed by women, for the spinners in the
painting are accompanied by infants. At the upper right-hand edge of the
painting, a standing woman dressed in blue uses a distaff and spindle. She feeds
the fibers into the forming thread from the distaff held in her left hand, while the
thread itself is twisted by the spinning motion of the wooden spindle which
dangles from her right hand. When the spindle reaches the ground, she will pick
it up and wind the length of thread around the shaft of the spindle. The spindle
itself is weighted by a circular flywheel, or whorl, made of wood, stone, terra-
cotta, or even ivory. Frequently, as in the case of number 77, the whorl was
decorated with circled dots or with concentric circles incised around the spindle
hole. In the center of the lower register of the miniature in the Genesis manuscript (color plate VI) a woman is seen spinning while sitting down. Like the
standing spinster, she holds up the distaff in her left hand. She rotates the
spindle with her right, inside a little metal bowl, which is suspended by means
of a looped handle from her right wrist. Possibly this bowl contained water,
with which she wetted the forefinger and thumb of her right hand before
drawing the fibers of flax from the distaff, as dampness made the fibers
stronger. Or she may have turned the spindle like a top inside the bowl, to
support some of its weight if she was spinning extremely fine and fragile thread.

The dyeing of unspun fiber and thread was a craft requiring
more complicated and permanent equipment than other stages of textile
production (Strong and Brown, pp. 175-77). Generally, it was carried out in spe-

141

cialized workshops, rather than at home. Color was greatly desired by consumers. "Be careful to have my tunic made properly," writes a brother to his sister, "and let them put good measure into it, and be large-handed with the coloring" (Hunt, pp. 225-26). The generosity of Early Christian dyers and weavers in this respect is amply demonstrated by the colorful textiles in this exhibition.

The weaving of the finished threads into textiles was carried out on looms of varying degrees of complexity and sophistication. Some of the weaving took place in the centralized government factories, but there was also a widespread industry of weavers operating in small workshops (Jones, pp. 187-90). A relatively simple type of loom was the warp-weighted loom, a vertical loom whose warp threads were attached to a cloth-beam at the top and held taut at the bottom by loomweights of stone or clay, similar to the weight that is number 78 in the exhibition. Another type of loom was the vertical two-beam loom, on which the warps were stretched between an upper and a lower

Fig. 42. Vatican Library, Cod. lat. 3225 (Poems of Vergil), fol. 58r. Circe Weaving beside Her Palace.

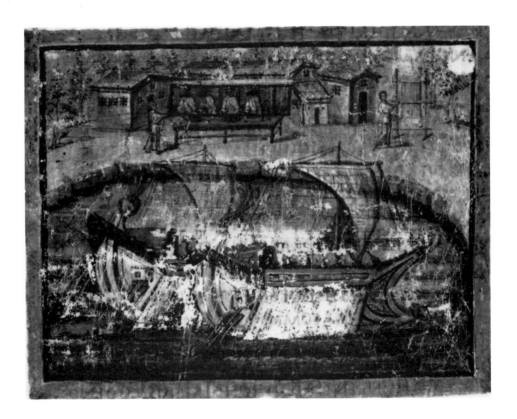

clothbeam (Strong and Brown, pp. 170-72). Such a loom is illustrated by a miniature in an early fifth-century manuscript of Vergil from Rome (fig. 42), where the witch Circe is seen beside her palace, singing "as she runs her piercing comb through the fine warps" (*Aeneid*, VII, 14). The painting shows the construction of the loom in some detail. At the bottom we see the two feet on which its tall uprights rested. Both the upper and the lower clothbeams are shown. In addition, there is a horizontal bar halfway up the loom; this is possibly the heddle-rod, attached to alternate warps, or a shed bar, enabling the weaver to open the shed through which the hank of weft could be passed. A row of vertical holes can be seen on each of the upright posts, which allowed the height of the brackets holding the heddle-rod to be adjusted upward as the work progressed. Circe's partially completed weaving is shown at the bottom of the loom.

The comb described by Vergil, which Circe ran through the warps of her loom, was a toothed instrument used to beat down the newly inserted weft threads against the existing web of cloth. Sometimes these tools were finely decorated. The wooden comb number 80 in the exhibition, for example, is carved with a seated lion. Other combs were marked with apotropaic motifs, such as crosses (Newark Museum, inv. no. 84.41) or concentric circles (our no. 79), which were possibly intended to guard against mishaps in the weaving.

The papyri demonstrate that men were employed in the production of textiles, as dyers, linen-weavers, and pattern-weavers (Rea, pp. 75-76; Roberts, pp. 101-2). But the scene presented by the miniature in the Vergil manuscript, of a woman plying a loom, was not unusual in the Late Roman world, for women as well as men worked at weaving (Jones, pp. 184, 188). The Egyptian papyri give a vivid picture of the part played by women in the production of fine textiles. In the late-third-century letter from a daughter to her mother which was cited above, the daughter says that she is sending two ounces of expensive purple wool so that her mother can make "the frocks and two veils" (Lobel, Wegener, and Roberts, pp. 153-54). The two ounces would have been sufficient material for the decorations that her mother would weave into these garments, which were presumably to be of linen. In the same letter, the daughter asks her mother to send her some linen cloths that she has made. Such documents suggest that women played an active role in the production and decoration of textiles, as well as in the spinning of their threads.

68
Tunic

Egypt (said to be from Tuna el-Gebel), 8th century

Wool

L. 126, W. 199

New York

The Metropolitan Museum of Art,
Gift of George D. Pratt, 1927, 12.185.3

Although this tunic may date from the eighth century, its overall appearance follows an earlier tradition of tunic decoration established in the fifth and sixth centuries. The tunic is woven of naturally light-colored wool. Wide in the body but with very narrow sleeves, it has been tacked at the waist. It is decorated with two sets of ornaments. One set, consisting of pendent *clavi*, two shoulder and four skirt *segmenta* (two in front and two at the back), and sleeve bands, is executed like the rest of the tunic in a tapestry weave. This set was woven directly into the fabric of the tunic in yellow, red, pink, purple, blue, and green wool. Most of its varied decorative figural and floral motifs are too abstract to be identified precisely. The *segmenta* are filled with haloed horsemen looming over haloed human figures and animals. All motifs are two-dimensional. An important role is played by outlines, which are often carried out by supplementary wefts wrapped around the warps (this technique is called soumak wrapping). The second set of ornaments consists of separately woven, brocaded woolen tapes, used as trimming of the hem, cuffs, and neck opening. The red-ground hem trim with its overall lozenge grid filled with stylized rosettes is the dominant decorative element of the tunic. Such brocaded and other types of separately woven tapes may have been initially introduced not only as decoration but more likely for protecting the edges of delicate and expensive silk garments as worn, for example, by the court ladies of Empress Theodora in the sixth-century mosaic in San Vitale in Ravenna (cf. also Thompson, 1986). Soon, however, they began to be used as another decorative element.

This tunic and another very much like it, also in the Metropolitan Museum of Art (Kajitani, no. 90, p. 65), are said to have been found in Tuna el-Gebel. They belong to a large number of similarly decorated tunics and tunic fragments now scattered in various museum and private collections.

For the motif of the horseman, see pp. 25-28.

Bibliography: Dimand, pp. 244-47, fig. 18

69
Tunic

Egypt, 7th century

Wool

L. 95.5, W. 105

New York

The Metropolitan Museum of Art, Gift of Maurice Nahman, 1912, 27.239

This child's all-wool dark-green tunic with a hood was executed in a tapestry weave, including the decoration—tan-and-purple *clavi* and double sleeve bands as well as plain tan stripes along the side seams and the cuffs. The wide *clavi*, framed by crested borders and filled with a laurel scroll and stylized figures with exaggerated heads and limbs, run the entire length of the tunic. The design of the sleeve bands is essentially the same as that of the *clavi*. This design is repeated on the right lower sleeve band; but the laurel scroll was omitted on the three others. Corded warp ends along the side seams and the sleeve ends and beside a hem fringe of the weft ends provide additional decorative touches.

The hood, still attached to the tunic, was woven separately in matching green wool with two tan-and-purple patterned medallions and two tan stripes along the hood's base and the crown seam. The latter is also finished with a long fringe of weft ends. Another red fringe is stitched around the front edge of the hood.

The laurel band and the figural motifs of the *clavi* and the sleeve bands are among the most commonly used decorative motifs of Roman and Early Christian art. Their bold and very stylized renditions seen in the Metropolitan Museum tunic represent a seventh- and eighth-century version of these motifs. For other examples of similarly decorated tunics, see Trilling, nos. 75, 94-95, pp. 77 and 87.

Bibliography: Kajitani, no. 92, p. 67.

145

70

Tunic ornaments

Egypt, 7th or 8th century

Wool and linen

Clavus L. 73, W. 8.8
Segmenta L. 25.5, W. 23; L. 19.1, W. 17.8

Boston

Museum of Fine Arts, 01.8339c, d, e

These red-ground *segmenta* and the pendent *clavus* once decorated a yellow-brown woolen tunic to whose fragments they are still attached as appliquéd ornaments. As is most often the case with such tunic appliqués, they are woven in a tapestry weave on plied linen warps with brightly colored woolen weft yarns. All three ornaments are decorated with a lozenge grid of stylized leaves and florets filled with animals, birds, fish, floral motifs, and baskets and framed by a border of scale pattern. In the two *segmenta* the grid design is interrupted by central medallions enclosing nimbed busts holding animals, while the *clavus* contains a panel with a standing richly attired female wearing a floral-petal crown on her head surrounded by a halo. Her arms are raised and she seems to hold a container or cross in her left hand. All figural motifs—the standing figure and the busts—resemble portrayals of personifications of seasons and benevolent powers, which were particularly popular in late-fifth- and sixth-century art. In textiles, such personifications continued to be represented in later centuries as well. The abstract style of the Boston ornaments points to the late seventh and eighth century as a possible date of their execution. For related examples see Errera, no. 297; Wulff and Volbach, no. 9085, pl. 35; du Bourguet, F51, pp. 266-67; Baginski and Tidhar, no. 144, p. 104. The Boston tunic ornaments also include a pair of sleeve bands (inv. no. 01.8339a & b).

Unpublished

71
Sleeve ornament

Egypt, 7th or 8th century

Wool and linen

L. 30.6, W. 14.7

University of Toronto

Malcove Collection, M82.46

This colorful sleeve band was applied to a tunic. It was woven separately as one of a set of tunic ornaments consisting of *clavi, segmenta,* and sleeve bands. It is all tapestry-woven on plied linen warps except for narrow strips of a plain weave along the warp endings which would have been tacked under the band when it was sewn onto the tunic.

The band has a five-part design composed of a central panel with a roundel enclosing a bust of a nimbed female. The panel is flanked on both sides by a pair of friezes, one above the other, filled with fierce-looking animals and stylized composite plants. The bust of the central roundel may represent a personification of Earth or one of four seasons. The animal and plant motifs are both fantastic and hybrid; for example, human masks were incorporated into the blossoms, and human heads were placed near the hind legs of the top-left and bottom-right animals. All motifs are executed in brightly colored woolen yarns which stand out from the red ground of the sleeve bands. They have distinct outlines carried out by supplementary wefts wrapped around the warps (soumak wrapping). The upper and lower sides of the band are finished with a border of red-and-white heart-shaped petals on a dark-blue ground.

Five-part designs were among the most popular sleeve decorations from the sixth century onward. Probably first introduced in the sixth century in silk-woven ornaments, they soon were adopted by tapestry weavers, who continued to make them in the following several centuries. In the process, the designs became increasingly stylized and abstract, as the Malcove Collection sleeve band illlustrates. For related examples see Thompson, no. 27, pp. 64-66; also Wulff and Volbach, no. 4588, pls. 29 and 105; no. 9190, pl. 105, no. 6955, pl. 108, and no. 9303, pl. 110; du Bourguet, F168 and F169, pp. 108-9; Baginski and Tidhar, no. 146, p. 106.

Bibliography: Campbell, 1985, no. 228, p. 161.

147

72
Sleeve band

Egypt, late 6th century

Wool and linen

L. 28.6, W. 10.8

Toronto

Royal Ontario Museum, 910.128.25

The combination of abstract, floral, and figural motifs of this sleeve band creates a colorful composite design. The sleeve band is woven in a tapestry weave in multicolored woolen weft yarns and undyed linen on group warps of undyed linen. It once decorated a sleeve of a linen tunic. The main element of the design is a yellow roundel containing a bust, most likely a female personification. The roundel is enclosed within a band consisting of a blue frieze with fish placed between two chains of floral buds. This colorful and varied band is framed along the top and the bottom by narrow red strips of delicate lozenge grid filled with fleur-de-lis motifs. While all the motifs of the Toronto sleeve band are commonly used individually in textile decoration (see also nos. 70 and 71), the specific arrangement of the motifs seen here is rare.

For a discussion of the personification, see pp. 13-14.

Unpublished

73
Tapestry panel

Egypt, 6th century

Wool and linen

L. 22, W. 22

University of Toronto

Malcove Collection, M82.45

This very fragmentary panel displays a roundel with a female figure on horseback moving to the right. Although not wearing a Phrygian cap the figure can still be identified as an Amazon wielding a double axe in her raised right hand. A colorful rider, she wears a short green tunic, a pink cloak, as well as a yellow belt and blue riding boots. Her galloping white mount is shown with its mane, saddle, and other trappings carefully indicated. Both horse and rider stand out from the purple ground of the roundel. The roundel was originally set in a square frame of which only corner spandrels filled with birds are preserved. The present border belongs to a different textile altogether and was added to the Amazon panel only very recently.

The Amazon panel is woven in a tapestry weave with woolen warps and woolen and linen weft yarns. The design runs parallel to the direction of the warp yarns. Because of its small size, the panel may have been used as a shoulder panel of a woolen tunic, as is indicated by the direction of the warps (tunics were usually woven in one piece lengthwise from hem to hem, the weaving starting with a sleeve), or a woolen shawl; its use in a domestic textile is also possible. Riders, warriors, hunters, and mythological figures, as in this case, represent an important and popular category of figural imagery used for household textiles and costumes. Stylistically, the Malcove mounted Amazon resembles a group of sixth-century weavings represented by the hanging with horses and warriors in Washington (Trilling, no. 17, p. 39) and the fragments with riderless horses in Baltimore (Brooklyn, p. 76, no. 240) and Cleveland (Weibel, p. 79, no. 14).

Bibliography: Campbell, 1985, no. 200, pp. 139-40.

74
Tapestry panel

Egypt, 6th century

Linen and wool

L. 25.7, W. 21.5

University of Michigan

Kelsey Museum of Archaeology, 10662

This tapestry panel is woven in a monochrome silhouette style on group warps of linen, with weft yarns of linen and of dark purple, almost black, wool. Its size suggests that it may have come from a household linen textile into which it was directly woven. The panel has an exterior border of cresting with corner trefoil finials. Internally, the design is composed of a central medallion enclosed by a wide circular frieze. The medallion displays the union of Leda and Zeus disguised as a swan. The surrounding frieze contains a variety of figures: some seem to be either nymphs or female deities, some are putti holding objects, while some others can be identified as shepherds (one on the left is shown seated playing a flute). The figures are surrounded by scattered foliate motifs suggesting a landscape setting. This busy and disjointed figural decoration is compositionally controlled by an open eight-lobed vine scroll whose points are finished with roundels containing birds and animals. The corner spandrels of the panel also contain animals.

The decorative effect of the design is enhanced by an alternating monochrome tonality of the ground and the figures between a hatching of simultaneously woven purple and white yarns (used as the ground around Leda with the swan and in the corner spandrels) and the off-white linen ground of the circular frieze.

The contrast between the dark silhouettes of the figures and the borders is also stressed by the linear effect of the detailing in a flying-shuttle technique of supplementary weft yarns used to clarify the outlines and internal articulation of the figures, such as facial details, costumes, and the plumage of the swan.

The Kelsey textile belongs to a vast group of tapestry-woven panels employed as decoration of household textiles and costumes and displaying mythological figures, putti, shepherds, and hunters. The specific composition of the Kelsey panel is, however, more unusual than most. It can be compared to a roundel with a similar, but reversed, internal scalloped band in London (Victoria and Albert Museum, inv. no. 1279.1888).

Unpublished

75

Tapestry panel

Egypt, late 5th-early 6th century

Wool and linen

L. 27, W. 26.5

Toronto

Royal Ontario Museum, 910.131.36

A five-roundel design is woven in the monochrome silhouette style in dark purple wool (with some touches of red and green) and in undyed linen wefts on group undyed linen warps in this tapestry panel. The roundels—the largest in the center with four smaller ones in the corners of the panel—are formed by narrow bands issuing from four vases, one in the middle of each side. Sprays of trefoil leaves fill the spaces around the vases. The central roundel encloses a galloping horseman. Nude, except for a cloak visible around his neck, he carries a missile in his raised left hand. A hare shown running alongside the horse identifies the scene as a hunt. The four corner roundels are filled with nude youths holding birds and baskets. The two inside the upper roundels are running toward each other, the two below away from each other. Although such youths are common in Late Antique art, these particularly resemble male personifications of the seasons or season-related imagery. Seasons can often be seen carrying symbols such as birds, animals, fruits, and flowers. The white ground inside the roundels is filled with dotting, which is a simplified version of the vegetal sprays used sometimes to suggest a landscape setting. The figures of the Toronto panel are executed with large heads and prominent eyes, but quite small bodies. The inner details of the figures are executed primarily in the flying-shuttle technique with a supplementary weft yarn, which was placed on the dark silhouettes of the design motifs, probably with a needle, simultaneously with the tapestry weaving of the panel. The panel has an exterior border of cresting with corner trefoils.

The Toronto panel is related to numerous other textiles decorated with similar roundel designs, including the hunting horseman and the naked youths. For the motifs of the seasons, see, for example, Badawy, fig. 4.80; Kendrick, no. 72; Wulff and Volbach, no. 9696, pl. 53; and an unpublished panel in Boston (Museum of Fine Arts, inv. no. 96.226). This type of decoration was used especially in household textiles, many of which were made of looped-pile cloths (see also cat. no. 5).

Unpublished

151

76
Woolen textile with tapestry roundel

Egypt, 4th century

Wool

L. 28.5, W. 24.5

Toronto

Royal Ontario Museum, 910.129.60

This fragment of a woolen cloth may have been used as a shawl. It is decorated with a tapestry-woven roundel. The roundel is framed by three-part filleted borders with the center fillets containing bands of interconnected discs. The main field of the roundel is covered with a dense geometric design composed of several overlapping and interlacing grids. The topmost grid of double-banded straps is rectangular; it interlaces with two diagonal grids of wide straps with internal braiding, one below the other. Together they turn the surface of the roundel into a mesh of diagonal and straight-armed cross motifs. Some of the crosses are also interlaced with rings, which also have internal braiding. The roundel is woven in dark purple wool. The geometric designs are executed in undyed wool in a tapestry weave and with a supplementary weft yarn in the flying-shuttle technique (see no. 5).

Interlace patterns and their endless variations, so common in Late Roman and Early Christian art, became widely used in textile decoration from the late third century onward. Particularly closely related to the Toronto piece are two textiles from Akhmim now in New York and London (Kajitani, no. 14, p. 41; Victoria and Albert Museum, inv. no. 1322.1888; Kendrick, no. 217), and a woolen roundel, provenance unknown, in London (Victoria and Albert Museum, inv. no. T.8.1960, unpublished).

For the significance of the crosses and the interlace, see pp. 3 and 21.

Unpublished

77
Spindle and whorl

Egypt

Wood

L. 11.4, Whorl D. 4

University of Illinois

World Heritage Museum, 14.5.166

This well-preserved spindle and whorl was used to spin wool, cotton, or linen fibers into thread. The spindle is made of a long, thin piece of wood with a round section. It tapers toward one end, and is weighted with a whorl at the other. The whorl is decorated with two incised lines around the circumference along the bottom edge, a series of dotted circles above, and two concentric circles around the spindle hole.

Thread for weaving textiles was spun mainly by women working in the home. The technique involved fastening a length of twisted fibers to the spindle, and allowing it to swing and drop to the ground as fibers were fed by hand to the spinning thread. The whorl acts as a weight to maintain the spin and produce a fine, even thread.

For similar spindles and whorls, see Rutschowscaya, pp. 44-48; Gazda, 1983a, p. 27, fig. 46; Paris, pp. 195-96, no. 142a; Petrie, 1927, pl. LIV, nos. 539-42; Petrie, 1917, p. 53, nos. 43-47, pl. LXV; Strzygowski, pl. IX, 7228.

Unpublished

78
Loom weight

Egypt

Clay

H. 6.8, Base D. 3

University of Illinois

World Heritage Museum, 26.2.102

Truncated conical weights of this type, made of clay or stone, were essential components of the warp-weighted loom. Warp threads were tied to a horizontal bar supported on two posts, and stretched and tightened by weights attached to groups of threads at the bottom. This example is pierced vertically with a hole through which a gathering of warp threads was guided and tied. The surface, marred by a large chip, is decorated with a branch motif consisting of a long incised vertical line with short, slightly oblique horizontal lines on either side.

For comparable loom weights, see Paris, pp. 195, 197, no. 143a, b; Petrie, 1917, nos. 138-39, pl. LXV; Strzygowski, p. 249, 7145a, b.

Unpublished

79
Weaver's comb

Egypt (Karanis), 1st-5th century

Wood

H. 22, W. 21.7

University of Michigan

Kelsey Museum of Archaeology, 3806

This large weaver's comb was made of five
sections of wood attached with dowels to form
a rectangular plaque. The handle, centrally
positioned on the long side, is an extension of
the middle section of the plaque. Opposite the
handle is a row of teeth, more deeply cut on the
face used to press the thread. Near the lower
edge of the plaque on the working side are three
sets of concentric circle designs with three, four,
and three circles in each set, respectively. The
handle has a thumb groove with one incised
line above it. Except for beveled edges at the
end of the handle and on three sides of the
plaque, the back of the comb is plain.

The comb was used to compress the weft
threads after each pass of the shuttle. This
technique in the weaving process controlled the
spacing and tightness of the weave.

Many examples of weaver's combs have been
found in Egypt, dating from the Roman and
Coptic periods. See Rutschowscaya, pp. 56-63,
Gazda, 1983a, p. 26, fig. 43, p. 27, fig. 46; Petrie,
1917, nos. 148-54, pl. LXV; Strzygowski, 8838,
pl. VIII.

Unpublished

80
Weaver's comb

Egypt (Fayoum), 1st-5th century

Wood

H. 14, W. 9.1

University of Michigan

Kelsey Museum of Archaeology, 92998

A weaver's comb similar in form to number 79, this piece was carved from a single piece of hard dark wood. Aside from the usual worn teeth, and minor cracking along the grain of the wood, it is in good condition. Unlike most weaver's combs, which, if they are embellished at all, have only simple designs such as incised circles and horizontal lines, this example has as its central motif a well-defined lion, seated and facing left, set in relief against a deeply carved rectangular background. The details of the lion's mane and anatomy are indicated with incised lines. A series of horizontal incised grooves decorates the handle. The back is plain and smooth.

Bibliography: Ann Arbor, no. 33.

81
Needle

Egypt

Bone

L. 12.2

University of Illinois

World Heritage Museum , 26.2.165

This sewing needle is slightly flattened at the
top around the eye, and tapers down to a point,
now broken off. This type continued in use
unchanged throughout the Roman period. For
similar examples in bone, see Gazda, 1983a, p.
27, fig. 46; Paris, p. 198, no. 145. Bronze and
wooden sewing needles were also commonly
used in the making of clothing and other
household goods, such as pillows, blankets, and
curtains (Rutschowscaya, pp. 54-55; Paris, p.
198, no. 145).

Unpublished

Fig. 43. Silistra, Tomb Painting.
Valet Bringing Trousers and Shoes to His Master.

Fig. 44. Silistra, Tomb Painting.
Valet Bringing a Cloak with an Attached Brooch to His Master.

Jewelry

At the end of the third century an Egyptian husband wrote to his wife, asking her to prepare to come and meet him if he should send for her. "When you come," he said, "bring all your gold ornaments, but do not wear them on the boat" (Winter, pp. 278-80). We do not know why this man was asking his spouse to bring her jewelry, but his admonition to beware of thieves on the crowded boat has a modern ring. The desire for jewelry is timeless; even the types of jewelry worn in the Early Christian period were, for the most part, the same as those worn today. There were rings, of gold (no. 82), of silver (nos. 86 and 87), and of bronze (nos. 84-85 and 88-89); there were necklaces (nos. 90 and 91), and earrings (no. 95); belt buckles (nos. 96-101) and brooches (nos. 102 and 103). Certainly people of that period took a delight in fine jewelry for its own sake, and even enjoyed its representation in textiles. The woman illustrated in the textile number 4, for example, shows off the pendants of her earrings and seems to shake her head to make them fly. In one important respect, however, the jewelry of the Early Christian world differed from many of the pieces worn in modern times. It was generally more than decorative; it was strongly functional, both in the physical and the supernatural sense. In part, this was in accord with Early Christian teaching, which frowned on the display of jewelry merely for the sake of ornament. "I desire," wrote St. Paul, "that . . . women should adorn themselves modestly and sensibly in seemly apparel, not with braided hair or gold or pearls or costly attire but by good deeds, as befits women who profess religion" (I Timothy 2:8-10). This stricture was echoed by St. Clement of Alexandria, who prohibited women from piercing their ears so that they could wear earrings, comparing those who did so to pigs with rings in their snouts (*Paedagogus*, III, 56). Clement did, however, permit the wearing of jewelry for specific approved purposes. He allowed that both women and men would need to wear finger-rings so that they could safeguard their possessions and their transactions by sealing them (*Paedagogus*, III, 57-58). Several sealing rings, with their designs engraved into flat-topped bezels, can be seen in the exhibition (nos. 84-86 and 88-89; for the motifs on the bezels, see pp. 86-87). Clement even went so far as to concede that women who had the misfortune of having "unchaste husbands" might adorn themselves in order make themselves more pleasing to their spouses (*Paedagogus*, III, 57). Thus the church father tacitly admits the power of jewelry over the senses, not only when he disapproves of its general use, but also when he suggests that Christian wives should wear jewelry to make themselves more alluring to husbands who were too prone to sensual temptation.

159

   Some of the jewelry was functional in the most obvious sense: it was designed to hold clothing together. Then, as now, there were ornamented buckles (nos. 96-101), whose use is graphically illustrated by the wall paintings in a fourth-century tomb at Silistra in Bulgaria, which depicts a wealthy couple apparently receiving the ministrations of their slaves at the baths (Dimitrov, pp. 35-52). Among the servants is a young valet bringing his master's shoes and trousers, the latter being an item of barbarian apparel that became increasingly popular in the Late Roman period (fig. 43). Dangling from the trousers is a belt with a large buckle at its end. Another slave brings his master his cloak (fig. 44), which has a large gold *fibula*, or brooch, pinned to it. The brooch was used to fasten the cloak at the right shoulder, in the manner shown by the aristocrat in figure 40. The exhibition includes two similar brooches, but probably made for less elevated individuals, since they are bronze and gilt bronze, not gold (nos. 102 and 103). Their arched profile was designed to accommodate the thick fold of cloth that had to be secured by the pin.

Many pieces of material value were designed to function immaterially, by providing supernatural protection. Crosses often were worn around the neck, as shown in color plate VIII, a small plaster statuette of a woman of the fifth or sixth century from Egypt. Such crosses could be either of gold (nos. 90 and 92), bronze (nos. 91 and 93), or wood (no. 94), depending upon the financial resources of the wearer. Other pieces of jewelry might incorporate crosses into their design, such as the crescent-shaped earrings, number 95, which are decorated in openwork with pairs of peacocks flanking crosses. Crosses also appeared on rings, such as number 83, a bronze marriage ring on which is engraved a cross between busts of the couple. In this case the cross embodies the power of Christ blessing the marriage. A literal image of this act of blessing is engraved upon the bezel of number 82, a gold marriage ring showing Christ in person standing between the bride and groom. Beneath the scene engraved on this more expensive ring is the inscription OMONV, or "Harmony."

Both of these marriage rings incorporate another feature, which is not Christian but magical in origin: their hoops are eight-sided, a shape that was believed to have protective powers over the womb (see pp. 9, 28). These Early Christian marriage rings, then, were intended to function in ways different than our own. More than a sign of commitment, they were intended to invoke the protection of Christ upon the marriage, and, more specifically, to safeguard the health of the woman in childbirth by means of an amuletic device. A similar mixture of the Christian with the magical may be represented by number 90, a gold necklace from which hangs a cross flanked by two hexagonal phylacteries, or amulet cases. These cases originally contained texts, now missing, which, like the cross, had the important function of protecting the wearer. In some examples the letters were chased with a stylus into thin sheets of gold, which were rolled up tightly so that they could be inserted into the phylacteries (Marshall, no. 3153; Ede, no. 28). The untarnishing gold sheet, invisible inside its case, preserved the words of the inscription free from corruption. The texts could have been canonical, such as the opening verse from the protective Psalm 91 ("He who dwells in the shelter of the Most High, will abide in the care of the God of Heaven"), or they could have been magical, such as the many spells against various demons given in the magical treatise, *The Testament of Solomon*. Typical of the magical recipes is the one directed against Saphthorael, who causes dissension. "If anyone will write these [names]: 'Iae, Ieo, sons of Sabaoth,' and wears them around his neck, I [Saphthorael] at once retreat" (McCown, p. 54*). The wearing of amuletic texts by Christians was condemned by several church fathers (Cabrol, 1907, cols. 1787-89). St. John Chrysostom, for

160

example, complained of women who hung from their persons the names of rivers (which were invoked as sources of life and fruitfulness) and who committed "a thousand other excesses of this nature," while professing to be Christians (*In epistolam ad Colossenses, Homilia VIII*, 5). As may frequently be suspected in the diatribes of the Early Christian fathers, the more insistent the complaints, the more established the practice.

82
Marriage ring

Constantinople ?, 6th-7th century

Gold

D. 1.6

Richmond

Virginia Museum of Fine Arts, Glasgow Fund, 66.37.7

This gold ring with a flat octagonal hoop and applied oval bezel belongs to a type of marriage ring popular in Byzantium during the sixth and seventh centuries. The scene engraved on the bezel depicts a specific moment in the marriage ceremony, the *dextrarum iunctio,* when the bride and groom join their right hands (Vikan, 1987, p. 34). A nimbed Christ, standing frontally between the nuptial couple, is shown in the act of bringing their hands together. The bride wears a diadem with pendilia (jeweled pendants), suggesting that she was a member of the Byzantine imperial family. Inscribed in the exergue, the space below the figural image, is the Greek word OMONV ("concord"), an invocation for a harmonious and productive marriage. This wish is reinforced by the salutary effects attributed to the eight-sided hoop, a type commonly associated with apotropaic bezel devices intended to convey harmony and health in marriage, especially with regard to successful childbirth (Vikan, 1987, p. 39).

Prototypes for this class of marriage ring may be seen in imperial marriage coins and medallions, such as a gold solidus showing Christ between the Emperor Marcian and his bride, Pulcheria (Ross, 1965, p. 56, no. 66, pl. XLII).

See Vikan, 1987, p. 36, no. 10 (Zucker Collection), and Ross, 1965, pp. 55-57, pl. XLII, nos. 64-66, for comparable rings. The *dextrarum iunctio* scene also appears on the central medallions of the finely crafted marriage belt in the Dumbarton Oaks collection (Weitzmann, 1979, p. 283, no. 262; Ross, 1965, pp. 37-39, pls. XXXI-XXXII, no. 38).

Bibliography: Weitzmann, 1979, p. 285, no. 263; Ross, 1968, p. 23, no. 27.

83
Marriage ring

Eastern Mediterranean, 4th-5th century

Base metal

D. Hoop, 2.1, D. Bezel .7

Private collection

The images engraved on the bezel of this base-metal ring place it among the earliest examples of Christian marriage rings, dated to the fourth and fifth centuries. The worn and schematically rendered images, derived from Roman prototypes, show a thin cross, centrally placed at the top, and a husband and wife on either side, facing each other en buste . The bezel is attached to an eight-sided hoop, a shape with apotropaic significance (see preceding entry, and Vikan, 1987, p. 39).

Related examples may be seen in Vikan, 1987, p. 34, figs. 7, 8; Ross, 1965, pp. 50-51, pl. XXXIX, nos. 50-52; Dalton, 1912, p. 21, no. 127

Unpublished

82

83

84
Ring

Eastern Mediterranean, 5th-7th century

Bronze

D. Hoop 2.06, Bezel 1.63

Toronto

Royal Ontario Museum, 986.181.125

This bronze ring is well preserved apart from slight bending of the hoop. The hoop is a narrow, flat band attached to either side of the bezel. The bezel is incised with a nimbed horseman, riding to the right and spearing a recumbent foe below. The rider is encircled by the apotropaic inscription EIS θEOC O NIKΩN ("One God who conquers").

For a discussion of the motif of the "holy rider," see pp. 25-28.

Unpublished

85
Ring

Eastern Mediterranean, 6th-7th century

Bronze

D. Hoop 2.57, Bezel 1.37

Toronto

Royal Ontario Museum, 986.181.18

A dark-green patina covers this well-preserved bronze ring. The plain hoop is circular in section. On the circular bezel are engraved the three words ΑΓΙΟC ΑΓΙΟC ΑΓΙΟC ("Holy, holy, holy").

For the significance of the inscription, see p. 87.

Unpublished

86
Ring

Eastern Mediterranean, 6th century

Silver

D. Hoop 2.01, Bezel 0.93

Toronto

Royal Ontario Museum, 986.181.12

The circular bezel of this well-preserved silver ring is engraved with the common acrostic formed of the two words ΦΩC and ZΩH ("Light" and "Life"). The ring's plain hoop is circular in section.

On the acrostic, see p. 21, above.

Unpublished

87
Ring

Eastern Mediterranean, 6th century

Silver

D. 2.84, L. extended 4.30

Toronto

Royal Ontario Museum, 986.181.98

This intact silver ring incorporates a miniature key. The circular hoop increases in thickness toward the barrel of the key, which is attached to the hoop by means of a ring. On either side of the barrel, the hoop is engraved with a stylized animal's head. A solid circular bit is soldered to the barrel of the key and is engraved with an equal-armed cross.

On the significance of the key, see p. 9 above. On the cross, see p. 2.

Unpublished

163

88
Ring

Eastern Mediterranean, 6th century

Bronze

D. Hoop 2.53, Bezel 1.51

Toronto

Royal Ontario Museum, 986.181.20

This is an intact bronze ring with a hoop that is flat on the inside face but curved in profile on the outside. On the circular bezel is incised an angel who stands holding a cross staff in the left hand.

For a discussion of the significance of the angel, see p. 87.

Unpublished

89
Ring

Eastern Mediterranean, 6th-7th century

Bronze

D. Hoop 2.27, Bezel L. 1.96

Toronto

Royal Ontario Museum, 986.181.26

The hoop of this well-preserved bronze ring is flat inside and rounded in profile on the outside. The oval bezel is engraved with a schematic rendering of the two holy women at the tomb of Christ. The tomb is cylindrical in shape, with a conical roof surmounted by a cross. The women approach on either side, with heads slightly bowed and arms lowered.

On the New Testament imagery, see p. 29.

Unpublished

90
Necklace

Eastern Mediterranean, 6th-7th century

Gold and glass

L. 54.35

Indiana University

Indiana University Fine Arts Museum, Burton Y. Berry Collection, 70.56.11

This striking gold necklace is made of a double quadruple loop-in-loop chain of thin twisted wire, closed at the ends with ringed terminals. The necklace is fastened by means of a clasp and a wire hook. The clasp is an openwork disc of sheet gold punched and stamped to form an inscribed floriated cross, a type commonly encountered in Byzantine necklaces from the sixth and seventh centuries. The focus of the necklace is a pendent cross flanked by two amulet cases. The cross, suspended from the chain by a small ring attached to the end of the upper arm, is solid cast gold with flat-ended conical arms tapering toward the center. A purple, translucent glass gem set in a high circular collet projects from the surface of the cross at the point where the arms meet (see no. 92 for a similar example). The amulet cases are long hexagonal tubes attached to the chain by two wide circular lugs.

Similar crosses in gold may be seen in Ćurčić and St. Clair, p. 88, no. 88; Bank, 1966, p. 349, no. 107a; Ross, 1965, p. 137, pl. XCVII, no. 179 (1); Amandry, p. 289, pl. XLIV, no. 232. For comparable clasps see Ross, 1965, p. 10, pl. XII, no. 6 b, pp. 16-17, pls. XVIII-XIX, no. 11; Zahn, p. 53, no. 108, p. 65, no. 131, both pl. 60 bis; Marshall, p. 319, pl. LX, no. 2741. Parallels of the amulet cases are illustrated in Ross, 1965, p. 137, pl. XCVII, no. 179 k; Marshall, 1911, p. 381, pl. LXXI, nos. 3155, 3156.

Bibliography: Rudolph and Rudolph, p. 188, no. 153.

Egypt, 6th-7th century

Bronze with traces of gilding

Cross, H. 7.3, W. 4.7, Discs D. 2.8

Richmond

*Virginia Museum of Fine Arts,
Williams Fund, 66.78.3*

This fragmentary necklace, made of bronze and
gilded to imitate the appearance of its more
costly counterparts in gold, is said to have come
from Egypt. The necklace is composed of single
wire links alternating with medallions, each
decorated with a cross and interstitial spirals of
imitation filigree. The centerpiece of the
necklace is a pendent cross suspended by
means of a small ring attached to the upper arm.
The surface of the cross is decorated with a
symmetrical arrangement of circled dots, and
five large circular insets, one in each arm and
one in the center, originally filled with glass.

For related bronze crosses, see Ćurčić and St.
Clair, p. 88, nos. 79, 81; Campbell, 1985, p. 115,
no. 154, 155; Strzygowski, pl. XXXIV, no. 9181.

Bibliography: Ross, 1968, p. 26, no. 34.

92
Pendent cross

Eastern Mediterranean, 6th-7th century

Gold with garnet

H. 3.8, W. 2.5

Richmond

Virginia Museum of Fine Arts, Gift of Mrs. Harris Dunscombe Colt, 82.64

An elegantly styled equal-armed pendent cross of solid cast gold, this piece is similar to catalogue number 90. The arms, tapering toward the center, are hexagonal in section and blunt-ended. At the point where the arms meet, a garnet is set in a high circular collet. The upper arm is fitted with a large plain suspension ring.

Comparative examples in gold may be seen in Ćurčić and St. Clair, p. 88, no. 88; Bank, 1966, p. 349, no. 107a; Ross, 1965, p. 137, pl. XCVII, no. 179, 1; Amandry, p. 289, pl. XLIV, no. 232.

Unpublished

167

93
Pendent cross

Egypt, 6th-8th century

Bronze

H. 9, W. 6.7

University of Toronto

Malcove Collection, M82.173

This pendent cross was made from a thin, flat sheet of bronze with a suspension ring attached to the top. The terminals of the arms are flared with disc-like extensions, each incised with concentric circles enclosing dots. The cross is further decorated with somewhat larger concentric circles, appearing singly on the lateral and upper arms, and paired on the lower arm. At the center, where the arms converge, a circular line suggests that an object, perhaps a glass bead, was glued to the surface (Campbell, 1985, p. 115, no. 156).

For related examples see Campbell, 1985, p. 114, nos. 149, 150, 152; Amandry, p. 290, pl. XLVI, no. 241; Strzygowski, pl. XXXIV, nos. 9177, 9181.

A discussion of the significance of the concentric circles is found on pp. 5-7.

Bibliography: Campbell, 1985, p. 115, no. 156.

94
Pendent cross

Egypt (Karanis), 4th-5th century

Wood

H. 7.5, W. 4.6

University of Michigan

Kelsey Museum of Archaeology, 7561

This small pendent cross from Karanis, Egypt, was crudely fashioned from one piece of wood. The arms of the cross are irregularly formed, and bear no decoration. The vertical extensions are broad, and widely flared at the ends, while the horizontal arms are short, rectangular projections. A hole was drilled through the top arm for the suspension rope, a piece of which still remains.

Bibliography: Haeckel, 1977, p. 101, no. 109; Gazda, 1983a, p. 43. fig. 75.

169

95
Earrings

Constantinople ?, early 7th century

H. 5.7, W. 4.2

Richmond

Virginia Museum of Fine Arts, Glasgow Fund, 66.15.7

This pair of crescent-shaped gold earrings with wire hoops is a fine example of a type widely distributed throughout the Byzantine empire. They were formed first by pressing a piece of sheet gold over a mold, and then punching and incising the surface to achieve the intricate openwork and detailing. The decoration on each consists of two lively, stylized peacocks in a lunette, confronting a floriated cross. The cross is inscribed in a medallion supported by two trefoil-leaved plants and intersected by a superimposed beaded post. Surrounding the lunette are bands of decoration, a fillet of gold grains, followed by zigzag openwork, and finally a border with punched dots. Soldered to the edge of the border are nine large, hollow pearls.

Similar earrings have been found in treasure and coin hoards buried during the period of Persian and Arab invasions in the late sixth and seventh centuries. The careful workmanship points to a workshop in a major artistic center, such as Constantinople, where comparable earrings have been found (Ross, 1968, p. 21).

For related examples with the peacock motif, see Ross, 1965, pp. 68-69, pl. XLVII, nos. 87, 90, p. 95, pl. LXVI, no. 138; Amandry, p. 84, pl. XLII, no. 203b; Orsi, pl. XI, fig. 4; Dalton, 1901, p. 45, pl. V, no. 276.

The meanings of the peacock are discussed on p. 11.

Bibliography: Weitzmann, 1979, p. 315, no. 290; Ross, 1968, pp. 20-21.

96
Buckle

Eastern Mediterranean, early 7th century

Gold

L. 5.2, W. 2.1

Richmond

Virginia Museum of Fine Arts, Glasgow Fund, 66.37.6

A beaded hinge joins the elongated lyre-shaped plate and kidney-shaped loop that make up this solid-cast gold buckle, a type fashionable in Byzantium during the late sixth and seventh centuries. The attachment plate has two beaded lugs for the hinge at one end, and a tip guard on the other. The lyre shape of the plate is formed by a drop-shaped panel surrounding a fleur-de-lis, followed by two confronting palmette leaves filled with a point-and-comma motif. Two independent leaves form the bridge adjacent to the hinge. On the underside of the plate, three studs served to fasten the buckle to the belt strap. The loop has a smooth, molded surface, a beveled interior, and two beaded lugs for the hinge. It is intersected through the center by a tongue consisting of round and oval bosses near the hinge, both pierced with triangular cavities as though to receive inlay, followed by a thick, curved tip, tapered upward to form a central ridge. The solid tip projects beyond the loop. The underside of the loop is hollow, except for the two tongue supports.

For similarly styled gold buckles, see Weitzmann, 1979, p. 326, no. 304; Bank, 1966, p. 348, no. 105; Ross, l965, p. 5, pl. VII, no. 2 c; Athens, no. 302; Amandry, p. 283, pl. XLI, no. 200; Schlunk, p. 25, pl. 13, no. 64.

Bibliography: Ross, l968, p. 22, fig. 24.

97
Belt buckle

Eastern Mediterranean, 6th century

Silver

L. 10.49, W. 3.11

Toronto

Royal Ontario Museum, 986.181.95

The patterning of the upper surface of the plate of this large silver belt-buckle consists of a tear-shaped panel at the end opposite the loop, and two pairs of highly stylized palmettes between it and the hinge. The ends of the tongue are cast in the shapes of a dolphin and a seahorse. Five rivets attached to the back of the plate once fastened it to the belt. The buckle is intact apart from some surface corrosion.

Unpublished

98
Buckle

Eastern Mediterranean, first half of the 7th century

Bronze and gilt

L. 7.05, W. 3.2

Richmond

Virginia Fine Arts Museum, Gift of Nash and Alice Heeramaneck, 68.13.3

This small buckle was cast in bronze and gilded to imitate similar buckles in gold (see catalogue no. 96). The plate has the lyre shape characteristic of many Byzantine buckles dating from the sixth and seventh centuries. On one end there is a tip guard, and on the other, two hinge lugs. The underside is fitted with three projections for fastening the buckle to the belt. The decoration of the upper surface consists of three components. The tip is formed by a tear-shaped panel framed by a densely striated border. The field of the panel is depressed with a cavity, also tear shaped, and surrounded by a raised band with small indented triangles. In the center, partially flanking the tear-shaped panel on either side, appear two half palmettes with a point-and-comma motif at the tip of the lobe and a large circular cavity at the base. All three cavities were probably filled with inlay. Between the palmettes and the loop is a narrow bridge filled with a zigzag design. The loop is kidney-shaped, smoothly rounded on the outside and beveled to a sharp edge on the inside. The tongue has a rectangular box-like panel near the hinge eye with a rectangular cavity, probably for inlay, and a ridged tip.

Many examples of gilded-bronze lyre buckles, dating from the sixth and seventh centuries, have been found throughout Byzantium and beyond its borders. They were worn by people of moderate means, or by the wealthy as copies of more valuable originals they wished to protect. For parallels, see Waldbaum, p. 118, pl. 44, no. 691; Chavane, pp. 163-65 pls. 46, 47, nos. 468, 473.

Bibliography: Ross, 1968, p. 22, fig. 25.

99
Buckle

Eastern Mediterranean, late 6th-7th century

Bronze

L. 6.5, W. 3.2

University of Illinois

World Heritage Museum, 22.1.86

The elements of this small bronze buckle—a lyre-shaped plate, narrow bridge, and elongated oval loop—form a single unit. The plate has a tip guard at the end opposite the loop, and three studs on the underside for attachment to the belt strap. Its lyre shape is defined by three elements unified by concentric grooves: a drop-shaped panel flanked by two leaf-like panels. The forms are open in the center. The bridge is integrated with the plate by scrolling grooves that emerge from the point where the leaf-like panels meet; the grooves extend outward, on either side, around a triangular opening in the center of the bridge. The loop is rounded on the outer surface and beveled on the inner. The area where the tip of the tongue rests on the loop is slightly flared and indented. The tongue is a thick rounded wire which loops at its base through the triangular hole in the bridge.

Related buckles may be seen in Waldbaum, p. 118, pl. 44, no. 691; Chavane, pp. 163-65, pls. 46, 47, nos. 468, 473; Ross, 1968, p. 22, fig. 25.

Unpublished

174

100
Belt buckle

Eastern Mediterranean, 6th century

Bronze with silver inlay

L. 4.32, W. 2.80

Toronto

Royal Ontario Museum, 986.181.47

This bronze belt buckle has an inlay of silver of which limited areas are missing. The plate is in the shape of a pomegranate. The ends of the loop form a pair of confronted dolphins with eyes and fins inlaid with silver. A small cross is inlaid into the plate on either side of the base of the tongue. The remainder of the plate is occupied by an inlaid wreath enclosing a monogram which reads ΠΑΥΛΟΥ ("Of Paul").

Unpublished

175

101
Square buckle plaque

France, 6th-7th century

Bronze

H. 1.7, L. 4.8, W. 4.62

University of Illinois

World Heritage Museum, 24.2.90

This square plaque was once silvered, but most of the silvering has worn away. The surface is generally scratched with slight corrosion, particularly near the areas of remaining silver. The plaque had four round-headed rivets or bosses, one of which remains, decorated with a raised rope border. They were used for fastening the plaque to the leather belt. Two rivet projections remain on one end of the reverse of the buckle, presumably for attachment of the buckle with a hinge-pin device. The incised design on the plaque consists of a central cross-shaped knot motif with rounded arm ends, the so-called Solomon's knot. This motif is framed by a large square with an L-shaped incision in each corner. The square, in turn, is framed by an incised dogleg motif.

The square buckle plaque is often called a dorsal plaque because it is worn near or on the back of the belt. When buckles are damascened, square buckles may serve as counterplaques. However, the silvered-bronze variety was more often used as a third plaque matching two multi-bossed trapezoidal buckle plates. The decoration on this buckle is crudely rendered, suggesting that it did serve a subsidiary position in a buckle-plaque ensemble. For comparative examples see Pilet, pl. 44 (from Frénouville); Barrière-Flavy, pl. LV, l, 2 (from Grancourt-le-Grand, Aisne) and pl. XLV, 5 (from Allenjoie, Doubs).

On the significance of the Solomon's knot, see p. 4.

Unpublished

102
Fibula

4th-5th century

Bronze

H. 2.4, L. 6.9, W. 5

University of Illinois

World Heritage Museum, 24.2.5

This bronze fibula of the onion-headed crossbow type consists of a hexagonal crossbar to which a pin is attached, a high arching bow, and a rectangular catchplate. The crossbar is simply decorated with onion-shaped knobs placed at the center on the front side, and one on each end. The other component to receive decoration is the catchplate, on which appear two incised parallel lines down the center, and triangular notches along the edges of the upper surface.

The crossbow fibula with onion knobs, popular during the fourth and fifth centuries, was an indispensable accessory of the chlamys, a free-hanging cloak pinned at the right shoulder, worn by military men and officials of the imperial bureaucracy. The geographical distribution of the archaeological finds is concentrated in territories that were densely populated with soldiers (Heurgon, pp. 21-23). Several representations of army officers and civilian officials wearing this type of fibula may be seen in Weitzmann, 1979, such as the missorium of Theodosius I (pp. 74-76, no. 64); the diptych of Probianus (p. 55, no. 53); and the diptych of an unknown patrician (p. 57, no. 54). They also appear on the court officials in the mosaics of Justinian and Theodora on the presbytery wall of San Vitale, Ravenna (Smith, 1977, pp. 82-83).

For comparative examples, see Paris, p. 307, no. 267; Mainz, p. 169, fig. 263a; Weitzmann, 1979, p. 303, no. 275a; Kent and Painter, p. 28, nos. 19, 21; Ross, 1968, p. 15, fig. 11; Heurgon, pl. XII; Marshall, p. 337, pl. LXII, nos. 2856, 2858; Dalton, 1901, p. 40, no. 256.

Unpublished

103
Fibula

4th-5th century

Bronze with gilt

H. 2.1, L. 4.7, W. 4.3

University of Illinois

World Heritage Museum, 24.2.528

This gilded-bronze crossbow fibula is intact except for the missing pin (see no. 102 for a related type). The crossbar has three spherical faceted knobs, one on each end and one on the front just below the bow. The sides of the bow taper upward to a narrow, flattened ridge. The rectangular catchplate has no decoration. As this example demonstrates, bronze fibulae were frequently gilded to achieve the rich effect of their more expensive counterparts in gold.

Fibulae of the crossbow type may be seen in Paris, p. 307, no. 267; Mainz, p. 169, fig. 263a; Weitzmann, 1979, p. 303, no. 275a; Kent and Painter, p. 28, nos. 19, 21; Ross, 1968, p. 15, fig. 11; Heurgon, pl. XII; Marshall, p. 337, pl. LXII, nos. 2856, 2858; Dalton, 1901, p. 40, no. 256.

Unpublished

Fig. 45. Kansas City, Nelson Gallery-Atkins Museum,
Bronze Lampstand.
Aphrodite Applies Her Cosmetics.

No less enduring than the allure of jewelry is the desire to make oneself attractive to others through personal care, the arranging of the hair and the application of cosmetics. Opposition to makeup was a constant theme in the writings of the Early Christian fathers, beginning with the advice of Tertullian to Christian women at the end of the second century. "For they who rub their skin with medicaments, stain their cheeks with rouge, and make their eyes prominent with antimony, sin against Him," he wrote. "Whatever is natural is the work of God. Therefore, whatever is painted on, that is the business of the devil." He advised women to make their virtues their cosmetics: to draw their whiteness from simplicity and their red cheeks from modesty, to paint their eyes with bashfulness and their lips with silence. "Thus painted," he concluded, "you will have God as your Lover" (*De cultu feminarum II*, 5 and 13 ; trans. after Roberts and Donaldson, pp. 20-25). Similar attitudes can be found in the writings of Tertullian's contemporary, Clement of Alexandria. He ridicules the woman who uses as cosmetics "the droppings of crocodiles, anointing herself with the scrapings of decayed wood, and rubbing charcoal into her eyebrows and white lead on her cheeks" (*Paedagogus*, III, 7; trans. Wood, p. 205). For the Christian, "the best beauty is that which is spiritual" (*Paedagogus*, III, 64).

Even cleanliness had its dangers; Clement of Alexandria complained at length of wealthy women who behaved immodestly at the public baths and who went there with an array of silver, which they put on display under the noses of the poor (*Paedagogus*, III, 31). A later Greek verse, a palindrome perhaps composed in the sixth century, advises more succinctly: "Wash (away) your sins, not only your face" (Trypanis, no. 223, p. 416).

Clement's description of the paraphernalia taken by the rich to the baths is strikingly illustrated in a fourth-century Roman work, the silver marriage casket of Projecta, who, as we know from the inscription on the lid, was a Christian (color plate I). The silver box is decorated around its body and lid with reliefs showing the bathing and dressing of the bride. Here may be seen Projecta going to the baths in the company of servants who bring silver jugs, bowls, basins, and mirrors, as well as round caskets containing bottles of oils and perfumes and rectangular caskets holding clothes and towels (Shelton, pls. 6-9).

It was not only members of the aristocracy in Rome who needed to make expensive preparations for weddings. In the same century, Papais, a bridegroom in provincial Egypt, wrote to his future mother-in-law in connection with provisions for his forthcoming marriage. He said that he was sending a "box for seven bottles filled with plain oil," presumably for the bride, and asked whether she had received a pearl and a gold ring, so that she could buy perfumes (Barns and Zilliacus, pp. 103-5).

The value and importance of perfumes and cosmetics in the Early Christian period is illustrated by the care that was lavished on the bottles

181

and jars made for their storage. These were fashioned in a variety of materials, including silver, ivory, bone, and wood. Some of the containers imitated the shapes of much larger storage vessels, such as the miniature glass amphoriskos, number 104, with its delicately pointed base that would have been supported upon a small stand. Other forms were specifically developed for cosmetics, such as the paired tubes (nos. 105 and 106), each of which would have held a different substance. Often the glass flasks were given multiple handles (nos. 107, 108, and 109), whose purpose was as much ornamental as functional.

Care was also given to the design of the instruments used to prepare and apply makeup. Some were of glass, like the spiral-twisted dipping rod, number 110, which was used to extract lotions from narrow-necked containers. The manner of application is shown in figure 45, a fifth- or sixth-century bronze lampstand from Egypt, the shaft of which probably represents Aphrodite at her toilet. The half-naked goddess applies makeup or perfume to her face with a rod held in her right hand, while she checks the results in a mirror held in her left hand. Other rods, made of less breakable materials than glass, such as wood or bronze, may have been used both for applying cosmetics and for mixing them. For example, the rod that is our number 111, which is topped by a finely crested rooster, has a rounded end that could have been used for either preparing or applying the cosmetic. Many substances, such as galena, the eyeshadow that was particularly popular in Egypt, came in powdered form (in the case of galena, as lead sulphide), and had to be mixed with a binding material such as water or gum before its application (Rutschowscaya, p. 37). The small bone spoon, number 112, with its handle delicately carved in the shape of a hand holding the bowl, may also have been been used in the preparation of cosmetics.

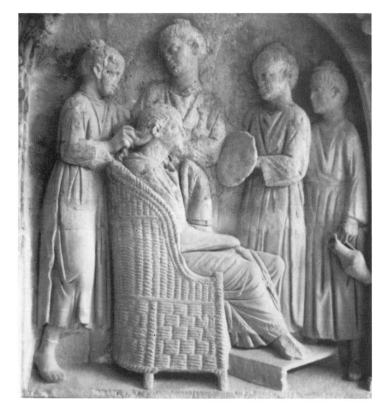

Fig. 46. Trier, Landesmuseum, Relief from a Tomb. A Lady Has Her Hair Done.

No less important than applying paints and perfumes was the care of the hair. Again, the complaints of the church fathers speak eloquently of the concerns that people had in this regard. "The women employ beauticians and handmaids, some to take care of their mirrors, others, the hairnets, others, their combs," said Clement of Alexandria (*Paedagogus*, III, 26; trans. Wood, p. 221). He might have been describing a third-century relief on a tomb at Neumagen, which shows a seated Roman matron having her hair fixed by a whole team of maids, one arranging the hair at the back of the woman's neck, one cradling a flask in the crook of her arm, one displaying a mirror before her mistress, and a fourth holding a ewer by its handle (fig. 46).

Hair combs have survived in considerable quantities from the Early Christian period, in ivory, bone, and wood. Although they have been discovered in all parts of the Roman world, the best preserved come from Egypt, where the dry climate has stabilized organic materials. In Egypt, many of the combs have been discovered in tombs, perhaps because the dead were groomed before their burial (Rutschowscaya, p. 26). Frequently the combs were provided with two rows of teeth; in one row the teeth were thick and widely spaced, to untangle knots in the hair, and in the other row the teeth were fine and set close together, to clean the hair and smooth it. Figure 47, another sixth-century bronze statuette of Aphrodite from Egypt, shows how these double-toothed combs were used. The bronze originally represented the goddess holding up a mirror in order to admire the locks which she had just arranged with the comb brandished in her left hand. The central part of such a comb, between the two rows of teeth, was often finely ornamented, either with relief carvings or with openwork. Among the motifs that appear are concentric circles (see no. 113), animals and birds (e.g., Rutschowscaya, nos. 33-37, pp. 34-35), and benificent inscriptions, such as ZŌĒ, or "Life" (New York, Metropolitan Museum of Art, inv. no. 12.182.89). Some combs were even inlaid with pieces of glass (see no. 114).

Pins were an essential aid to the creation of elaborate hairstyles. Both Tertullian (*De cultu feminarum II*, 7) and Clement of Alexandria spoke out against extravagant coiffures, particularly those requiring the addition of wigs. Clement condemned those women who preened themselves by scratching their heads with hairpins of ivory or tortoiseshell, and he pointed out that the wearing of another's hair would vitiate a priest's blessing: "On whom does the priest lay his hands? Whom does he bless? Not the woman who is so dressed up [with spurious locks], but the artificial hair that belongs to someone else, and through it the other head." His recommendation to Christian women was that they bind up their hair simply at the neck with a plain hairpin (*Paedagogus*, III, 62, 63, and 71; trans. Wood, 248, 253).

Large numbers of hairpins have survived from the Late Roman world. These range from the plain pins sanctioned by Clement, to more decorative pins topped by elaborately turned finials (see no. 116 for both types), by birds such as cocks (no. 117), or even by female busts (see, for example, Paris, no. 241, pp. 277-79).

In the Early Christian period, just as today, many who were dissatisfied with their natural hair color resorted to dyes. Tertullian inveighed against dark-haired women who tried to make themselves look like Germans or Gauls by dying their dark hair blond with saffron (*De cultu feminarum II*, 6). He

Fig. 47. Paris, Louvre Museum, Bronze Statuette. Aphrodite Combing Her Hair.

also condemned those who tried to hide their age by dying their grey hair black (ibid.). Clement said that grey hair should not be concealed as it is God's mark of honor, a splendid sight which instills sobriety in the young (*Paedagogus*, III, 63). Nevertheless, the desire to conceal the signs of aging survived unabated, for the physician Alexander of Tralles, writing in the sixth century, gives no less than three recipes for darkening the hair (Puschmann, p. 453; Stannard, p. 207). This branch of ancient medicine was the equivalent of cosmetic surgery today.

Finally, for the approval of the improvements that art had wrought over nature, whether on the face or in the hair, mirrors were necessary. These were manufactured of glass or polished metal (nos. 118 and 119). At the higher levels of society, mirrors would be of silver, like number 118, which is provided at the back with an elaborately fashioned wire handle. The handle is twisted into the shape of a Hercules knot, to bring prosperity and good luck (see p. 3, above). It was designed to be held by a servant (see fig. 46) or in the manner illustrated by color plate IV, a ceiling fresco from the imperial palace in Trier, which depicts a richly dressed woman adjusting the veil that sets off her well-coiffed hair. By showing us what the lady saw in her mirror, this painting helps us to visualize the effect that much artistry with combs and cosmetics created nearly seventeen centuries ago.

104
Thread-decorated amphoriskos

Eastern Mediterranean, 3rd-4th century

Glass

H. 13.5, Rim D. 1.9

University of Illinois

World Heritage Museum, 22.1.183

This amphoriskos of "colorless" glass, used to hold an unguent or cosmetic, has some evidence of milky weathering. The ovoid body, tapered to a solid, pointed base, has a long, narrow, tubular neck. Near the rim, the neck is incised with a groove. The rim is flattened and rounded off. Trailed threads spiral around the body.

Related types may be seen in Auth, p. 204, no. 359.

Unpublished

105
Double cosmetic tube with multiple handles

Eastern Mediterranean, 4th-5th century

Glass

H. 9.6 (with handle, 14.7), Rim D. 1.3

University of Illinois

World Heritage Museum, 16.8.1

A free-blown, blue-green cosmetic container of "colorless" glass, this piece features two phials that were formed from a single bubble of glass by pressing the sides to form a diaphragm. Milky and iridescent weathering is evident on the exterior surface. One tube is broken near the bottom. The irregular, slightly bulging bases of the tubes are solid and flattened. The rim is rounded. Spiral threading of a darker blue-green decorates the upper half of the vessel, but once covered the entire surface. The dark blue-green trailed threads form a basket handle over the top, and two small loop handles at the sides.

Similar examples may be seen in Matheson, p. 120. no. 325; Auth, p. 146, no. 187; Hayes, 1975, p. 101, no. 360, pl. 28, no. 361, pl. 22

Unpublished

106
Double cosmetic tube

Eastern Mediterranean, 4th-5th century

Glass

H. 11.2, Rim D. 1.6

University of Illinois

World Heritage Museum, XX.11.2

This free-blown, bluish green double cosmetic tube of "colorless" glass is similar in form and technique to catalogue number 105. The surface deformation reveals evidence of incrustation and iridescent weathering. The bases of the tubes, bulging slightly, are rounded off and flattened. The rim is molded inward. Fragments of the trailed thread decoration that once spiraled down the entire length of the tubes still adhere to the sides.

Unpublished

107
Flask with multiple handles

Eastern Mediterranean, 5th century

Glass

H. 12, (with handle, 18.4), Rim D. 5.2, Base D. 5.8

University of Illinois

World Heritage Museum, 17.2.27

This blue-green flask of "colorless" glass has a squat body with vertical sides, rounded shoulders, and a tall funnel-shaped neck. The rim is rounded. The vessel rests on a concave base, and has nine trailed handles, four sets of dark blue-green double loops symmetrically arranged around the neck, and a basket handle over the top.

For a related example with a basket handle, see Hayes, 1975, p. 100, no. 356, pl. 23.

Unpublished

187

108
Flask with multiple handles

Eastern Mediterranean, 4th-5th century

Glass

H. 13, Base D. 4.5

University of Illinois

World Heritage Museum, 17.2.31

This small blue-green flask of "colorless" glass has a spherical body with spiral ribbing, a pushed-in base, and a tall, cylindrical neck. Two sets of thick double-looped trailed handles of a darker blue-green are attached to the rim, neck, and shoulders. The wide, flat rim is poorly crafted and folded inward. When the liquid content of the flask was poured out, the flow was controlled by a flange with a narrow opening located at the base of the neck. The flange was formed by fusing the neck to the body in a separate process. Incrustation and iridescent weathering are apparent on the outer surface of the vessel.

An example similar in form, but resting on a thick pad base, may be seen in Sotheby, p. 118, no. 205.

Unpublished

109
Lentoid flask

Syro-Palestinian, mid- or late 4th century

Glass

H. 15, Rim D. 4.5

University of Illinois

World Heritage Museum, 17.2.29

This is a pale bluish green flask, with a circular flat-sided body, a long, thin tubular neck, and a slightly flattened, pushed-in base. The body is covered with a light mold-blown ribbing, twisted spirally. The tapering neck flares out at the top to form a wide mouth. The rim is folded inward. The neck is decorated with a single trailed thread of a dark, peacock blue. Two symmetrically placed loop handles of the same color extend from the midpoint of the neck to the shoulders. The vessel shows evidence of iridescent weathering.

Similar flat-sided flasks may be seen in Auth, p. 36, no. 171, and Hayes, 1975, p. 106, no. 389, pl. 22. For related pilgrim flasks in glass, see Auth, p. 220, nos. 455-59.

Unpublished

188

110
Dipping rod

Eastern Mediterranean, 1st or 2nd century

Glass

L. 16, Ring D. 2.8

University of Illinois

World Heritage Museum, 22.1.163

Dipping rods, such as this example, were commonly used throughout the Mediterranean to extract cosmetics and unguents from narrow-mouthed bottles. This one has a straight, slender, pale blue-green shaft, twisted spirally, with a circular ring at one end, and a button-like dipper, partially broken, at the other.

For similar examples, see Sotheby, p. 117, nos. 200, 201; Auth, p. 229, no. 521; Hayes, 1975, fig. 21, no. 656b.

Unpublished

111
Cosmetic applicator with rooster finial

Egypt, 5th-7th century

Bronze

L. 13.2

Private collection

This handsome bronze cosmetic applicator would have figured among a woman's toiletry items in late antiquity. It is composed of a cylindrical shaft, rounded and slightly bulbous at the tip, and a rooster finial. The rooster is defined in profile and mounted on a baluster section. The design is generally comparable to bone and ivory hairpins decorated with the rooster motif (see no. 117). A parallel to the highly stylized, geometrically rendered rooster may be found in a wooden hairpin in the Metropolitan Museum of Art, New York, inv. no. 08.202.18, a, d, or o.

Unpublished

189

112
Cosmetic spoon

Egypt (Karanis) 1st-4th century

Bone

H. 1.3-2.5, L. 9.6, W. 2.8

University of Michigan

Kelsey Museum of Archaeology, 21869

This intriguing bone cosmetic spoon was carved in the form of a hand. The pear-shaped bowl, still retaining traces of pigment, rests in the palm and fingers. The handle, which is hollow in the center and smoothly carved, is formed by the wrist and forearm. The end of the handle is incised with a band of irregular lines. On the back of the hand, care was taken to carve the details of the fingers naturalistically. The spoon is in good condition, except for a break in the arm shaft.

Bibliography: Gazda, 1983a, p. 27, fig. 44; Gazda, 1983b.

113
Double-tooth hair comb

Egypt

Wood

L. 25.5, W. 8

University of Michigan

Kelsey Museum of Archaeology, 24966

This long, rectangular hair comb made from a light brown wood with a smooth, polished surface has two sets of teeth located on the narrow ends of the plaque. The coarse teeth were used to disentangle the hair, and the fine ones to arrange and smooth it. The decorative design on the plaque is the same on both sides. Two bands of interlocking triangles at the base of the teeth frame a symmetrical arrangement of dotted circles consisting of a large circle in the center, inscribed by a chain of tiny circles, and four smaller circles, one placed in each corner. The general condition of the comb is good, although the plaque is slightly warped, and the teeth are worn.

Combs of this type were in use in Roman Egypt over a long period of time. A great number have been discovered in the tombs of Antinoe, sometimes placed on the chest of the dead. Due to the longevity of the type and the absence of stratigraphic evidence, they are difficult to date.

Similar examples from Egypt may be seen in Rutschowscaya, pp. 29-31, nos. 14-19, 21; Badawy, p. 342, no. 5.45; Strzygowski, p. 146, pl. VIII, 8831, 8832.

For the significance of concentric circles, see p. 5.

Unpublished

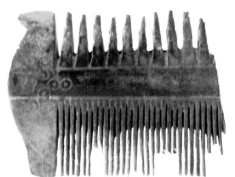

114
Double-tooth hair comb

Egypt

Wood

L. 23, W. 6.5

University of Michigan

Kelsey Museum of Archaeology, 24964

This comb, like catalogue no. 113, has two rows of teeth, one fine and one coarse, on the narrow ends of a rectangular plaque. It is made of a smooth blond wood, and decorated on one side with five large excised circles arranged in an X-pattern. Each circle was once filled with a pentagonal piece of pale green glass set in plaster, similar to those in the plaster mirror frames of Gheyta (Petrie, 1927, pl. XXIX). One piece of glass still remains in place. Smaller incised circles provide additional decoration. Petrie suggests that the mirrored combs were showpieces of the bridal trousseau (Petrie, 1927, p. 26). For the significance of the mirror see p. 7.

Similar combs are illustrated in Rutschowscaya, p. 29, no. 13, p. 35, no. 38; and Petrie, 1927, p. 26, pl. XXI, nos. 52-53.

Unpublished

115
Double-tooth hair comb

Egypt

Wood

L. 5.9, W. 5.2

University of Illinois

World Heritage Museum, 14.5.160

This hair comb is styled differently from catalogue numbers 113 and 114. The sets of coarse and fine teeth are placed on the long sides of a narrow rectangular plaque, and bracketed by end pieces with curving profiles. The plaque is decorated on one side only with a scattered arrangement of dotted circles.

Examples of this type may be seen in Rutschowscaya, p. 33, nos. 31, 32; Gazda, 1983a, p. 27, fig. 44; Petrie, 1927, p. 26, pl. XX, nos. 21, 29, pl. XXI, nos. 43, 46.

Unpublished

116
Hairpins

Egypt, 1st-4th century

Bone

L. 9.6, 5.2, 9.4, 6.2

University of Illinois

World Heritage Museum, 14.5.181; 14.5.182; 14.5.184; 14.5.185

Bone hairpins, like these examples found in Egypt, were used by women to hold their coiffures in place. The smooth, rounded shafts taper to a point at one end, and terminate with simple spherical or faceted knobs on the other. One example, no. 14.5.182, is slightly more elaborate, with three molded cylindrical knobs projecting from the head.

Numerous bone hairpins have been found in the sarcophagi of women and young girls, many featuring finials with human busts, hands, animals, as well as geometric designs. A variety of examples in bone and ivory may be seen in Hartmann, p. 41; Paris, p. 277, no. 241; Petrie, 1927, pl. XIX; Strzygowski, pl. XIX

Unpublished

117
Hairpin

Egypt (Karanis) 1st-4th century

Bone

L. 12.5

University of Michigan

Kelsey Museum of Archaeology, 3488

This bone hairpin, like the pins of catalogue number 116, has a rounded shaft tapered to a point, and, like number 111, has a head decorated with a rooster perched on a notched post. The rooster is shown in profile, roughly carved without interior details.

Similar examples with the rooster motif may be seen in Petrie, 1927, p. 24, no. 55, pl. XIX; Strzygowski, pl. XIX, 8882, 8883; Metropolitan Museum of Art, New York, inv. no. 08.202.18, a, d, or o.

Bibliography: Gazda, 1983a, p. 27, fig. 44.

193

118
Mirror

Syria, 3rd-4th century

Silver

D. 34.6, H. 2.2

Cleveland

The Cleveland Museum of Art, Purchase J. H. Wade Fund, 56.31

This handsome mirror comes from a treasure of eleven pieces of silver acquired by the Cleveland Museum of Art, after they had reportedly been found together in Syria (Milliken, pp. 35-37). The mirror comprises a circular dish and a handle which is soldered onto the back. A raised ridge with a flattened top runs in a circle inside the edge of the reflecting face of the mirror. Inside this ridge, and congruent with it, is another forming an arc on the quadrant. The two ridges are joined to one another by four more ridges, which radiate outward from the inner quadrant forming three curved coffers, perhaps designed to help with the proper alignment of sections of the hair. The back of the mirror is incised with six concentric circles. The handle is made of two pieces of thick silver wire which are intertwined to form a knot of Hercules. The wires end in four flattened terminals shaped as ivy leaves with curved and pointed tips, which act as soldering plates where the handles join the surface. The ivy metaphor is strengthened by tendril-like loops in the stems outside the knot.

This type of mirror, with the handle on the reverse, was introduced by the second century A.D. (M. M. Mango, p. 212). It can be seen in use in color plate IV, which reproduces a ceiling fresco of the early fourth century from the imperial palace at Trier, and in figure 46, which reproduces a third-century tomb sculpture from the same region. A similar silver mirror, probably of the early third century, was found at Wroxeter in England (Toynbee, pp. 334-35, pl. 78C; Strong, p. 179). Like the mirror in Cleveland, it has a handle applied to the back, and the handle is fashioned of two pieces of wire twisted into a knot of Hercules and ending in leaf terminals. The apotropaic significance of this knot is discussed on pp. 3-4.

Bibliography: Milliken, pp. 35-37, plate following p. 41; M. M. Mango, p. 212.

119
Mirror

Roman, 1st to early 2nd century

Bronze

D. Disc 11.2, L. Handle tab 3

Private collection

This bronze hand-mirror consists of a flat disc to which is attached at one point along the circumference a short rectangular tab with the two corners drawn out at the bottom to form pointed extensions. The tab once served to attach the mirror to a handle, probably either a turned baluster grip, or the single or multiple loop type. One side of the disc was burnished to a fine reflective surface; the other was decorated with lathe-turned concentric rings. This motif was a favorite decorative device on mirrors, continuing into the Early Christian period. For its significance, see p. 6.

The abundance of mirrors and the range of types found at domestic and cemetery sites dating to the period of the Julio-Claudians suggest that the manufacture of mirrors greatly expanded at this time. By the late third century the production was reduced to four main types. This variety of hand mirror, with the handle attached to the circumference, was in general use during the first and early second centuries. It is a simpler version of the more elaborate silver mirrors of the type found at Pompeii and Herculaneum. These luxury items of the wealthy were carefully tended and handed down from one generation to the next (Lloyd-Morgan, p. 145).

Examples of related hand mirrors may be seen in Waldbaum, p. 109, nos. 650, 651, 653; Paris, pp. 274-75, no. 239 a, b.

Unpublished

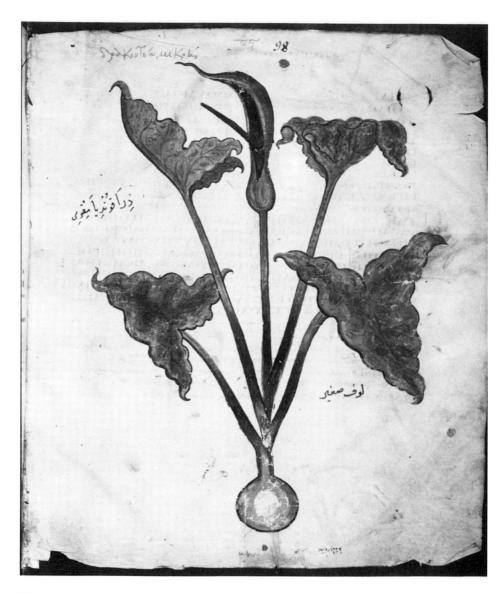

Fig. 48. Vienna Nationalbibliothek, Cod. med. gr. 1 (Herbal of Dioscurides), fol. 98.
Arum Maculatum.

Nowhere in the culture of the early Christians is the intersection of the physical and the supernatural more apparent, and more paradoxical, than in the fields of health and medicine. Then, as today, there were medical schools, there was surgery, and there was a science of pharmacology (Duffy, pp. 21-27). But coexisting with empirical medicine were the magical cures of amulets and the spiritual healing dispensed by holy men and holy women. All three types of medicine are evidenced in the material culture of the time, in the surgical instruments and textbooks of doctors, in the amulets of magicians, and in the keepsakes and reliquaries of the saints.

Relations between the empirical and the supernatural healers tended to be strained, for the two were often in competition with each other. A holy man of the sixth century, St. Nicholas of Sion, chastised a blind man who had spent all his money on doctors without finding a cure: "Why did you not put your faith in the saints?" he asked. "You would have been cured [by us] free of charge" (Ševčenko, p. 58). Nevertheless, in spite of the invective of the saints' lives against doctors, supernatural and physical medicine interpenetrated. A few saints, such as Theodore of Sykeon, who died in A.D. 613, even acted as referral services, sending patients who came to them to the appropriate specialists in physical healing, to surgeons or to doctors skilled in prescribing medicines (Magoulias, p. 128). Holy men themselves were not averse to going to doctors, and doctors, for their part, occasionally recommended magical aids to health, if not the services of the saints. Thus St. Theognios, who fell off an ass in Palestine, was willing to have recourse to a specialist in bone setting in order to have his broken leg set between reed splints (Magoulias, p. 144). Another holy man, the ascetic Aaron, suffering from a terrible case of gangrene in the loins, was cured by doctors who healed the ulcer by applying drugs and bandages, and who even inserted a lead pipe so that he could urinate. The operation was successful, for the saint lived with the tube in place for another eighteen years (Ashbrook Harvey, pp. 88-89). On the other hand, Alexander of Tralles, a distinguished physician of the sixth century, included an account of magical amulets in his treatise on medicine. Writing about the treatment of colic, he said that many of his patients, especially the wealthier ones, objected to physical remedies such as enemas, forcing him to prescribe amulets, which he characterized as being effective, though unnecessary, cures (Duffy, p. 26). The mixture of the physical and the supernatural can also be found in medical papyri from Egypt, where pharmacological recipes appear alongside the texts of charms, the two kinds of remedy being given equal value (Grenfell and Hunt, 1915, pp. 238-41).

Aesthetically, the most spectacular products of physical medicine were the illustrated herbals, such as the sumptuously illustrated volume that was made in Constantinople at the beginning of the sixth century for presentation to the princess Anicia Juliana. This manuscript originally

197

contained 435 full-page paintings of the plants whose medicinal uses are described by the author of the text, the famous pharmacologist Dioscurides, who lived in the second century A.D. (fig. 48).

Fig. 49. New York, Metropolitan Museum of Art, Stone Sarcophagus, Detail.
A Doctor with his Books and Case of Medical Instruments.

Less spectacular visually, but no less evocative of medical conditions of the time, are the instruments used by surgeons and physicians (see nos. 120-24). A collection of instruments is illustrated on the marble sarcophagus of a fourth-century doctor, which was found near Ostia (fig. 49). Here we see the physician seated in front of a cupboard which holds the equipment of his surgery: on the lower shelf is a bowl, on the upper shelf the scrolls containing his medical reference works, and on top of the cupboard his open case of instruments. Among the instruments in the case can be seen one with a leaf-shaped blade, similar to number 120 in the exhibition, and another with a long curved tapering tip, similar to number 121.

Often the physicians' cases were ornamented, as were the instruments they contained, such as number 121, which has an elaborately turned baluster handle. The motivation for such apparently unfunctional decoration was possibly to inspire confidence, as would an expensively decorated doctor's consulting room today. Unanaesthetized patients, who could see all too well what was going on during the course of their surgery, could be assured of the doctor's successful status by his costly looking tools. Also, it seems that many surgeons made a kind of public display out of their operations (Bliquez, p. 194), perhaps as a form of insurance against accusations of malpractice. St. John Chrysostom describes these public operations: "For the wise doctors, when they are about to amputate putrid limbs, or to cut out stones obstructing the passages, or to correct any other ill of nature, do not take the sick man into a corner in order to do this [operation], but they set him out in the middle of the market place and create a theater around him from the passers-by, and in this manner they set about the surgery" (*Ecloga de adversa valetudine et medicis, Homilia XIII*). One can see that, in such circumstances, an impressively formed and decorated set of instruments would have greatly enhanced the spectacle. Nevertheless, for sensitive spectators these procedures were an ordeal, as they surely were for the patients. "At these operations," says John Chrysostom, "you can see the flesh being cut, the blood flowing, gangrene being removed: and one has to endure a good deal of unpleasantness arising from the spectacle and a good deal of pain and grief, not only from the sight of the wounds, but also from the suffering of those being cauterized and cut. For no one is so made of stone that, as he stands by those undergoing these operations and hears their cries, he does not break down, feel troubled, and become despondent in his soul" (*In paralyticum demissum per tectum*, 4; trans. Bliquez, p. 194).

It is small wonder that many people preferred to be cured by the holy doctors, whose methods were not only cheaper but also considerably less painful. How much better to have the experience of one patient, who, having visited the relics of St. Artemios, was miraculously operated upon by the saint while he slept, and awoke completely cured of his infirmity. "What have you to say to me, swaggering surgeon?" crowed the author of the life of the saint when he had finished this tale. ". . . Your profit making is diminished, your scalpels are being consumed by rust, your two-seater chairs and your blunt-hooked surgical instruments are of no use!" (Papadopoulos-Karameus, mir. 25, 35-36; trans. Magoulias, p. 139).

As the story of St. Artemios implies, spiritual healing was usually effected by contact, with the holy man himself, with his relics if he were dead, or with some article or substance connected with his person. For example, according to the Life of St. Symeon the Younger, the stylite saint who lived on top of a column near Antioch, a priest from Georgia visited the holy man and asked him for some of his hair. Returning to his homeland, the priest enclosed the hairs in a cross, which he placed in a shelter, so that all who visited it were cured of diverse diseases and infirmities (van den Ven, p. 130). Such a keepsake, endowed with the miraculous powers of the holy person, was called a *eulogia*, or "blessing." These blessings made it possible for the spiritual healers to effect their cures at a distance, even from beyond the grave, for their tombs retained the special powers that the saints had possessed during life. A *eulogia* might take various forms. It could be a piece of the saint's clothing, or even, in the case of ascetic saints such as the Elder Symeon Stylites, one of the maggots that fell from the sores in his flesh. A pilgrim lucky enough to obtain a blessing of the latter variety might discover that the worm turned into a pearl as he held it in his hand (Antonius, *Vita*, 18; ed. Lietzmann, p. 45). Usually, as in the case of the hairs of St. Symeon, the blessings were generic in their application. They were capable

199

of curing all manner of diseases, and frequently their efficacy was not limited to matters of health; they could, for example, protect people from the perils of travel.

As the number of supplicants to the saints and their shrines increased, it became necessary to find substitute blessings that could be dispensed in greater quantities than personal items such as hair or clothing. One solution was to give pilgrims tokens made of baked earth, or "dust," associated with the saint or his shrine. Often these tokens, such as numbers 126 and 127, which were probably made at the site of the column of St. Symeon the Younger, show the saint's image as an assurance of their origin and efficacy. On their reverse sides the tokens frequently bear the imprints of the palms in which they were formed (see no. 127). These palm prints may have been more than an accidental result of the process of manufacture; they may have had the conscious intent of conveying to the recipient the idea that the saint himself had touched or blessed the token (Vikan, 1982, pp. 38-39). The earth was believed to carry the miraculous powers of the saint and could be put to use in a variety of ways. It could, for example, be rubbed into the limbs of a paralytic, or it could be drunk by a man with an ulcer (Vikan, 1982, p. 31). The token could simply be worn as a general prophylactic by those who were well. According to the Life of St. Symeon the Younger, the saint apparently operated an ingenious welfare system, giving dust which he had blessed to the poor people of Antioch, who gave it to others in exchange for food (van den Ven, p. 163). By this means, he succeeded in turning his immaterial powers into material nourishment for the needy.

Earth was also collected from the holy places associated with the life of Christ. An anonymous sixth-century pilgrim to the Holy Land from Piacenza, in northern Italy, says that earth was brought to the tomb of Christ and put inside it, so it could subsequently be taken away as a blessing by pilgrims (*Peregrinatio*, 18; trans. Wilkinson, 1977, p. 83). It is possible that the token number 129, which shows the Entry of Christ into Jeruslam, is from a site in the Holy Land.

Another type of object associated with the practice of spiritual medicine was the *ampulla,* or flask, made for holding holy oil, water, or loose dust associated with a holy person or shrine. These flasks could either be worn suspended from the neck, in the manner illustrated by figure 50, a tenth-century fresco from Faras Cathedral in Nubia, or they could be placed over a bed in order to protect the sleeper from harm brought on by demons (Vikan, 1982, p. 12).

An interesting passage in the diary of the pilgrim from Piacenza relates how he visited the basilica at Golgotha and witnessed flasks full of oil being touched to the wood of the Holy Cross. When the mouth of one of the flasks touched the wood, the oil started to bubble over (*Peregrinatio*, 20; trans. Wilkinson, 1977, p. 83). The practice of giving to pilgrims substances such as oil which had been in contact with the object of veneration was a way of protecting the relic itself. An earlier pilgrim, Egeria, who visited Jerusalem around the year 380, wrote that in her day people were allowed to kiss the wood itself, but only under the watchful gazes of the bishop and deacons, because someone had already stolen a piece of the relic by biting off a chunk of it (*Peregrinatio,* XXXVII, 2; trans. Wilkinson, 1971, p. 137). Several flasks from the

Fig. 50. Faras Cathedral, Fresco. The Anchorite Aaron Wearing an Ampulla.

Holy Land of the type described by the Piacenza pilgrim have survived. One of them, a metal ampulla in Bobbio, bears the words: "Oil of the wood of life, which guides on earth and sea" (Grabar, 1958, p. 33, pl. 32). The implication of the inscription is that the relic, and by its power the oil, acted as a protection for travellers, to prevent their going astray or falling into danger, for many of their potential misfortunes might be demonic in origin. The oil also had curative properties, for in the sixth century it is recorded that oil of the True Cross was used to exorcise evil spirits (Vikan, 1982, p. 12). The flasks containing the oil were manufactured in terra-cotta, lead, silver, or gold; but even a bishop, such as St. Spiridon of Trimithon on Cyprus, might not be ashamed to wear an ampulla made out of clay, as we know from his panegyric, composed in 655 (Frolow, pp. 174-75).

Ampullas were also manufactured at the shrines of major saints, so that visitors could carry away substances connected with their tombs. Number 130 in this exhibition is a terra-cotta flask attributed to the shrine of St. John the Evangelist in Ephesus, who was thought to be sleeping there in his tomb until he should awake at the Second Coming. The ampulla, which shows the saint in the act of writing, once contained the dust, or "manna," which the slumbering saint, in a miraculous sneeze, blew up through the holes in the top of his tomb every year on his feast day, the eighth of May (Duncan-Flowers, 1989). An ampulla of this type has been found in a private house at Aphrodisias in Turkey, indicating that these flasks from Ephesus, like those from the Holy Land, were kept at home for the protection of the household (Campbell, 1988, p. 541, fig. 3a-c).

Number 131 is a flask from a different shrine, the grave of the popular St. Menas, southwest of Alexandria in Egypt. It would have contained either oil from the lamps burning over the martyr's grave, or holy water from his shrine (Weitzmann, 1979, p. 576). In either case, the substance had beneficial properties, which might extend even into the afterlife, for people were buried with these flasks (Breccia, p. 306; Campbell, 1988, p. 545).

Most of the objects associated with spiritual medicine, the tokens and the substances in the ampullas, were generic in their application. Magical remedies, on the other hand, were more specific. For example, number 132, a green stone engraved with rayed serpents, may have been a remedy specifically for the stomach, while the tentacled head on number 133, a conflation of the Chnoubis with the Gorgon, may have been a protective device directed at the womb (see pp. 7-8, above). Magical amulets of this kind were not to the liking of the church fathers, who associated them with paganism and with Judaism (St. John Chrysostom, *In epistolam ad Colossenses, Homilia VIII,* 5; St. Jerome, *Commentaria in Evangelium S. Matthaei,* XXIII, 6). Nevertheless, their popularity among Christians is evidenced by the large number of amulets combining magical with Christian subject matter (see number 134, with the enthroned Christ, and number 136, with a rider holding a cross-headed spear). We have the previously cited testimony of the sixth-century doctor Alexander of Tralles, most of whose clients must have been Christians, that the demand for magical cures was not restricted to the poorer classes; indeed, he says that it was his wealthier patients who were unwilling to submit themselves to the discomforts and indignities of empirical medicine, and who sought relief in amulets. It could be said that people at the upper levels of society were more oriented toward the future in their thinking, in that they were more willing to put their faith in supernatural cures such as those provided by magical amulets and spiritual healers, and less trusting in merely physical remedies from the classical past.

The last object in this section of the exhibition, the censer that is number 138, might at first sight not appear to be connected with health at all. Yet one of the functions of incense in the Early Christian house was to serve as an accompaniment to prayers on behalf of the sick. The life of St. Symeon the Younger contains several accounts of healings being granted to supplicants who invoked the saint at home while burning incense (Vikan, 1982, p. 30; *idem,* 1984, p. 71). More than any other substance, the smoke of incense would be seen to unite the visible with the invisible, by mingling with and then dissipating into the ambient air.

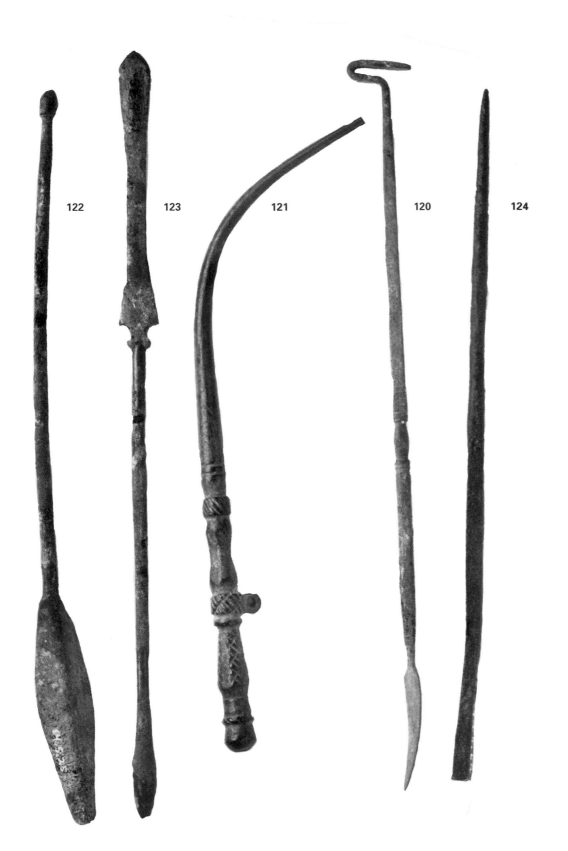

122   123   121   120   124

203

120
Curved hook-spatula probe

Egypt, 1st-4th century

Bronze

L. 18

University of Illinois

World Heritage Museum, 14.5.38

As its name suggests, this instrument is composed of two elements attached to the ends of a shaft. The curved hook dissector, which Galen speaks of as an "eyed hook" (Milne, p. 87), served to seize and raise small pieces of tissue around wounds and lesions and to draw out the tonsils for amputation with the fistula knife. The pointed spatula was both a pharmacological and a surgical instrument. Like most spatulas, it was used for the mixing and spreading of medicaments, and the scraping away of discharges. It could also serve as a semi-sharp dissector to lance and clean fistulas.

For related examples see Künzl, p. 65, fig. 35 (Musée des Antiquités Nationales, Saint-Germain-en-Laye); Milne, pp. 87-88, pl. XXIII, no. 1 (author's collection), no. 2 (St. Germain-en-Laye), no. 3 (British Museum), no. 4 (St. Germain-en-Laye).

Unpublished

121
Surgical instrument

Egypt, 1st-4th century

Bronze

L. 18

University of Illinois

World Heritage Museum, 14.5.130

This surgical instrument of uncertain use is composed of a short baluster handle and a curving shaft tapered to a point. The tip is broken off. The round section and large calibration of the shaft, along with its pronounced curve, suggest that it may be a variation of the handled needle. This type was not suitable for suturing tissue, being too blunt and thick, but was used for fixing the bandages of dressings and splints.

Comparable examples may be seen in Waldbaum, p. 112, nos. 667, 668, pl. 42 (Sardis).

Unpublished

122
Cyathiscomele

Egypt, 1st-4th century

Bronze

L. 18

University of Illinois

World Heritage Museum, 14.5.25

The cyathiscomele, a combination of olivary probe and elongated, narrow spoon, was used by Egyptians to apply cosmetic ointments and pigments, and was probably adopted by medical men for their own purposes. The spoon was used to withdraw medicinal powders and ointments from containers; the olivary (the oval enlargement) to mix and apply them. The olivary could be used, alternatively, in a manner similar to catalogue number 123 as a probe and cautery.

Numerous examples of the cyathiscomele have been found at sites throughout Europe and the Mediterranean. See Künzl, p. 72, fig. 46, no. 4 (Rheinisches Landesmuseum, Trier), p. 91, fig. 69, nos. 2, 3 (Rheinisches Landesmuseum, Bonn), p. 98, fig. 78 (Rheinisches Landesmuseum, Bonn), p. 104, fig. 83, no. 6 (Museo Civico di Brescia), p. 106, fig. 85, no. 5 (Luzzi), p. 115, fig. 90, no. 4 (Museo Carolino-Augusteum, Salzburg), p. 123, fig. 97 (private collection); Tabanelli, pl. XXXVII (Museo Romano Germanico di Magonza); Milne, pp. 61-63, pls. XIV, 3, XV, 1.

Unpublished

123
Spathomele

Egypt, 1st-4th century

Bronze

L. 19

University of Illinois

World Heritage Museum, 14.5.35

The spathomele, or spatula probe, used extensively by medical doctors, consists of a probe with an olivary at one end of a long shaft, and a thick, blunt, oar-shaped blade on the other. Mentioned by almost every medical writer, it had multiple pharmacological and surgical applications. The olivary probe could be used to stir medicaments and ointments, and apply them to the affected area. It could also be employed as a sound for large cavities, and as a cautery to destroy the roots of hair after epilation. The spatula could be used for spreading ointments, applying plaster to casts, depressing the tongue, dissecting, and cauterizing.

The use of the spathomele was not confined to medical men. It was employed by painters in the preparation and mixing of pigments and by women in the application of cosmetics. Large numbers of the spatula probes have been found, all with the characteristic oar-shaped blade, though varying greatly in outline. For comparative examples, see Künzl, p. 58, fig. 26, no. 3 (Musée Crozatier, Le Puy), p. 65, fig. 35, no. 23 (Musée des Antiquités Nationales, Saint Germain-en-Laye), p. 72, fig. 46, no. 3 (Rheinisches Landesmuseum, Trier), p. 83, fig. 57, no. 11 (Heimatmuseum, Bingen), p. 90, fig. 68, no. 6 (Römisch-Germanisches Museum, Cologne); Tabanelli, pp. 78-79, nos. 8-10, pl. LIV (Museo Romano-Germanico di Magonza); Milne, pp. 58-61, pl. XII, no. 1 (Naples), no. 4 (Athens), pl. XIII. no. 1 (Naples), no. 2 (Römisch-Germanisches Zentralmuseum, Mainz).

Unpublished

124
Specillum

Egypt, 1st-4th century

Bronze

L. 17

University of Illinois

World Heritage Museum, 14.5.64

The specillum, or pointed probe, composed of a simple shaft with a square section tapered to a point, is one of the most common medical instruments to survive from antiquity. Numerous examples have been uncovered at Pompeii and Herculaneum. Like most well-designed medical instruments, it continued in use until the end of the Empire with form and decoration remaining basically unchanged.

Among the surgical procedures for which it was employed is the opening and exploration of fistulas, and the examination of the ear. When wrapped in wool, it could be used to wipe away discharges, or to apply fluid medicaments to the eye or ear. In the latter procedure, a piece of wool would be soaked with the medicine, and gently squeezed around the shaft to allow the fluid to run down and drip off the tip.

The versatile instrument was used equally in the domestic setting. Often found among the troves of ancient toiletry articles, it was used to extract kohl from cosmetic tubes, and to apply it to the eyes. As a writing stylus, it was used to inscribe and erase characters in wax tablets.

For other examples of the specillum, many combined with a small flat disk at one end for cleaning the ears, see Künzl, 1983, p. 48, fig. 16, nos. 30-35 (Römisch-Germanisches Zentralmuseum, Mainz), p. 49, fig. 17, nos. 3, 6 (Private Collection, Meyer-Steineg, Jena), p. 98, fig. 78, p. 99, fig. 79 (Rheinisches Landesmuseum, Bonn); Tabanelli, pl. XLI (Museo Romano-Germanico di Magonza), XLIII (Biblioteca Ambrosiana di Milano); Milne, pl. XVIII (author's collection).

Unpublished

125
Tongue depressors

Bronze

(Left-a) L. 13.5, disc W. 5.4, (middle-b) L. 11.7, disc W. 4.2, (right-c) L. 13.2, disc W. 4.2

University of Illinois

World Heritage Museum
(a) 24.2.32, (b) 24.2.34, (c) 24.2.35

These three tongue depressors are in good condition. All three are similar in form, but have varied handle designs. Example (a) has a flat rounded disc beveled on the upper edge. The shaft has a diamond-shaped section, and is terminated with a pinecone finial articulated only on the upper side. The disc shape of example (b) is identical to (a), but with an unbeveled edge. The shaft is rounded on the front, and decorated with incised lines, horizontal near the bowl, oblique above, and herringbone just below the finial. The back of the shaft is flat and undecorated. The finial is in the form of a bust. The handle section of (c) is of the baluster type terminated with a knob finial incised with torqued oblique lines. The disc is rounded and slightly beveled on the upper edge.

Surgeons used tongue depressors to control the tongue when lancing an abcess, sectioning the frenulum, or excising tonsils. They could also be utilized as cauteries to arrest hemorrhages, remove tumors, and sterilize wounds and lesions. Some examples with the disc burnished to a high polish suggest they may have functioned as small mirrors.

A similar instrument is illustrated in Milne, p. 79, pl. XX, no. 6 (after Védrènes).

Unpublished

126
Pilgrim token

Syria (Antioch), 6th century

Earthenware

D. 3.10, max. thickness 1.10

Toronto

Royal Ontario Museum, 986.181.78

This brown terra-cotta pilgrim token of St. Symeon Stylites the Younger was supposedly made from earth around the base of his column on the "Miraculous Mountain," southwest of Antioch. The token was originally circular, but there is now a crack in the upper left side and chips are missing around the edge. The surface is worn. The imprinted image shows the bust of St. Symeon on his column, wearing the hooded cloak of a monk and a large encolpion on his chest. A cross appears above his head. On either side of the saint are flying angels holding out crowns of victory. A ladder leans against the column on its right side; below the saint, to the left, a monk holding a censer venerates the stylite. Two small crosses flank the supplicant.

For a discussion of portraits of Saints Symeon the Younger and Symeon the Elder, see p. 24.

Unpublished

127
Pilgrim token

Syria (Antioch), 6th century

Earthenware

D. 3.17, max. thickness 0.80

Toronto

Royal Ontario Museum, 986.181.84

An irregularly shaped token of light brown terra-cotta, this piece bears a worn imprint depicting St. Symeon the Younger on his column. Like the previous example, it was manufactured out of earth taken from near the base of the pillar. The stylite wears a monastic cloak with a hood. A nimbed angel hovers on each side of the saint, while below two supplicants with raised arms stand on each side of the column. A ladder leans against the left side of the pillar, and to its right there is a Syriac inscription.

The back of the token bears the imprint of a human palm.

On images of St. Symeon, see p. 24. On the significance of the palm print, see p. 200.

Unpublished

128
Pilgrim token

Syria (Antioch?), 6th century

Earthenware

D. 3.52, max. thickness 1.42

Toronto

Royal Ontario Museum, 986.181.81

This circular token of black terra-cotta has several chips missing, especially at the top right edge, and the surface is worn. The imprint shows the Virgin Mary, nimbed and seated on a cushioned, lyre-backed throne. She holds the infant Christ on her lap. The Child is nimbed and seated in a frontal pose, holding a scroll in his left hand and blessing with his right. The throne is flanked by two nimbed angels above, and two kneeling supplicants below.

For the image of Mary, see p. 24.

Unpublished

129
Pilgrim token

Eastern Mediterranean, 6th century

Earthenware

D. 3.44, max. thickness 1.55

Toronto

Royal Ontario Museum, 986.181.80

The imprint of this circular terra-cotta token shows the Entry into Jerusalem. In the center of the image is Christ, sitting sidesaddle on a long-eared donkey and holding a cross-headed staff. An angel, striding to the left but with his body turned to face the viewer, leads the donkey by a rein held in his left hand. Behind the donkey, on the right, is a group of palm branches. The pattern below the ground line is too indistinct to be read. The token is abraded around its edges. It has some hairline cracks and slight surface wear.

For a discussion of the significance of the Entry into Jerusalem, see p. 29.

Unpublished

130
Ampulla with evangelist

Asia Minor, 6th century

Earthenware

H. 6.9, W. 4.8, T. 1.9

University of Illinois

World Heritage Museum, 22.1.207

This ampulla belongs to a small group of clay pilgrim flasks found in the region around Ephesus in western Asia Minor. Characteristic of the ampullas from this area, it is small, oval in form, and devoid of handles. The string holes piercing the shoulders allowed the flask to be suspended from the neck or belt of the pilgrim.

The flask is in fair condition. The images are worn, and a large chip in the neck and shoulder has partially destroyed the image on one side. There are two different images shown on this flask. On one side, a male figure is shown in three-quarter view seated in a chair with a high back and with crossed legs under an aedicula abbreviated as a spiral column. In his right hand he is holding a stylus, and in his left a codex or diptych. On the other side, a male figure, standing frontally and flanked by two stylized trees, holds a book decorated with the cross of St. Andrew against his chest. He has a cap of short hair, a long pointed beard, and wears a long-sleeved tunic.

These images are compared to the standing and seated evangelist portraits in the sixth-century Rabbula Gospels. The seated portrait was a type especially associated with the evangelists in the Byzantine tradition. From the Early Christian period until the fall of Byzantium, Ephesus was the cult center of St. John the Evangelist. According to popular legend, St. John lay sleeping in his tomb until the Second Coming. Once a year on his feast day, he affirmed his living presence by blowing dust up to the surface of his tomb. A portion of this "manna" was carried away by the pilgrims who visited his shrine, for it was attributed with the power to heal and protect. Given the popularity of St. John in western Asia Minor, it is likely that this ampulla originated from St. John's shrine in Ephesus and contained his miraculous dust.

Similar examples of this type may be seen in Campbell, 1988, p. 541, fig. 3; Ćurčić and St. Clair, pp. 120, no. 148; Metzger, pp. 45-46, figs. 95-97; Zalesskaja, 1976, p. 153, no. 1003; Hanfmann, pp. 16-17; Dalton, 1901, p. 159, no. 912; and in the Yale University Art Gallery, New Haven, inv. no. 1913.592.

Unpublished

131
Ampulla with St. Menas

Egypt, 6th-7th century

Earthenware

H. 9.5, W. 7, T. 2

University of Chicago

Divinity School

A pilgrim flask from the Shrine of St. Menas at Abou Mena near Alexandria, Egypt, this ampulla was formed of a pale brownish clay in a two-part mold. It has a round, flattened body to which was joined a neck and two vertical handles. Like catalogue number 130, it would have been filled with a miraculous substance, possibly oil from the lamps burning in the tomb of the saint, or water from the sacred spring nearby.

The flask is decorated with relief images of St. Menas, the same on both sides. Inscribed by a wide circular band filled with raised dots, the saint is shown standing frontally with his arms extended in the orans pose. As a martyred soldier, he is shown in the traditional Roman military costume: a short, belted tunic, a long chlamys hanging from the shoulders down the back, and high boots. Although the images are worn, it appears that the saint has no nimbus, but flanking his head are two small Greek crosses. Below his arms are two kneeling camels.

The numerous examples of Menas flasks found in Egypt and throughout the Mediterranean attest to the popularity of the saint's sanctuary during the Early Christian period (Kaufmann, pp. 59-78). Examples of this iconographic type have been dated by Kiss on the basis of stratigraphic evidence to the seventh century, during the reign of Heraclius (Kiss, p. 144).

For comparable Menas flasks, see Ćurčić and St. Clair, p. 119, no. 145; Metzger, pp. 70-73, figs. 15-22, p. 74, fig. 24; Weitzmann, 1979, p. 576, no. 515; Strzygowski, pp. 224-25, pl. XXI, nos. 8969, 8970, 8973, p. 302, no. 9169 (bronze).

Unpublished

210

132
Amulet

Eastern Mediterranean

Stone

H. 1.1, L. 2.6, W. 1.5

Private collection

This amulet, a four-sided prism carved of green steatite, is bored longitudinally so that it can be worn on a string. Each of the four long faces has an incised motif. Side (a) depicts a snake with a scrolled tail and short rays projecting from its body. The rays at the back of the head are longer, forming a crest. Side (b) has the inscription AΓIE ("O Holy One!"). Side (c) shows another similar snake, also with short rays. Side (d) carries the inscription IAΩ ("Jehovah").

The amulet is of interest in that it corresponds to Galen's description of the wearing of green jasper stones engraved with radiate serpents as charms to benefit the stomach (see pp. 7-8).

For similar examples, see Goodenough, p. 281, figs. 1179 and 1181 (both with IAΩ); Bonner, p. 314, no. 359 (Walters Art Gallery, inv. no. 42.731, with an engraved snake and IAΩ), and pp. 172-73, 314, no. 360 (Seyrig collection no. 26, with ZEY AΓIE).

For discussion of the inscription IAΩ, see also p. 18.

Unpublished

133
Amulet

Eastern Mediterranean, 7th-8th century

Lead

H. (with ring) 6.99, D. 5.90

Toronto

Royal Ontario Museum, 986.181.74

This circular amulet, cast from lead, has a ring for suspension added at the top. The edge of the disc is now uneven, its surfaces are worn, and there are several perforations. The shallow relief on the obverse shows a "holy rider" galloping to the right and spearing a demon with a human head and a snake-like body. A small cross appears above the rider's head. Between the demon and the hooves of the horse is the stretched-out body of a snake. A winged angel stands to the right of the horseman, beneath another small cross. The circular border around the medallion contains an inscription, which is too worn to be read.

The reverse of the medallion depicts a Chnoubis or Gorgon with a circular head from which radiate seven curled snake-like tentacles. This design is superimposed upon a cross shape which divides the field of the medallion into four quadrants. Each arm of the cross is delineated by three vertical lines, with a series of transverse bars running across them. Indistinct letters appear in the field, between the arms of the cross and the tentacles of the Chnoubis. The circular border contained an inscription, now also indistinct.

For the motif of the rider, and for the possible identity of his foe, see pp. 25-28. The forms and significance of the Chnoubis are discussed on pp. 7-8.

Unpublished

214

134
Amulet

Syria or Palestine, 5th-6th century

Bronze

D. 5.4

University of Michigan

Kelsey Museum of Archaeology, 26119

This large, well-preserved round amulet was cast in bronze and engraved. It has a drilled suspension hole that was provided for during manufacture, since the last syllable of the inscription in the rim of the obverse side was omitted to allow space for the perforation. The image on the obverse shows a nimbed rider on a galloping horse spearing a prostrate demon in the form of a lioness with a woman's head. The top of the spear is a cross with a penant waving to the left. To the right of the horse is a nimbed angel, standing on a ladder, holding a staff and gesturing toward the vanquished demon. Above the angel's head is an eight-rayed star. An inscription in the field to the left of the horse reads EIC θC O NIKON TA KAKA ("One God who conquers evils"). In the border of the medallion is the first verse of Psalm 91 and the first three words of the second verse: O KATOIKON EN BOHθIA TOY YΨISTOY EN SKEΠH TOY θY TOY OURANOY AYLICθ– ICETAI EPI TO KΩ ("He who dwells in the shelter of the Most High, will abide in the care of the God of heaven. He will say to the Lord . . ."). This psalm above all others is the one chosen to invoke divine protection.

The designs on the reverse of the medallion can be divided into three horizontal bands. The upper band is Christian, the lower two are purely magical. At the top, immediately beneath the suspension hole, appears the enthroned Christ, cross-nimbed and holding a book in his left hand, while he raises his right. He sits enclosed by an almond-shaped mandorla. Flanking the mandorla are the Four Beasts of the Apocalypse, the winged man and the ox on the left, the eagle and the lion on the right. Below them is an inscription in one line running acrss the medallion: AΓIOC AΓIOC AΓIOC KC SABAΩθ ("Holy, holy, holy, Lord God of Sabaoth"). The central band of the medallion is taken up with six large magical signs with ring-shaped terminals. The lower third contains an assortment of magical symbols: several small letters or characters, a roaring lion running to the right, a snake beneath the lion, and a scorpion (or possibly a crab) in front of it. In the margin runs the following inscription: CΦPAΓIC θY ZONTOC ΦYΛAΞON AΠO ΠANTOC KAKOY TON

ΦOPOYNTA TO ΦYΛAKTHPION TOY ("Seal of the living God, guard from all evil the one who wears this charm").

The intended function of this amulet, to protect from all evils, is clearly indicated by its inscriptions. The significance of the word CΦPAΓIC, or "seal," in Early Christian thought and practice has been discussed by Danielou, pp. 54-69, and Hahn, 1989. The imagery is notable for its frank admixture of Christian and magical motifs, for the composition of Christ with the Four Beasts is also known from the apses of churches (see p. 32). A similar amulet in the Dumbarton Oaks collection is published by Ross, 1962, pp. 53-54, no. 60.

For the motif of the "holy rider," see pp. 25-28.

Bibliography: Bonner, pp. 219-20, no. 324; Godwin, pp. 68-69, no. 33; Nees, p. 210, fig. 69.

135
Amulet

Syria or Palestine, 4th-7th century

Bronze

H. 4.5, W. 3.00

University of Chicago

Divinity School

An integral suspension loop protrudes from the top of this thin, pear-shaped bronze amulet. The suspension loop is set at right angles to the plaque, to prevent its twisting at the end of the string. The plaque is considerably worn, especially on the obverse, and a portion is missing at the lower left.

The design engraved on the obverse face showed a rider spearing a now invisible foe. Comparisons with similar amulets indicate that the enemy would have been a recumbent human figure or a lion. Above is the inscription NIKΩN" ("Victorious"). The design on the reverse is better preserved. It shows, at the bottom center, the evil eye being attacked by a trident above and by a dagger or spear on either side. Below are the indistinct forms of several noxious animals which attack the eye; on other comparable amulets these include a rearing lion, a pecking ibis, a snake, a scorpion, a dog, or a leopard. Above is the inscription IAΩ CA / BAΩθ MIX / AHΛ BOHθ I ("Jehovah, Sabaoth, Michael, help!").

Amulets of this type are relatively common. Similar examples are discussed by Bonner, pp. 211-12, and catalogued by him, pp. 302-3 (nos. 298-303). Other members of this group can be found in Goodenough, p. 227, no. 1049 (Palestine Archaeological Museum, inv. no. 38.1091), and in Ćurčić and St. Clair, p. 81, no. 64.

For a discussion of the significance of the evil eye, see pp. 4-5. For the motif of the rider, see pp. 25-28.

Unpublished

136
Amulet

Syria or Palestine, 4th-7th century

Bronze

H. 4.5, W. 1.5

University of Chicago

Divinity School

This bronze amulet is cast in the form of an eye (compare the shape of the eye engraved on the reverse of the preceding amulet, no. 135). It is provided with an integral suspension ring at the top, which is set at right angles to the faces of the plaque. The design cut into the obverse shows a schematic image of a rider holding a cross-headed spear, with which he pierces a prostrate foe indicated only by a few indistinct strokes. The reverse bears the inscription O KATYK, for O KATOIKΩN, the first words of Psalm 91 ("He who dwells in the shelter of the Most High"), a common apotropaic formula (see no. 134).

For a similar example, see Bonner, p. 306, no. 319, with discussion on pp. 218-19.

On the significance of the "holy rider," see pp. 25-28.

Unpublished

137

Mirror plaque

Syria or Palestine, 5th century

Earthenware

H. 15.01, W. 10.00

University of Chicago

Divinity School

This terra-cotta mirror plaque is in the shape of a gabled shrine. Apart from the loss of its two mirrors, it is in good condition. The principal mirror was set into a depression framed by a narrow circular molding. The circle is enclosed by a rectangular frame marked with diagonal ridges. In the corners between the circle and the rectangle there are small raised circles enclosing dots. Two more circled dots are set at the junctions of the uprights of the rectangular frame with its base. Above the rectangle is a shallow semicircular niche with a decoration of rays created by raised lines radiating from a semicircle at the base. Some of the rays still contain traces of paint: one ray is painted blue, two are red, four others contain blue dots. Above the niche is a triangular gable which originally enclosed another, smaller, circular mirror. This mirror, also, was framed by a narrow molding, and was flanked on each side by a pair of concentric rings enclosing a dot. Inside each of the two circular frames is a ring of holes that once retained the prongs attached to the back of the mirror.

Similar mirror plaques have been found in Syria, Palestine, and Egypt (New York, pp. 238-40; Rahmani, pp. 54-59, pl. 16; Michon, pp. 161-65, figs. 1-4). For their function, and for the significance of the circled dot motif, see pp. 5-7.

Unpublished

218

138
Censer

Eastern Mediterranean, 5th-6th century

Bronze

H. 15.20, Chain and ring L. 6.90

Toronto

Royal Ontario Museum, 986.181.110

This remarkable bronze censer, in the form of a female head, is intact. It is composed of two parts. The lower portion is cast in the shape of the woman's head and neck; the neck flares out to make the base of the object. The woman wears a necklace, the jewels of which are indicated by incised circled dots. The upper part of the censer is a high domed lid, attached by a hinge at the back and secured by a hook at the front. The lid is perforated at the front and the back to allow the smoke of the incense to escape and is decorated at intervals by encircled dots. At the top of the lid there is an equal-armed cross, to which a suspension chain is attached.

On the significance of the shape, see p. 14. For the use of censers in domestic contexts, see p. 202.

Unpublished

Fig. 51. Cleveland Museum of Art, Fragment of a Hanging.
Dancer with a Flute.

220

No survey of the domestic life of the Early Christian period would be complete without a look at the entertainments the people enjoyed. Some of these were public spectacles on a grand scale—the chariot races in the circus and the extravagant productions in the theaters. Other performances took place in people's houses, including music and dancing, whose popularity among Christians is confirmed by the vehemence of the church fathers' diatribes against them. We can be sure that whatever the preachers condemned with the most regularity had the greatest appeal for their flocks. At the end of the second century, for example, Clement of Alexandria commanded Christians: "Leave the pipe to the shepherd, the flute to the men who are in fear of [pagan] gods and are intent on their idol-worshipping. Such musical instruments must be excluded from our wineless feasts, for they are more suited for beasts . . . than for men. . . . Truly, the devious spells of syncopated tunes . . . corrupt morals by their sensual and affected style, and insidiously inflame the passions (*Paedagogus*, II, 41; trans. Wood, p. 130). In the fourth century, the Syrian writer Ephrem declared that the steps of the road to hell included: "lute playing, theatrical spectacles, piping, dances, the baths, soft clothing, sumptuous eating, . . . prolonged sleep, and soft beds" (Toal, p. 307). Much of the ecclesiastical opposition to secular music was on account of its association with the theater, to which the church authorities were particularly opposed. Speaking of stage performances in Antioch during the late fourth century, St. John Chrysostom wrote: "There [you will find] obscene language, and even more obscene postures, and the same kind of hairstyles, gaits, clothes, and voices, as well as softness of limbs, sidelong glances, pipes and flutes, plays and pantomimes, and, in short, everything full of the utmost licentiousness" (*In Matthaeum Homilia XXXVII*, 6).

It is possible that the clergy attacked the secular entertainments of the theaters because they were in competition with their own services. John Chrysostom complained that theatrical performances were held at Constantinople even on Holy Saturday (Quasten, p. 453). He himself was moved to preach a sermon denouncing such spectacles when he found his church deserted because many of his congregation were at the circus (*Contra circenses ludos et theatra*).

In spite of the diatribes of the church fathers, performances of music and dancing continued to be an important feature of home entertainment during the Early Christian period. In wealthy households, banquets were accompanied by concerts, as can be seen in a painting of Pharoah's feast which is preserved in a sixth-century manuscript illustrating scenes from Genesis (Vienna, Nationalbibliothek, Cod. theol. gr. 31, p. 34; Gerstinger, p. 105). Here the guests are serenaded by two female musicians, one playing a double flute, the other an arrangement of water-filled bowls set upon a table (color plate VII). A mosaic depicting a musical performance in some detail has survived from the dining-room floor of a house at Mariamîn in Syria. In this portrayal, which probably dates to the late fourth century, the time of John Chrysostom, there are five female musicians in rich costumes standing on a wooden stage and playing a variety of instruments, including an organ, a cithara (a type of lyre), clappers, and a pair of flutes somewhat similar to those shown in our exhibition (nos. 139 and 140). A sixth woman dances in step to the music, holding castanets in her hands (Balty, 1977, pp. 94-98, figs. 42-44). Although this mosaic comes from a well-to-do house, we know from contracts preserved in Egyptian papyri of the Late Roman period that such bands were employed during festivals to perform in more humble village houses. The contracts usually specify that during the period of their employment the musicians will receive room and board, a per diem allowance, and travel expenses to and from the village. In addition, the employers provided for insurance against the loss of the musicians' instruments, costumes, and stage jewelry. For example, a letter written in the third century by Artemisia, the mistress of a house in Philadelphia, reads: "To Isidora, castanet dancer, from Artemisia of the village of Philadelphia. I wish to engage you with two other castanet dancers to perform at the festival at my house for six days. . . . You will receive as pay 36 drachmas for each day, and for the entire period 4 artabas of barley and 20 pairs of bread loaves. And whatsoever garments or gold ornaments you may bring down, we will guard these safely; and we will furnish you with two donkeys when you come down to us and a like number when you go back to the city" (Westermann and Kraemer, pp. 56-58). Other contracts engaged musicians, usually flautists, to accompany the dancers (e.g., Ingrams, pp. 115-16).

The mosaic from Mariamîn and the Egyptian papyri help to bring to life the musical instruments such as flutes (nos. 139 and 140), lutes, and clappers that have been preserved by archaeology (Badawy, pp. 354-57, fig. 6.1). Another vivid illustration of music and dance in Early Christian Egypt is the splendid weaving shown in figure 51, a fragment of a large hanging executed in looped-knot technique, with a woolen pile on a linen ground. This textile, which is now in the Cleveland Museum of Art, was discovered in Egypt (Shepherd, pp. 336-38); it shows a female dancer, dressed in a costume ornamented with strips and panels (*clavi* and *segmenta*) at the shoulders, and with a diaphanous skirt through which her legs are visible in a dancing pose. As she dances, she holds her flute to her mouth, and with her eyes casts a sidelong glance, perhaps of the flirtatious type condemned by Chrysostom, or perhaps merely to keep in time with other members of the troupe who may have been represented in the missing portion of the hanging.

Besides music and dancing, other favored pastimes drawing the disapproval of preachers were gaming and gambling. Again, the frequency of the church fathers' complaints leads us to suspect that these activities were widespread among their congregations. Clement of Alexandria warned his flock that "playing with dice is to be stopped; so is the love of gain associated with the game of knucklebones, which many like to pursue. For such things bring an inordinate delight to these idlers. Laziness is the cause of it. Those who are severed from the truth love inanities. For they cannot obtain joy in any way other than by mischief" (*Paedagogus*, III, 11). Two centuries later, John Chrysostom cautioned the people of Antioch against playing with dice, not so much because the games were evil in themselves, but because they encouraged a host of other, greater sins: "A fondness for dice often causes blasphemy, losses, anger, abuse, and a thousand other evils graver than these. Let us shun not only outright sins, but also those practices which seem morally neutral, but which little by little lead us to these transgressions" (*Ad populum Antiochenum homilia XV*, 4).

In spite of John Chrysostom's authority, the good people of Antioch evidently did not heed his warnings. The continuation of gaming can be seen in the topographical border of a floor mosaic which was laid in a villa in the vicinity of Antioch sixty to seventy years after John spoke. The border, which illustrates a selection of daily activities from Antioch and its suburbs, includes no less than two dice games (fig. 52). In each game, the two players are shown sitting on folding chairs, facing each other across a table. One player holds a cup upside down over the table, throwing the dice onto the board. The other player indicates the score by extending the fingers of his raised hand (Levi, pp. 330-31, pl. 79b and c). Apart from confirming the continued popularity of dice games into the fifth century, the mosaic helps us to visualize how the dice and the bone cup shown in this exhibition (nos. 141 to 144) might have been used. More evidence for the popularity of board games comes from the discovery of the boards themselves, which sometimes have been preserved because they were incised into stone blocks such as stylobates, or even set in mosaic. One mosaic board, of the fourth or fifth century, was discovered at Antioch (Levi, pp. 291-95, fig. 123).

It is fitting to close this exhibition with some objects which more than any others bring home to the modern viewer the domestic life of the early Christians, namely the toys of their children. Then, as today, babies in their cribs were entertained by rattles, as is shown by the woman and child depicted in the upper right-hand portion of color plate VI, a miniature from the sixth-century manuscript of Genesis. (The square object held by the woman is probably a rattle, similar to the Egyptian sistrum, rather than a mirror; see Mazal, p. 152; Badawy, fig. 6.1.) Older children played with dolls (nos. 145 and 146), some of which were wrapped with cloth to represent swaddled infants. Other toys represented animals, such as the model goose, number 148, and the tiny dog, number 149. Children would play with live dogs too, as can be seen from figure 53, a vignette of a boy holding a puppy from a mosaic floor in the Great Palace of the Byzantine emperors at Constantinople (Brett, p. 76, pl. 33). Many of the toys were diminutive reproductions of household objects like those seen in this exhibition. We find miniature dishes, as well as doll-sized furniture such as the armchair, number 150. There were also small copies of the tools used by grownups at their work; number 151 is a miniature version of a full-sized weaver's comb similar to number 79. In such toys we can see the children preparing themselves for the roles that they were to play later in adult society.

Fig. 52. Antioch, Border of a Floor Mosaic. Two Dice Players.

Fig. 53. Constantinople, Great Palace, Floor Mosaic, Detail. Boy Playing with a Puppy.

139
Flute

Egypt (Karanis)

Wood

L. 17.4

University of Michigan

Kelsey Museum of Archaeology, 26997

This flute of dark wood is in good condition.
The cylindrical shaft is pierced by three holes on
the top, and one on the bottom. At one end, the
shaft is terminated with a knob-like element; at
the other, there is a broken fitting for the
mouthpiece, which is missing. The decoration
consists simply of two parallel incised lines near
the knob. A reed flute from Egypt of similar
form, but with a double shaft, is illustrated by
Petrie, 1927, p. 68, no. 311, pl. L.

Unpublished

140
Flute

Egypt (Karanis)

Bone

L. 17.9, D. 1.7

University of Michigan

Kelsey Museum of Archaeology, 8504

This hollow cylindrical fragment of a bone flute, tapered at one end, is pierced by three holes: two on the top, and one on the bottom. One of the holes on the top, nearest the broad end, is surrounded by a depression. The general condition of the flute is poor, the shaft being cracked, and pieces are missing from the top. Another example of a flute from Egypt may be found in Petrie, 1927, p. 58, no. 311, pl. L.

Unpublished

141
Cylindrical box

Egypt (Karanis)

Bone

H. 5.9, D. 3.5, Lid D. 2.8

University of Michigan

Kelsey Museum of Archaeology, 10030 a,b

This tapered cylindrical box has an unattached disk lid. The base is affixed with glue. The lid is raised by a small knob handle set in a depression. Incised lines, one at the base and near the rim, and two at the center, accent the smooth, polished surface. Except for chips on the rim, lid, and base, the box is in good condition. Carefully crafted bone boxes like this example were employed as throwing cups in games involving dice. Gambling was a favorite pastime at banquets and other social occasions in the Late Roman world. After invoking the name of the deity or a loved one for good luck, the dice would be shaken in the cup to guarantee fair play and thrown onto a gaming table (Paoli, pp. 234-35). In addition, these boxes have been found among toiletry items in domestic settings, and thus must also have served as cosmetic containers for powders and rouge.

Related examples may be seen in Gazda, 1983a, p. 30, fig. 53; and Paris, p. 272, no. 234. For turned wooden boxes, see Petrie 1927, p. 62, no. 562, pl. LIV; and Strzygowski, p. 158, no. 7226, pl. IX.

Unpublished

142
Dice

Egypt

Bone

H. 0.8, W. 0.8

University of Michigan

Kelsey Museum of Archaeology, 66.1.18-19

These bone dice were employed in games of chance. The values, one to six, are marked with dotted circles. For comparative examples, see Martin, pp. 42-43, fig. 59; Stryzgowski, pl. XX, 8944; Petrie, 1927, pl. XLIX.

Unpublished

143
Dice

Egypt

Bone

University of Illinois

World Heritage Museum, 14.5.161-4

Like catalogue number 142, these roughly
cubical dice, two large and two small, are
incised with dotted circles to mark the value of
each surface. See Martin, pp. 42-43, fig. 59;
Stryzgowski, pl. XX, 8944; and Petrie, 1927, pl.
XLIX for similar examples.

Unpublished

144
Dice

Egypt (Karanis)

Bone

University of Michigan

Kelsey Museum of Archaeology, 22765-66

These bone dice from Karanis are similar to
examples seen in catalogue numbers 142 and
143. For comparisons, see Martin, pp. 42-43, fig.
59; Stryzgowski, pl. XX, 8944; Petrie, 1927, XLIX.

Unpublished

145
Doll

Egypt

Bone and cloth

H. 12.5, W. 6.8

University of Michigan

Kelsey Museum of Archaeology, 66.1.113

This is a crude bone doll swaddled in a bundle of cloth. The doll has incised eyes and an incised left eyebrow, highlighted with black paint (bitumen). The ears are indicated by slight projections. A mass of tricolored yarn hair (blonde, red, and black) is insecurely attached to the doll's head. The body, a simple tapering rectangular extension of the head, was inserted through a hole in the cloth and tied at the back with green yarn.

Unpublished

146
Doll

Egypt, Roman

Cloth

H. 8.1, W. 2.2

University of Michigan

Kelsey Museum of Archaeology, 26413

A tiny rag doll, this toy represents a swaddled infant with a round, black face wrapped in alternating strips of yellow and black cloth. The swaddling is tied at the neck and lower body with black yarn. Other examples of dolls found in the homes of Karanis, and other towns in the Fayoum, may be seen in Petrie, 1927, pl. LV.

Bibliography: Gazda, 1983a, p. 29, fig. 52.

147
Doll

Egypt (Karanis)

Wood

H. 12.7, W. 4.7

University of Michigan

Kelsey Museum of Archaeology, 7501

This so-called "ankh-shaped" doll, in excellent condition, is one of many examples found at Karanis. It is a simple children's toy, carved from a flat piece of dark wood. Incised lines loosely articulate the hair, neck, and waist. Incised concentric circles mark the eyes, mouth, arms, and knees. A hole pierces the body at the navel. Above it, three holes are filled with wooden dowels.

Similar dolls may be seen in Petrie, 1927, p.62, nos. 600, 601, pl. LV.

Bibliography: Gazda, 1983a, p. 29, fig. 52.

148
Toy goose

Egypt

Clay

H. 4.8, W. 2.8, L. 4.5

University of Michigan

Kelsey Museum of Archaeology, 6598

This miniature goose, a child's toy, was modeled in reddish clay, and detailed with incised lines to create a naturalistic appearance. The feathers of the neck and body are marked with short lines, the wings with a herringbone pattern. A ring around the base of the neck is impressed with dots. Many examples of terra-cotta and mud-formed toy animals survive from the Roman period, especially in the Egyptian towns of the Fayoum. See Paris, p. 187, No. 124; Gazda, 1983a, p. 29, fig. 52; Petrie, 1927, pl. LIII.

Unpublished

229

149
Toy dog

Egypt

Clay

H. 4.5, L. 3.9, W. 1.8

University of Michigan

Kelsey Museum of Archaeology, 6597

A toy dog shown sitting in the grass, this piece represents one of many species of domestic and wild animals reproduced in miniature for children's amusement. The dog, made of a yellowish-buff clay in a two-part mold, has long hair, a short tail, and a ribbon around its neck. Other examples of naturalistically modeled toy dogs in varying poses may be seen in Paris, p. 187, nos. 124 d and e; Gazda, 1983a, p. 29, fig. 52.

Unpublished

150
Toy chair

Egypt (Karanis), Roman

Wood

H. 9.5, L. 4.5, W. 4.9

University of Michigan

Kelsey Museum of Archaeology, 26412

This toy chair, a cathedra, was carved from a light brown wood, worn and cracked by weathering. The deep seat is enveloped by a high rounded back, and armrests. Three rounded legs at the base raise the chair slightly off the floor. The panel in front of the seat is decorated with an incised saltire cross. In the domestic setting, the cathedra was considered a woman's chair, although it was also probably used by men (Paoli, p. 80).

Bibliography: Gazda, 1983a, p. 29, fig. 52.

151

Toy weaver's comb

Egypt (Karanis)

Wood

H. 1.1, L. 7.1, W. 5.3

University of Michigan

Kelsey Museum of Archaeology, 7571

The tools employed by adults in their crafts and trades often found their counterparts in children's toys. This toy weaver's comb, carved from a single piece of wood, is a miniature reproduction of larger prototypes used to compress the weft threads of the fabric being woven. It is in good condition, although in ancient times it had been broken and repaired with a string tightened by a fragment of bone. The back of the comb is plain, and tapers at the handle and comb ends. The front is flat and decorated with six concentric dotted circles, four on the plate and two on the handle, a decoration similar to that found on the adult's weaving comb, number 79. The circle nearest the end of the handle was pierced to allow the comb to be suspended.

Bibliography: Gazda, 1983a, p. 29, fig. 52.

Bibliography

Amandry, P. 1963. *Collection Hélène Stathatos*. Vol. III. *Objets antiques et Byzantines*. Strasbourg.

Ann Arbor. 1980. *The Art of the Ancient Weaver* (exh. cat.). Kelsey Museum of Archaeology, University of Michigan.

Ashbrook Harvey, S. 1984. "Physicians and Ascetics in John of Ephesus: An Expedient Alliance." *Dumbarton Oaks Papers* 38: 87-93.

Athens. 1964. *Byzantine Art. An European Art: Ninth Exhibition Held under the Auspices of the Council of Europe*.

Auth, S. 1976. *Ancient Glass at the Newark Museum*. Newark, N.J.

Badawy, A. 1978. *Coptic Art and Archaeology: The Art of the Christian Egyptians from the Late Antique to the Middle Ages*. Cambridge, Mass.

Baginski A., and Tidhar, A. 1980. *Textiles from Egypt, 4th-13th Centuries C.E.* L. A. Mayer Memorial Institute for Islamic Art, Jerusalem.

Bailey, D. M. 1975. *A Catalogue of the Lamps in the British Museum II*. London.

Baltimore. 1947. *Early Christian and Byzantine Art* (exh. cat.). The Walters Art Gallery.

Balty, J. 1977. *Mosaïques antiques de Syrie*. Brussels.

———. 1984. *Apamée de Syrie: Bilan des recherches archéologiques 1973-1979. Actes du 3e Colloque tenu à Bruxelles du 29 au 30 mai 1980: aspects de l'architecture domestique d'Apamée*. Brussels.

Bank, A. 1966. *Byzantine Art in the Collections of the USSR*. Leningrad and Moscow.

———. 1978. *Byzantine Art in the Collections of Soviet Museums*. New York.

Baramki, D. C. 1933. "An Early Christian Basilica at 'Ein Hanniya." *Quarterly of the Department of Antiquities in Palestine* 3: 113-17.

———. 1940-42. "The Pottery from Khirbat el-Mefjer." *Quarterly of the Department of Antiquities in Palestine* 10: 65-103.

Baramki, D. C., and Avi-Yonah. 1933. "An Early Christian Church at Khirbat Asida." *Quarterly of the Department of Antiquities in Palestine* 3: 17-19.

Barns, J. W. B., and Zilliacus, H., eds. 1960. *The Antinoopolis Papyri*. Vol. II. London.

Barrière-Flavy, C. 1901. *Les arts industriels des peuplades barbares de la Gaule du Ve - VIIIe siècles*. 3 vols. Toulouse.

Beckwith, J. 1972-74. "An Early Christian Bronze Lamp." *Archivo Español de Arqueologia* 45-47: 463-65.

Berger, L. 1960. *Römische Gläser aus Vindonissa*. Basel.

Bliquez, L. J. 1984. "Two Lists of Greek Surgical Instruments and the State of Surgery in Byzantine Times." *Dumbarton Oaks Papers* 38: 187-94.

Bonner, C. 1950. *Studies in Magical Amulets, Chiefly Graeco-Egyptian*. Ann Arbor.

Bouras, L. 1982. "Byzantine Lighting devices." *Jahrbuch der Österreichischen Byzantinistik* 32 (3) (= *XVI. Internationaler Byzantinistenkongress, Akten*, vol. II, 3): 479-91.

Bourguet, P. du. 1964. *Catalogue des étoffes coptes: Musée National du Louvre*. Paris.

Brandenburg, H. 1983. "Greif." In *Reallexikon für Antike und Christentum*, ed. T. Klauser. Vol. XII, pp. 951-95. Stuttgart.

Breccia, E. 1938. "Le prime ricerche italiane ad Antinoe." *Aegyptus* 18: 285-310.

Brett, G., Macaulay, W. J., and Stevenson, R. B. K. 1947. *The Great Palace of the Byzantine Emperors: First Report*. Oxford.

Broneer, O. 1930. *Terracotta Lamps: Corinth. Results of Excavations Conducted by the American School of Classical Studies at Athens*. Vol. IV, part 2. Cambridge, Mass.

Brooklyn. 1941. *Pagan and Christian Egypt: Egyptian Art from the First to the Tenth Century A.D.* (exh. cat.). The Brooklyn Museum.

Browne, G. M., et al., eds. 1972. *The Oxyrhynchus Papyri*. Vol. XLI. London.

Budge, E. W. 1904. *The Book of Paradise*. Vol. I. London.

Cabrol, F. 1907. *Dictionnaire d'archéologie chrétienne et de liturgie*. Vol. I, 2. Paris.

Cabrol, F., and Leclercq, H. 1925. *Dictionnaire d'archéologie chrétienne et de liturgie*. Vol. VI, 2. Paris.

Cahn, H. A., and Kaufmann-Heinimann, A., eds. 1984. *Der spätrömische Silberschatz von Kaiseraugst*. 2 vols. Derendingen.

Cameron, A., ed. and trans. 1976. Flavius Cresconius Corippus, *In laudem Iustini Augusti minoris*. London.

Campbell, S. D., ed. 1985. *The Malcove Collection: A Catalogue of the Objects in the Lillian Malcove Collection of the University of Toronto*. Toronto.

———. 1988. "Armchair Pilgrims: Ampullae from Aphrodisias in Caria." *Mediaeval Studies* 50: 539-45.

Chavane, M. J. 1975. *Salamine de Chypre VI, les petits objets*. Paris.

Cledat, J. 1904-6. *Le Monastère et la Nécropole de Baouît*. Mémoires de l'Institut Français d'Archéologie Orientale, 12. Paris.

Cleveland. 1978. *Handbook of the Cleveland Museum of Art*. Cleveland.

Coche de la Ferté, E. 1957. *Collection Hélène Stathatos*. Vol. II. *Les Objets byzantins et post-byzantins*. Limoges.

———. 1958. *L'Antiquité chrétienne au Musée du Louvre*. Paris.

Cochrane, C. N. 1940. *Christianity and Classical Culture*. Oxford.

Coles, R. A., et al., eds. 1970. *The Oxyrhynchus Papyri*. Vol. XXXVI. London.

Colt, H. D. 1962. *Excavations at Nessana*. Vol. I. London.

Crowfoot, G. M., and Harden, D. B. 1931. "Early Byzantine and Later Glass Lamps." *Journal of Egyptian Archaeology* 17: 196-208.

Crum, W. E., and Evelyn White, H. G. 1926. *The Monastery of Ephiphanius at Thebes*. 2 vols. New York.

234

Ćurčić, S., and St. Clair, A. 1986. *Byzantium at Princeton: Byzantine Art and Archaeology at Princeton University*. Princeton.

Dalton, O. M. 1901. *Catalogue of Early Christian Antiquities and Objects from the Christian East in the Department of British and Medieval Antiquities and Ethnography of the British Museum*. London.

———. 1912. *Catalogue of the Finger Rings in the British Museum*. London.

Daltrop, G. 1969. *Die Jagdmosaiken der römischen Villa bei Piazza Armerina*. Hamburg and Berlin.

Danielou, J. 1956. *The Bible and the Liturgy*. Notre Dame.

Day, F. 1942. "Early Islamic and Christian Lamps." *Berytus* 7: 65-79.

Deichmann, F. W. 1958. *Frühchristliche Bauten und Mosaiken von Ravenna*. Baden-Baden.

Delivorrias, A., ed. 1987. *Greece and the Sea* (exh. cat.). De Nieuwe Kerk, Amsterdam.

Dimand, M. S. 1930. "Coptic Tunics in the Metropolitan Museum of Art." *Metropolitan Museum Studies* 2: 239-52.

Dimitrov, D. P. 1962. "Le système décoratif et la date des peintures murales du tombeau antique de Silistra." *Cahiers archéologiques* 12: 35-52.

Dinkler, E. 1978. "Der Salomonische Knoten in der Nubischen Kunst und die Geschichte des Motivs." *Études Nubiennes* 77: 73-86.

Dodd, E. C. 1961. *Byzantine Silver Stamps*. Washington, D.C.

———. 1973. *Byzantine Silver Treasures*. Bern.

Dölger, F. J. 1928. *IXθYC*. Vol. I. Münster.

Drake, H. A. 1976. *In Praise of Constantine: A Historical Study and New Translation of Eusebius' Tricennial Orations*. Berkeley.

Drewer, L. 1981. "Fisherman and Fish Pond: From the Sea of Sin to the Living Waters." *Art Bulletin* 63: 533-47.

Driston, E., ed. 1944. *Exposition d'Art Copte*. Cairo.

Duffy, J. 1984. "Byzantine Medicine in the Sixth and Seventh Centuries: Aspects of Teaching and Practice." *Dumbarton Oaks Papers* 38: 21-27.

Dunbabin, K. M. D. 1978. *The Mosaics of Roman North Africa*. Oxford.

Duncan-Flowers, M. 1989. "A Pilgrim's Ampulla from the Shrine of St. John the Evangelist." In *The Blessings of Pilgrimage*, ed. R. Ousterhout. Urbana, Ill.

Duval, N. 1985. Review of J. Balty, ed., *Apamée de Syrie: Bilan des recherches archéologiques 1973-1979. Actes du 3e Colloque tenu à Bruxelles du 29 au 30 mai 1980: aspects de l'architecture domestique d'Apamée* (Brussels, 1984). *Bulletin Monumental* 143: 290-94.

Ede, C. 1988. *Writing and Lettering in Antiquity*, XII . London.

Elbern, V. H. 1986. "Per speculum in aenigmate. Die 'imago creationis' an einem frühchristlichen phylakterion." In *Studien zur spätantiken und byzantinischen Kunst Friedrich Wilhelm Deichmann gewidmet*, ed. O. Feld and U. Peschlow. Vol. 3, pp. 67-73.

Ellis, S. P. 1988. "The End of the Roman House." *American Journal of Archaeology* 92: 565-76.

235

Engemann, J. 1972. "Anmerkungen zu spätantiken Geräten des Alltagslebens mit christlichen Bildern, Symbolen und Inschriften." *Jahrbuch für Antike und Christentum* 15: 154-73.

———. 1975. "Zur Verbreitung magischer Übelabwehr in der nichtchristlichen und christilichen Spätantike." *Jahrbuch für Antike und Christentum* 18: 22-48.

Ennabli, A. 1976. *Lampes chrétiennes de Tunisie: Musées du Bardo et de Carthage.* Paris.

Errera, I. 1916. *Collection d'anciennes étoffes égyptiennes.* Brussels.

Ferrua, A. 1970. "Una nuova regione della catacomba dei SS. Marcellino e Pietro." Rivista di Archeologia Cristiana 46: 7-83.

Fitzgerald, G. M. 1931. *Beth-shan III: Beth-shan Excavations. 1921-23, the Arab and Byzantine Levels, III.* Philadelphia.

Forbes, R. J. 1966. *Studies in Ancient Technology.* Vols. V and VI. Leiden.

Forsyth, G. H., and Weitzmann, K. 1973. *The Monastery of Saint Catherine at Sinai: The Church and Fortress of Justinian.* Ann Arbor.

Friedlander, P. 1945. *Documents of Dying Paganism.* Berkeley.

Frolow, A. 1961. *La Relique de la Vraie Croix.* Paris.

Fulford, M. G., and Peacock, D. P. S. 1984. *Excavations at Carthage: The British Mission.* Vol. I, 2. Sheffield.

Galavaris, G. 1970. *Bread and Liturgy: The Symbolism of Early Christian and Byzantine Bread Stamps.* Madison, Wis., and London.

Gazda, E. K., ed. 1983a. *Karanis: An Egyptian Town in Roman Times* (exh. cat.). Ann Arbor.

———. 1983b. *In Pursuit of Antiquity* (exh. cat.). Ann Arbor.

Gerstinger, H. 1931. *Die Wiener Genesis.* 2 vols. Vienna.

Gervers, V. 1977. "An Early Christian Curtain in the Royal Ontario Museum." In *Studies in Textile History in Memory of Harold B. Burnham,* ed. V. Gervers, pp. 56-81. Toronto.

Godwin, J. 1981. *Mystery Religions in the Ancient World.* San Francisco.

Gombrich, E. H. 1979. *The Sense of Order: A Study in the Psychology of Decorative Art.* Ithaca.

Gonosová, A., and Kondoleon, C. 1985. "Art of Late Rome and Byzantium." *Apollo* 122: 34-39.

Goodenough, E. R. 1953. *Jewish Symbols in the Greco-Roman Period.* Vol. II. New York.

Grabar, A. 1958. *Ampoules de Terre Sainte (Monza-Bobbio).* Paris.

———. 1967. *The Golden Age of Justinian: From the Death of Theodosius to the Rise of Islam.* New York.

Grant, R. M. 1977. *Early Christianity and Society: Seven Studies.* San Francisco.

Graziani Abbiani, M. 1969. *Lucerne fittili paleocristiane nell'Italia settentrionale.* Bologna.

Grenfell, B. P., and Hunt, A. S. 1915. *The Oxyrhynchus Papyri.* Vol. XI. London.

Grenfell, B. P., Hunt, A. S., and Bell, H. I. 1924. *The Oxyrhynchus Papyri.* Vol. XVI. London.

Griffing, R. P. 1938. "An Early Christian Ivory Plaque in Cyprus and Notes on the Asiatic Ampullae." *Art Bulletin* 20: 266-79.

Haeckel, A. 1977. *The Gods of Egypt.* Ann Arbor.

Hamilton, R. W. 1959. *Khirbat al Mafjar.* Oxford.

Hanfmann, G. M. A. 1966. "The Eighth Campaign at Sardis: 1965." *Bulletin of the American Schools of Oriental Research* 182 (April): 2-54.

Harcum, C. G. 1921. "Roman Cooking Utensils in the Royal Ontario Museum of Archaeology." *American Journal of Archaeology* 25: 37-54.

Harden, D. B. 1936. *Roman Glass from Karanis.* University of Michigan Studies, Humanistic Series, 41. Ann Arbor.

Hardy, E. R. 1952. *Christian Egypt: Church and People.* New York.

Hartmann, M. 1985. "Spätrömisches aus Kaiseraugst-Schmidmatt." *Archäologie der Schwiez* 8 (part 1): 39-43.

Hayes, J. W. 1972. *Late Roman Pottery.* London.

———. 1975. *Roman and Pre-Roman Glass in the Royal Ontario Museum.* Toronto.

———. 1980. *Ancient Lamps in the Royal Ontario Museum I: Greek and Roman Clay Lamps.* Toronto.

———. 1984. *Greek, Roman, and Related Metalware in the Royal Ontario Museum: A Catalogue.* Toronto.

Heurgon, J. 1985. *Le trésor de Ténès.* Paris.

Hölscher, U. 1954. *The Excavations of Medinet Habu V: Post-Ramessid Remains.* The University of Chicago Oriental Institute Publications, 66. Chicago.

Hooper, F. A. 1961. *Funerary Stelae from Kom Abou Billou.* Ann Arbor.

Hunt, A. S. 1910. *The Oxyrhynchus Papyri.* Vol. VII. London.

Husselman, E. M. 1979. *Karanis Excavations of the University of Michigan in Egypt, 1928-1935: Topography and Architecture.* Ann Arbor.

Ingrams, L., et al. 1968. *The Oxyrhynchus Papyri.* Vol. XXXIV. London.

Johnson, B. 1981. *Pottery from Karanis: Excavations of the University of Michigan.* Ann Arbor.

Jones, A. H. M. 1960. "The Cloth Industry under the Roman Empire." *Economic History Review,* 2nd series, 13 (no. 2): 183-92.

Kähler, H., and C. Mango. 1967. *Hagia Sophia.* New York.

Kajitani, N. 1981. "Coptic Fragments." *Textile Art* (in Japanese) 13: 6-77. Kyoto.

Kalavrezou-Maxeiner, I. 1985. "The Byzantine Knotted Column." In *Byzantine Studies in Honor of Milton V. Anastos,* ed. S. Vryonis, pp. 95-103. Malibu.

Kaufmann, C. M. 1910. *Ikonographie der Menas-Ampullen.* Cairo.

Kendrick, A. F. 1920. *Catalogue of Textiles from Burying Grounds in Egypt.* Vol. I. *Graeco Roman Period.* Victoria and Albert Museum, London.

Kennedy, C. A. 1963. "The Development of the Lamp in Palestine." *Berytus* 14 (2): pp. 67-115.

Kent, J. P. C., and Painter, K. S. 1977. *Wealth of the Roman World.* London.

Kiss, Z. 1973. "Les Ampoules de St. Menas découvertes à Kôm el-Dikka (Alexandrie) en 1969." *Études et travaux* 7 (Travaux du Centre d'Archéologie Méditerranéenne, 14): 137-54

237

Kitzinger, E. 1954. "The Cult of Images in the Age before Iconoclasm." *Dumbarton Oaks Papers* 8: 83-150.

———. 1970. "The Threshold of the Holy Shrine: Observations on Floor Mosaics at Antioch and Bethlehem." *Kyriakon: Festschrift J. Quasten.* Vol. II, pp. 639-47. Munster.

———. 1980. "Christian Imagery: Growth and Impact." In *Age of Spirituality: A Symposium,* ed. K. Weitzmann, pp. 141-63. New York.

Kraemer, C. J. 1958. *Non-Literary Papyri* (=H. O. Colt, *Excavations at Nessana.* vol. III). Princeton.

Künzl, E. 1983. *Medizinische Instrumente aus Sepulkralfunden der römischen Kaiserzeit.* Cologne.

Kybalová, L. 1967. *Coptic Textiles.* London and Prague.

Laurent, V. 1936. "Amulettes byzantines et formulaires magiques." *Byzantinische Zeitschrift* 36: 300-315.

Leclant, J. 1978. "La grenouille d'éternité des pays du Nil au monde méditerranéen." In *Hommages à Maarten J. Vermaseren.* Vol. II, pp. 561-72. Leiden.

Levi, D. 1947. *Antioch Mosaic Pavements.* 2 vols. Princeton.

Lietzmann, H., ed. 1908. *Das Leben des Heiligen Symeon Stylites.* Leipzig.

Lloyd-Morgan, G. 1981. "Roman Mirrors and the Third Century." In *The Roman West in the Third Century: Contributions from Archaeology and History,* ed. A. King and M. Henig. Part I (*British Archaeological Reports, International Series,* 109, 1).

Lobel, E., Wegener, E. P., and Roberts, C. H. 1952. *The Oxyrhynchus Papyri.* Vol. XX. London.

Loeschcke, S. 1909. "Antike Lanternen und Lichthäuschen." *Bonner Jahrbücher* 118: 370-430.

Lyon-Caen, C., and Hoff, V. 1986. *Musée du Louvre: Catalogue des lampes en terre cuite grecques et chrétiennes.* Paris.

McCown, C. C., ed. 1922. *The Testament of Solomon.* Leipzig.

Magoulias, H. J. 1964. "The Lives of the Saints as Sources of Data for the History of Byzantine Medicine in the Sixth and Seventh Centuries." *Byzantinische Zeitschrift* 57: 127-50.

Maguire, H. 1987a. *Earth and Ocean: The Terrestrial World in Early Byzantine Art.* University Park, Pa.

———. 1987b. "The Mantle of Earth." *Illinois Classical Studies* 12 (2): 221-28.

Mainstone, R. J. 1988. *Hagia Sophia: Architecture, Structure and Liturgy of Justinian's Great Church.* London.

Mainz. 1980. *Gallien in der Spätantike von Kaiser Constantin zu Frankenkönig Childerich* (exh. cat.). Römisch-Germanisches Zentralmuseum.

Maloney, C., ed. 1976. *The Evil Eye.* New York.

Mango, C. 1972. *The Art of the Byzantine Empire, 312-1453: Sources and Documents.* Englewood Cliffs.

Mango, M. M. 1986. *Silver from Early Byzantium: The Kaper Koraon and Related Treasures.* Baltimore.

Marshall, F. H. 1911. *Catalogue of the Jewellery in the British Museum.* London.

Martin, M. 1982. *Objets quotidiens de l'époque romaine.* Augster Blaetter zur Roemerzeit, 3. Augst.

Mat'e, M., and Ljapunova, K. 1951. *Khudozestvennye tkani koptskogo Egipta.* Moscow.

Matheson, S. B. 1980. *Ancient Glass in the Yale University Art Gallery*. New Haven.

Matz, F. 1968. *Die dionysischen Sarkophage* (*Die antiken Sarkophagreliefs*, Vol. 4) Part I. Berlin.

Mazal, O. 1980. *Kommentar zur Wiener Genesis*. Frankfurt.

Menzel, H. 1969. *Antike Lampen im Römisch-Germanischen Zentralmuseum zu Mainz*. 2nd ed. Mainz.

Metzger, C. 1981. *Les ampoules à eulogie du Musée du Louvre*. Paris.

Michon, E. 1924. "Miroirs et non custodes eucharistiques." In *Strena Buliciana: commentationes gratulatoriae Francisco Bulić*, pp. 161-65. Zagreb.

Migne, J.-P., ed. 1862. *Patrologiae cursus completus, Series graeca*. Vol. LXI. Paris.

Milliken, W. M. 1958. "Early Byzantine Silver." *Bulletin of the Cleveland Museum of Art* 45: 35-41.

Milne, J. S. 1907. *Surgical Instruments in Greek and Roman Times*. New York.

Milojčić, V. 1968. "Zu den spätkaiserzeitlichen und merowingischen Silberlöffeln." *Berichte der Römisch-Germanischen Kommission des Deutschen Archäologischen Instituts* 49: 111-48.

Mitten, D. G. 1975. *Museum of Art, Rhode Island School of Design, Catalogue of the Classical Collection: Classical Bronzes*. Providence.

Nees, L. 1987. *The Gundohinus Gospels*. Cambridge, Mass.

New York. 1986. *Treasures from the Holy Land: Ancient Art from the Israel Museum* (exh. cat.). The Metropolitan Museum of Art.

———. 1987. *Carthage: A Mosaic of Ancient Tunisia* (exh. cat.). The American Museum of Natural History.

Orsi, P. 1942. *Sicilia bizantina*. Vol. I. Rome.

Ostrogorsky, G. 1969. *History of the Byzantine State*. Trans. J. Hussey. New Brunswick.

Paoli, U. E. 1963. *Rome, Its People, Life, and Customs* . Harlow.

Papadopoulos-Kerameus, A., ed. 1909. *Varia graeca sacra*. St. Petersburg.

Paris. 1983. *La civilisation romaine de la Moselle et la Sarre* (exh. cat.). Musée du Luxembourg.

Parlasca, K. 1982. "Pseudokoptische 'Reiterheilige.' " In *Studien zur spätantiken und frühchristlichen Kunst und Kultur des Orients*, ed. G. Koch, pp. 19-30. Wiesbaden.

Perdrizet, P. 1921. *Les terres cuites grecques d'Égypte de la collection Fouquet*. Nancy.

———. 1922. *Negotium permabulans in tenebris: études de démonologie gréco-orientale*. Strasbourg.

Petrie, W. F. M. 1905. *Roman Ehnasya* (plate and text supplement to *Roman Ehnasya*, 1904). Egypt Exploration Fund, Special Extra Publication. London.

———. 1917. *Tools and Weapons*. London.

———. 1927. *Objects of Daily Use*. British School of Archaeology in Egypt. London.

Piccirillo, M. 1986. *I mosaici di Giordania*. Rome.

Pilet, C. 1980. *Le nécropole de Frénouville: Étude en population de la fin du IIIe à la fin du VIIIe siècle* (*British Archaeological Reports* , 83). Vol. III. Oxford.

239

Pitra, J. B., ed. 1858. *Spicilegium solesmense complectens Sanctorum Patrum Scriptorumque ecclesiasti-corum anecdota hactenus opera.* Vol. IV. Paris.

Poulou-Papadimitriou, N. 1985. *Samos paléochrétienne: l'apport du matérial archéologique.* Thesis, Paris I.

Puschmann, T., ed. and trans. 1878-79. *Alexander von Tralles.* Vol. I. Vienna.

Quasten, J. 1960. *Patrology.* Vol. III. Utrecht.

Rahmani, L. Y. 1964. "Mirror-plaques from a Fifth-century A.D. Tomb." *Israel Exploration Journal* 14 (nos. 1-2): 50-60.

Randall, R. H., Jr. 1985. *Masterpieces of Ivory from the Walters Art Gallery.* Baltimore.

Rea, J. R. 1978. *The Oxyrhynchus Papyri.* Vol. XLVI. London.

Reine, F. J. 1942. *The Eucharistic Doctrine and Liturgy of the Mystagogical Catecheses of Theodore of Mopsuestia.* Washington, D.C.

Renner, D. 1982. *Die koptische Textilien in den Vatikanischen Museen. Pinacoteca vaticana, Kataloge.* Vol. II. Wiesbaden.

Richter, G. 1926. *Ancient Furniture: A History of Greek, Etruscan and Roman Furniture.* Oxford.

———. 1956. *Catalogue of Greek and Roman Antiquities in the Dumbarton Oaks Collection.* Cambridge, Mass.

Roberts, A., and Donaldson, S. 1907. *The Ante-Nicene Fathers.* Vol. IV. New York.

Roberts, C. H. 1950. *The Antinoopolis Papyri.* Vol. I. London.

Robinson, H. S. 1959. *The Athenian Agora.* Vol. V: *Pottery of the Roman Period.* Princeton.

Root, M. C. 1982. *Wondrous Glass: Reflections on the World of Rome.* Ann Arbor.

Rosenthal, R., and Silvan, R. 1978. *Ancient Lamps in the Schloessinger Collection (Quedem* 8). Hebrew University of Jerusalem.

Ross, M. C. 1960. "Byzantine Bronze Peacock Lamps." *Archaeology* 13: 134-36.

———. 1962. *Catalogue of the Byzantine and Early Mediaeval Antiquities in the Dumbarton Oaks Collection.* Vol I: *Metalwork, Ceramics, Glass, Glyptics, Painting.* Washington, D.C.

———. 1965. *Catalogue of the Byzantine and Early Mediaeval Antiquities in the Dumbarton Oaks Collection.* Vol. II: *Jewelry, Enamels, and Art of the Migration Period.* Washington, D.C.

———. 1968. "Jewels of Byzantium." *Arts in Virginia* 9: 12-31.

———. 1970. "Byzantine Bronzes." *Arts in Virginia* 10: 32-43.

Rudolph, W. 1979. *Highlights of the Burton Y. Berry Collection.* Bloomington, Ind.

Rudolph, W., and Rudolph, E. 1973. *Ancient Jewelry from the Collection of Burton Y. Berry.* Bloomington, Ind.

Russell, J. 1982. "The Evil Eye in Early Byzantine Society: Archaeological Evidence from Anemurium in Isauria." *Jahrbuch der Österreichischen Byzantinistik* 32 (3) (XVI. Internationaler Byzantinistenkongress, Akten, Vol. 2, 3): 539-48.

Rutschowscaya, M.-H. 1986. *Musée du Louvre: Catalogue des bois de l'Égypte copte.* Paris.

Salomonson, J. W. 1960. "The 'Fancy Dress Banquet': Attempt at Interpreting a Roman Mosaic from El Djem." *Bulletin Antieke Beschaving* 35: 25-55.

———. 1962. "Late-Roman Earthenware with Relief Decoration Found in Northern-Africa and Egypt." *Oudheidkundige Mededelingen* 43: 53-95.

———. 1968. "Études sur la céramique romaine d'Afrique. Sigillée claire et céramique commune de Henchir el Ouiba (Raqqada) en Tunisie Centrale." *Bulletin Antieke Beschaving* 43: 80-145.

———. 1969. "Spätrömische rote Tonware mit Reliefverzierung aus nordafrikanischen Werkstätten. Entwicklungsgeschichtliche Untersuchungen zur reliefgeschmückten Terra Sigillata Chiara 'C.' " *Bulletin Antieke Beschaving* 44: 4-109.

———. 1979. *Voluptatem spectandi non perdat sed mutet: Observations sur l'iconographie du martyre en Afrique romaine*. Amsterdam.

Schiemenz, G. P. 1982. "ΚΥΡΟΥ ΙΩΑΝΝΟΥ in Umm er-Rus. Zur Bedeutung eines frühbyzantinischen Fussbodenmosaiks." In *Studien zur spätantiken und frühchristlichen Kunst und Kultur des Orients*, ed. G. Koch, pp. 72-114. Wiesbaden.

Schiller, G. 1972. *Iconography of Christian Art*. Vol. II. London.

Schlumberger, D. 1939. "Les fouilles de Qasr el-Heir el-Gharbi (1936-38). Rapport préliminaire." *Syria* 20: 324-73.

Schlumberger, G. 1895. *Mélanges d'archéologie byzantine*. Paris.

Schlunk, H. 1939. *Kunst der Spätantike im Mittelmeerraum* (exh. cat.). Kaiser Friedrich Museum, Berlin.

Schneider, L. 1983. *Die Dömane als Weltbild: Wirkungsstrukturen der spätantiken Bildersprache*. Wiesbaden.

Segall, B. 1938. *Katalog der Goldschmiedearbeiten*. Benaki Museum, Athens.

Ševčenko I., and Ševčenko, N. 1984. *The Life of Saint Nicholas of Sion*. Brookline.

Shelton, K. J. 1981. *The Esquiline Treasure*. London.

Shepherd, D. G. 1974. "Saints and a Sinner on Two Coptic Textiles." *Bulletin of the Cleveland Museum of Art* 61: 331-38.

Shier, L. 1949. "A Roman Town in Egypt." *The Classical Outlook* 26: 61-63.

———. 1972. "The Frog on Lamps from Karanis." In *Medieval and Middle Eastern Studies in Honor of Aziz Suryal Atiya*, ed. S. A. Hanna, pp. 349-58. Leiden.

———. 1978. *Terracotta Lamps from Karanis, Egypt: Excavations of the University of Michigan*. Ann Arbor.

Sijpesteijn, P. J. 1977. *The Wisconsin Papyri*. Vol. II. Zutphen.

Simiaka Pacha, M. 1937. *Guide sommaire du Musée Copte*. Cairo.

Simon, E. 1962. "Zur Bedeutung des Greifen in der Kunst der Kaiserzeit." *Latomus* 21 (1962): 749-80.

Smith, C. 1977. *Ravenna: I secoli d'oro*. Ravenna.

Smith, R. W. 1957. *Glass from the Ancient World: The Ray Winfield Smith Collection, a Special Exhibition*. Corning Museum of Glass, Corning.

Soren, D. 1985. "An Earthquake on Cyprus: New Discoveries from Kourion." *Archaeology* 38 (2): 52-59.

Sotheby, Parke-Bernet. 1979. *The Constable-Maxwell Collection of Ancient Glass*. London.

Stannard, J. 1984. "Aspects of Byzantine Materia Medica." *Dumbarton Oaks Papers* 38: 205-11.

Steenbock, F. 1983. "Ein fürstliches Geschenk." In *Festschrift Yvonne Hackenbroch*, ed. J. Rasmussen, pp. 25-33. Munich.

Stern, H. 1948. "Nouvelles recherches sur les images des conciles dans l'église de la Nativité à Bethléem." *Cahiers archéologiques* 3: 82-105.

Strong, D. E. 1966. *Greek and Roman Gold and Silver Plate*. London.

Strong, D., and Brown, D. 1976. *Roman Crafts*. New York.

Strzygowski, J. 1904. *Catalogue général des antiquités égyptiennes du Musée du Caire: Koptische Kunst*. Cairo.

Sussman, V. 1985. "Lighting the Way through History: The Evolution of Ancient Oil Lamps." *Biblical Archaeology Review* 11 (2): 42-56.

Tabanelli, M. 1958. *Lo strumento chirurgico e la sua storia*.

Thompson, D. 1971. *Coptic Textiles in the Brooklyn Museum*. Brooklyn.

———. 1986. "The Evolution of Two Traditional Coptic Tape Patterns: Further Observations on the Classification of Coptic Textiles." *Journal of the American Research Center in Egypt* 23: 145-56.

Toal, M. F. 1959. *The Sunday Sermons of the Great Fathers*. Vol. III. Chicago.

Toynbee, J. M. C. 1964. *Art in Britain under the Romans*. Oxford.

Trilling, J. 1982. *The Roman Heritage: Textiles from Egypt and the Eastern Mediterranean 300 to 600 A.D.* (*Textile Museum Journal* 21). Washington.

Trowbridge, M. L. 1930. *Philological Studies in Ancient Glass*. (University of Illinois Studies in Language and Literature, 13). Urbana.

Trypanis, C. A., ed. and trans. 1971. *The Penguin Book of Greek Verse*. Harmondsworth.

van den Ven, ed. and trans. 1962-70. *La vie ancienne de S. Syméon Stylite le Jeune (521-592)*. Subsidia Hagiographica, 32. Brussels.

Viaud, G. 1978. *Magie et coutumes populaires chez les Coptes d'Égypte*. Sisteron.

Vienna. 1964. *Frühchristliche und koptische Kunst* (exh. cat.). Akademie der bildenden Künste.

Vikan, G. 1982. *Byzantine Pilgrimage Art*. Washington, D. C.

———. 1984. "Art, Medicine, and Magic in Early Byzantium." *Dumbarton Oaks Papers* 38: 65-86.

———. 1987. "Early Christian and Byzantine Rings in the Zucker Family Collection." *The Journal of the Walters Art Gallery* 45: 32-43.

Vikan, G., and Nesbitt, J. 1980. *Security in Byzantium: Locking, Sealing, and Weighing*. Washington, D. C.

Volbach, W. F. 1958. *Frühchristliche Kunst: Die Kunst der Spätantike in West- und Ostrom*. Munich.

———. 1969. *Early Decorative Textiles*. London.

Waage, F. O. 1941. "Lamps." In *Antioch-on-the-Orontes*. Vol. III: *The Excavations of 1937-1939*, ed. R. Stillwell, pp. 55-87. Princeton.

Waldbaum. J. C. 1983. *Metalwork from Sardis: The Finds through 1974.* Cambridge, Mass.

Ward, A., Cherry, J., Gere, C., and Cartlidge, B. 1981. *Rings through the Ages.* New York.

Weibel, A. C. 1952. *Two Thousand Years of Textiles.* New York.

Weitzmann, K. 1977. *Late Antique and Early Christian Book Illumination.* London.

———, ed. 1979. *Age of Spirituality. Late Antique and Early Christian Art, Third to Seventh Century* (exh. cat.). The Metropolitan Museum of Art, New York.

Wells, C. M., Freed, J., and Gallagher, J. 1988. "Urban and Rural Housing in Ancient Tunisia: Houses of the Theodosian Period at Carthage." *American Journal of Archaeology* 92: 248-49.

Wells, C. M., and Wightman, E. M. 1980. "Canadian Excavations at Carthage, 1976 and 1978: The Theodosian Wall, Northern Sector." *Journal of Field Archaeology* 7 (1): 43-63.

Westerman, W. L., and Kraemer, C. J. 1926. *Greek Papyri in the Library of Cornell University.* New York.

Wilkinson, J. 1971. *Egeria's Travels.* London.

———. 1977. *Jerusalem Pilgrims before the Crusades.* Warminster.

Winter, J. G. 1936. *Michigan Papyri.* Vol. III. Ann Arbor.

Wipszycka, E. 1965. *L'Industrie textile dans l'Égypte romaine.* Warsaw.

Wood, S. P., trans. 1954. *Clement of Alexandria: Christ the Educator.* New York.

Wroth, W. 1908. *Imperial Byzantine Coins in the British Museum.* London.

Wulff, O. 1909. *Altchristliche und mittelalterliche byzantinische und italienische Bildwerk.* Part I, *Altchristliche Bildwerk.* Berlin.

Wulff, O., and Volbach, W. F. 1926. *Spätantike und koptische Stoffe aus ägyptischen Grabfunden in den Staatlichen Museen.* Berlin.

Zahn, R. 1929. *Sammlung Baurat Schiller, Berlin.* Auction catalogue. Berlin.

Zalesskaja, V. N. 1976. "Amulettes byzantines magiques et leurs liens avec la litterature apocryphe." *Actes du XIVe Congrès International des Études Byzantines.* Vol. III, pp. 243-47. Bucharest.

———. 1977. *Iskusstvo Vizanti v. sobraniyakh SSSR: Katalog Vistavki.* Vol. III. Moscow.

Zischka, U. 1977. *Zur sakralen und profanen Anwendung des Knotenmotivs als magisches Mittel, symbol oder Dekor.* Munich.

Index of Household Objects by Type

246

DATE DUE

DEMCO 38-297